The Collegeville Chant Psalter

for Sunday, Solemnities, and Major Feast Days

Anthony Ruff, OSB

LITURGICAL PRESS
Collegeville, Minnesota

www.litpress.org

Reprint Policy

For your assistance, image files of the assembly responses are available online for you to download and reproduce in aids for worship. In order to reproduce these image files legally, you must either (1) purchase the Liturgical Press annual music reprint license (reporting the use of titles is not required) or (2) have a membership with the licensing agent Onelicense.net (reporting the use of titles is mandatory).

The image files can be found at the following web address: www.litpress.org/tccp-responses.

ACKNOWLEDGMENTS

The cover design is by Monica Bokinskie. Photo by Michael Becker.

The English translation of Psalm Responses from *Lectionary for Mass* © 1969, 1981, 1997, International Commission on English in the Liturgy Corporation (ICEL). All rights reserved.

Verse texts copyright © 1970, 1986, 1997, 1998, 2001 Confraternity of Christian Doctrine, Inc., Washington, D.C. All rights reserved. No part of this work may be reproduced or transmitted in any form or by any means, electronic or mechanical, including photocopying, recording, or by any information storage and retrieval system, without permission in writing from the copyright owner.

Antiphon music set by Anthony Ruff, OSB, © 2019, Order of Saint Benedict, Saint John's Abbey, Collegeville, MN. Published and administered by Liturgical Press, Box 7500, Collegeville, MN 56321. All rights reserved.

The *Saint Meinrad Psalm Tones* based on the eight Gregorian modes © 1973, 1993, Saint Meinrad Archabbey, Saint Meinrad, IN 47577. All rights reserved. Reprinted with permission.

© 2019 by Order of Saint Benedict, Collegeville, Minnesota. All rights reserved. No part of this book may be reproduced in any form, by print, microfilm, microfiche, mechanical recording, photocopying, translation, or by any other means, known or yet unknown, for any purpose except brief quotations in reviews without the previous written permission of Liturgical Press, Saint John's Abbey, PO Box 7500, Collegeville, Minnesota 56321-7500. Printed in the United States of America.

ISBN: 978-0-8146-4430-0

FOREWORD

This collection offers simple chanted settings of the Responsorial Psalm for every Sunday and major feast day of the liturgical year. Responsorial Psalms in this style were first conceived for unaccompanied singing led by a single cantor at daily Mass at Saint John's Abbey. But for those who desire it, keyboard accompaniments are provided in this collection.

These settings are text-based in every respect, intentionally simple and unornamented. The refrain melodies are only slightly more than inflected speech, with primary scale degrees bringing out the natural accentuation of the text, and infrequent two-note groups highlighting important words or defining syntactical units. The melodic settings are in the eight Gregorian chant modes as found in the psalm tones of Saint Meinrad's Archabbey. Type melodies, one for each mode, are employed repeatedly for varying antiphon texts, making it easier for cantor and congregation to pick up the refrain melodies over time. The Saint Meinrad's psalm tones are used not only for their simple beauty, but especially because they are well suited to the rhythm and accentuation of the English language. Attention is drawn to the pointing. The first word or syllable to leave the reciting note is indicated by underlining.

To the singer: It is important to remember that these settings are speech-based. They must not drag or be turned into a metrical setting. Singers should follow the natural accentuation of spoken English. The singer might find it helpful first to recite the text of the refrain and verses, and then to sing them with approximately the same rhythm and tempo. To proclaim the psalm verses effectively, the singer should become as familiar as possible with the modal melodies of the eight psalm tones, committing them to memory if possible. Before singing the melody of the refrain, it is suggested that the singer first internalize the melody of the psalm tone, since the refrain melodies are based upon and grow out of the psalm tone formulas.

To the keyboard player: It is important to vary the volume between refrain and verses, playing more loudly to stimulate and support the congregation, but playing as quietly as possible for the verses, while still offering necessary support to the cantor, so as to allow the text of the verses to be heard clearly. As much as possible, the accompaniment for the psalm tone should be committed to memory so that one can follow and support the cantor without delay or hesitation. It is advisable to memorize the first chord of the antiphon as well so that the transition from verse to antiphon can be made smoothly. Some organists might wish to help the congregation by soloing out the antiphon melody with a louder registration on a separate manual.

Piano players should account for the fact that the piano is percussive and does not sustain sounds like the organ. In order to provide continuous support, chords should be repeated more often than is written. For both refrain and verses, such repetition should occur on accented syllables. Especially on the verses, the reiteration of chords might take the form of gentle arpeggiation.

Fr. Anthony Ruff, OSB
Saint John's Abbey
Holy Thursday, April 18, 2019

Psalm 1

6th Sunday in Ordinary Time, Year C

Bless-ed are they who hope in the Lord.

Psalm Tone

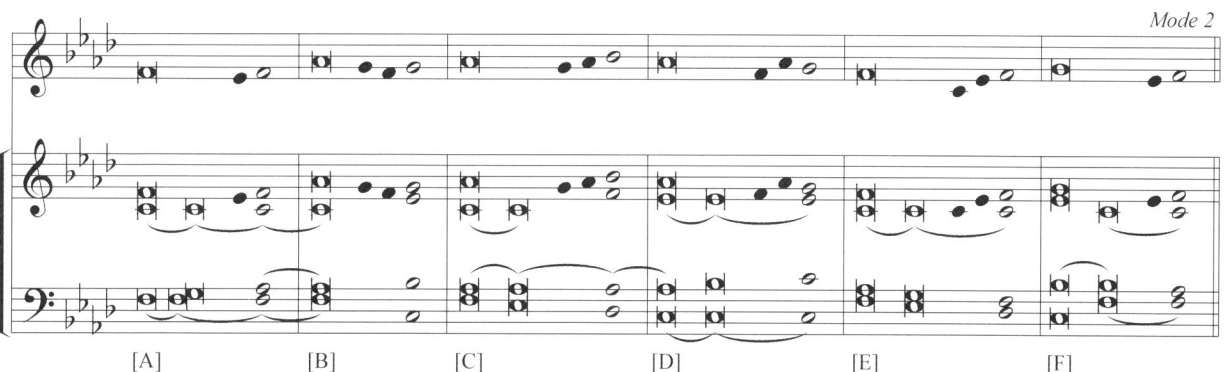

Mode 2

[A] [B] [C] [D] [E] [F]

Psalm 1:1-2, 3, 4 and 6. R/ 40:5a

1. Blessed the man who fol<u>lows</u> not
   the counsel <u>of</u> the wicked,
   nor walks in the <u>way</u> of sinners,
   nor sits in the company <u>of</u> the insolent,
   but delights in the law <u>of</u> the Lord
   and meditates on his law day <u>and</u> night.   *R/*

2. He is like <u>a</u> tree
   planted near <u>running</u> water,
   that yields its fruit <u>in</u> due season,
   and whose leaves <u>never</u> fade.
   [omit E]
   Whatever he <u>does</u>, prospers.   *R/*

3. Not so the wicked, <u>not</u> so;
   they are like chaff which the wind <u>drives</u> away.
   For the Lord watches over the way <u>of</u> the just,
   [omit D, E]
   but the way of the wick<u>ed</u> vanishes.   *R/*

Text: Refrain, *Lectionary for Mass,* © 1969, 1981, 1997, ICEL; verses, *Lectionary for Mass*/New American Bible, © 1970, 1986, 1991, 1997, 2001, 2010, CCD. All rights reserved.
Music: *The Collegeville Chant Psalter,* © 2019, Order of Saint Benedict, Collegeville, MN. Published and administered by Liturgical Press, Collegeville, MN 56321. All rights reserved.

Psalm 4

3rd Sunday of Easter, Year B

Lord, let your face shine on us.

3rd Sunday of Easter, Year B, *alternate response*

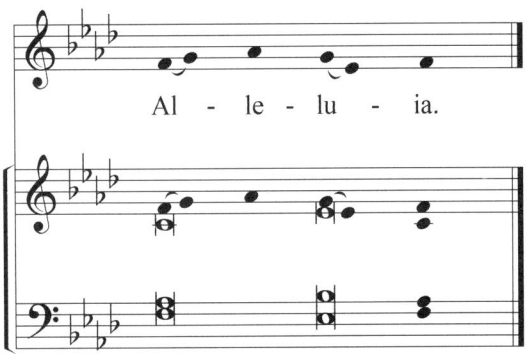

Al - le - lu - ia.

Psalm Tone

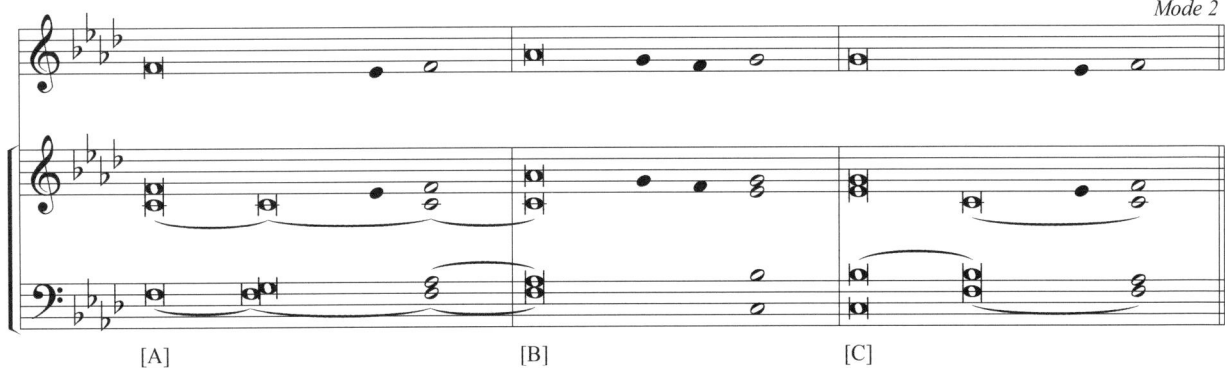

Mode 2

[A] [B] [C]

Psalm 4:2, 4, 7-8, 9. R/ v. 7a

1. When I call, answer me, O my <u>just</u> God,
   you who relieve me when I am <u>in</u> distress;
   have pity on me, and hear <u>my</u> prayer! R/

2. Know that the Lord does wonders for <u>his</u> faithful one;
   [omit B]
   the Lord will hear me when I call <u>upon</u> him. R/

3. O Lord, let the light of your countenance
   shine <u>upon</u> us!
   [omit B]
   You put gladness into <u>my</u> heart. R/

4. As soon as I lie down, I fall peacefully <u>asleep</u>,
   for you a<u>lone</u>, O Lord,
   bring security to <u>my</u> dwelling. R/

Text: Refrain, *Lectionary for Mass,* © 1969, 1981, 1997, ICEL; verses, *Lectionary for Mass*/New American Bible, © 1970, 1986, 1991, 1997, 2001, 2010, CCD. All rights reserved.
Music: *The Collegeville Chant Psalter,* © 2019, Order of Saint Benedict, Collegeville, MN. Published and administered by Liturgical Press, Collegeville, MN 56321. All rights reserved.

Psalm 8

Trinity Sunday, Year C

Psalm Tone

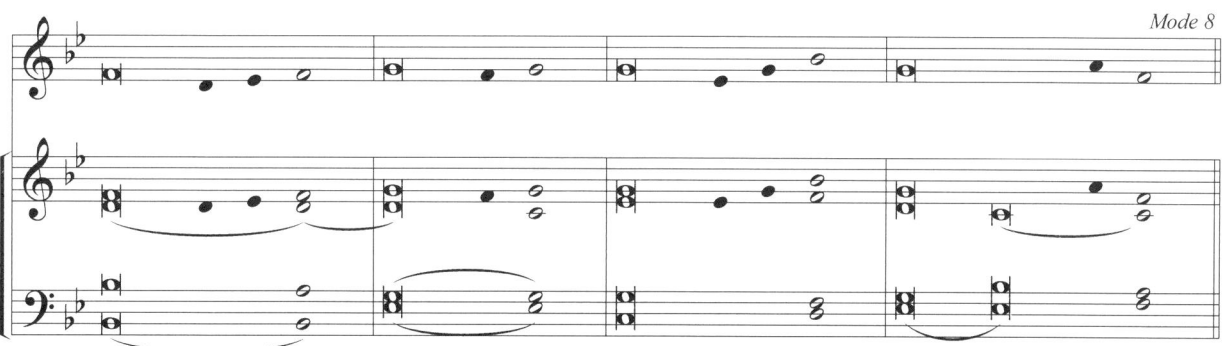

Psalm 8:4-5, 6-7, 8-9. R/ v. 2a

1. When I behold your heavens, the work <u>of</u> your fingers,
   the moon and the stars which you set <u>in</u> place —
   what is man that you should be mind<u>ful</u> of him,
   or the son of man that you should care <u>for</u> him? *R/*

2. You have made him little less <u>than</u> the angels,
   and crowned him with glory <u>and</u> honor.
   You have given him rule over the works <u>of</u> your hands,
   putting all things under <u>his</u> feet. *R/*

3. All <u>sheep</u> and oxen,
   yes, and the beasts of <u>the</u> field,
   the birds of the air, the fishes <u>of</u> the sea,
   and whatever swims the paths of <u>the</u> seas. *R/*

Text: Refrain, *Lectionary for Mass,* © 1969, 1981, 1997, ICEL; verses, *Lectionary for Mass*/New American Bible, © 1970, 1986, 1991, 1997, 2001, 2010, CCD. All rights reserved.
Music: *The Collegeville Chant Psalter,* © 2019, Order of Saint Benedict, Collegeville, MN. Published and administered by Liturgical Press, Collegeville, MN 56321. All rights reserved.

Psalm 15

22nd Sunday in Ordinary Time, Year B

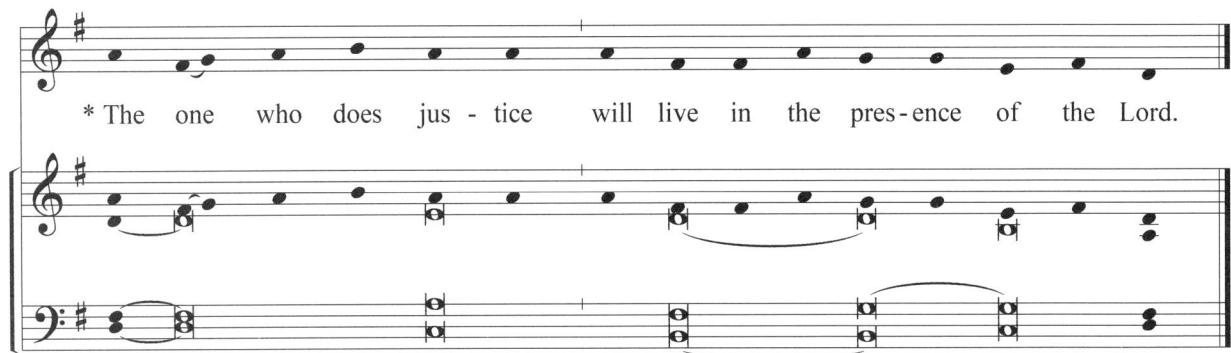

* *Some editions of the Lectionary begin this response "One who does justice..."*

16th Sunday in Ordinary Time, Year C

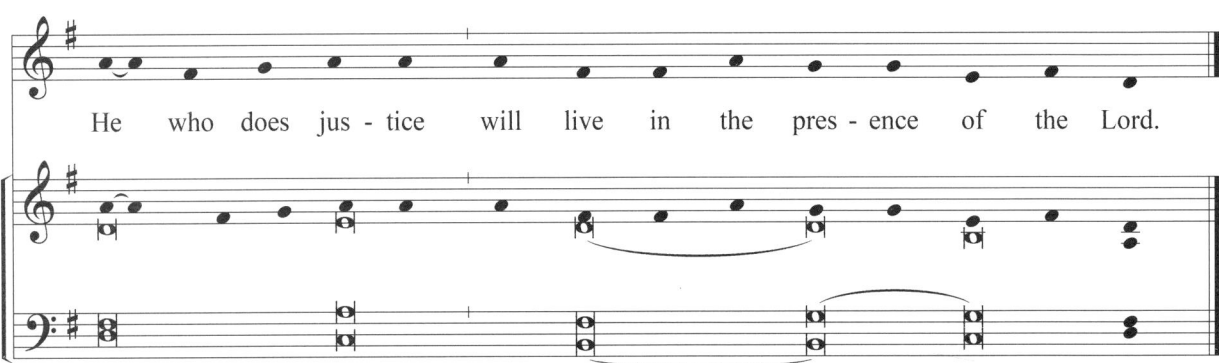

Psalm Tone

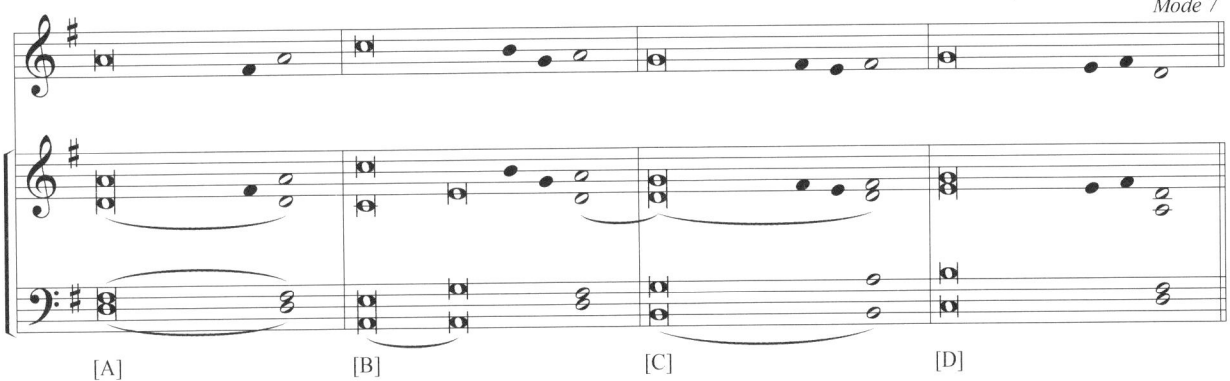

[A] [B] [C] [D]

Psalm 15:2-3, 3-4, 4-5. R/ v. 1a

22 OT B only

1. Whoever walks blamelessly and <u>does</u> justice;
   who thinks the truth <u>in</u> his heart
   [omit C]
   and slanders not <u>with</u> his tongue. *R/*

2. Who harms not his fel<u>low</u> man,
   nor takes up a reproach a<u>gainst</u> his neighbor;
   by whom the reprobate <u>is</u> despised,
   while he honors those who <u>fear</u> the Lord. *R/*

3. Who lends not his money <u>at</u> usury
   and accepts no bribe a<u>gainst</u> the innocent.
   Whoever <u>does</u> these things
   shall never <u>be</u> disturbed. *R/*

16 OT C only

1a. One who walks blamelessly and <u>does</u> justice;
    who thinks the truth <u>in</u> his heart
    [omit C]
    and slanders not <u>with</u> his tongue. *R/*

Text: Refrain, *Lectionary for Mass*, © 1969, 1981, 1997, ICEL; verses, *Lectionary for Mass*/New American Bible, © 1970, 1986, 1991, 1997, 2001, 2010, CCD. All rights reserved.
Music: *The Collegeville Chant Psalter*, © 2019, Order of Saint Benedict, Collegeville, MN. Published and administered by Liturgical Press, Collegeville, MN 56321. All rights reserved.

Psalm 16

Easter Vigil 2 • 33rd Sunday in Ordinary Time, Year B • 13th Sunday in Ordinary Time, Year C

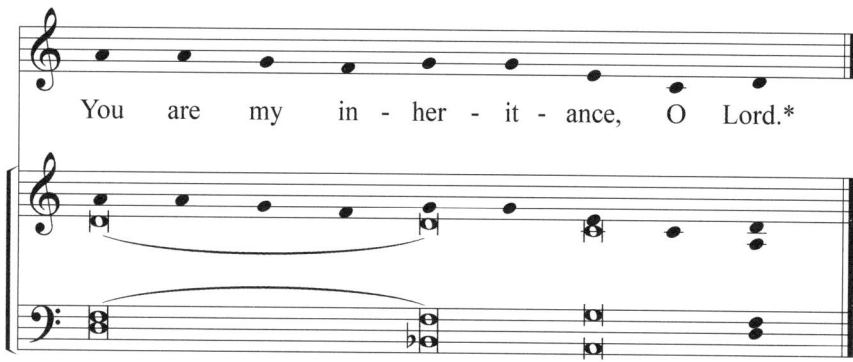

* 33 OT B has an exclamation point at the end of the Response instead of a period.

3rd Sunday of Easter, Year A

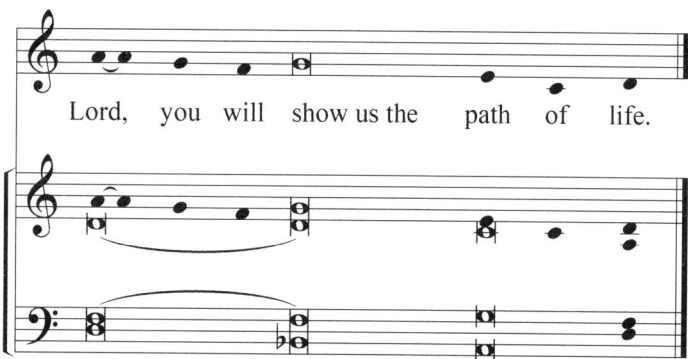

3rd Sunday of Easter, Year A, *alternate response*

Psalm Tone

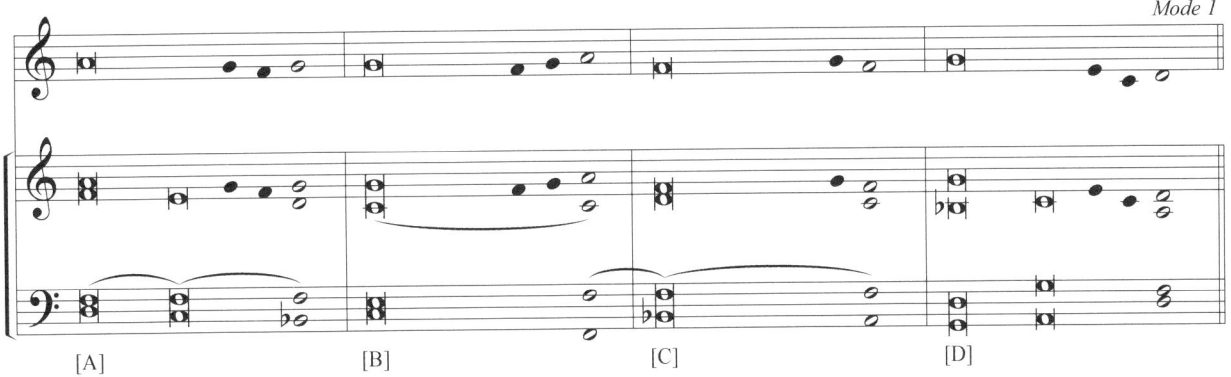

Psalm 16:5, 8, 9-10, 11. R/ v. 1

Easter Vigil 2 and 33 OT B only
1. O Lord, my allotted portion <u>and</u> my cup,
    you it is who hold <u>fast</u> my lot.
    I set the Lord ever <u>be</u>fore me;
    with him at my right hand I shall not <u>be</u> disturbed.   *R/*

Psalm 16:1-2, 5, 7-8, 9-10, 11. R. v. 1; v. 11a

3 Easter A and 13 OT C only
1. Keep me, O God, for in you <u>I</u> take refuge;
    I say to the Lord, "My <u>Lord</u> are you.
    O Lord, my allotted portion and <u>my</u> cup,
    you it is who hold <u>fast</u> my lot."   *R/*

1a. I bless the <u>Lord</u> who counsels me;
    even in the night my <u>heart</u> exhorts me.
    I set the Lord ever <u>be</u>fore me;
    with him at my right hand I shall not <u>be</u> disturbed.   *R/*

2. Therefore my heart is glad and my <u>soul</u> rejoices,
    my body, too, <u>a</u>bides in confidence;
    because you will not abandon my soul to <u>the</u> netherworld,
    nor will you suffer your faithful one to under<u>go</u> corruption.   *R/*

3. You will show me the <u>path</u> to life,
    fullness of joys <u>in</u> your presence,
    [omit C]
    the delights at your right <u>hand</u> forever.   *R/*

Text: Refrain, *Lectionary for Mass,* © 1969, 1981, 1997, ICEL; verses, *Lectionary for Mass/New American Bible,* © 1970, 1986, 1991, 1997, 2001, 2010, CCD. All rights reserved.
Music: *The Collegeville Chant Psalter,* © 2019, Order of Saint Benedict, Collegeville, MN. Published and administered by Liturgical Press, Collegeville, MN 56321. All rights reserved.

Psalm 17

32nd Sunday in Ordinary Time, Year C

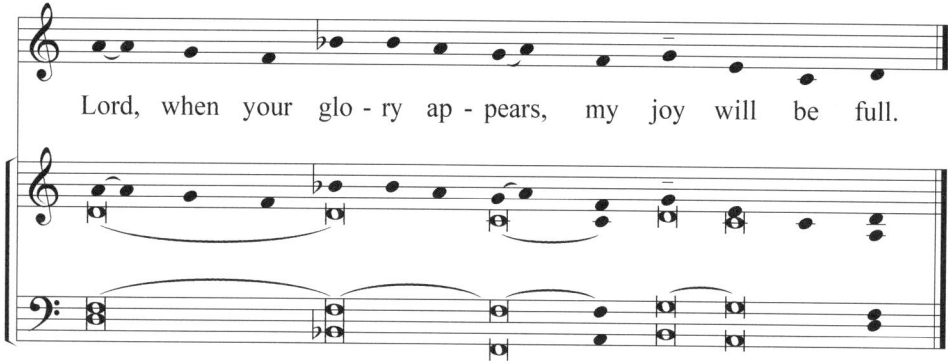

Lord, when your glory appears, my joy will be full.

Psalm Tone

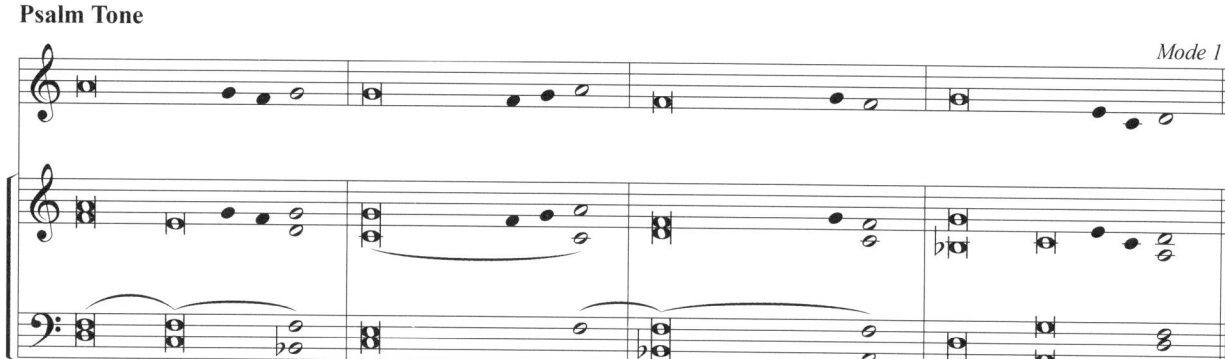

Mode 1

Psalm 17:1, 5-6, 8, 15. R/ v. 15b

1. Hear, O Lord, <u>a</u> just suit;
   attend <u>to</u> my outcry;
   hearken to <u>my</u> prayer
         from lips with<u>out</u> deceit. *R/*

2. My steps have been steadfast <u>in</u> your paths,
   my feet <u>have</u> not faltered.
   I call upon you, for you will answer me, <u>O</u> God;
   incline your ear to me; <u>hear</u> my word. *R/*

3. Keep me as the apple <u>of</u> your eye,
   hide me in the shadow <u>of</u> your wings.
   But I in justice shall behold <u>your</u> face;
   on waking I shall be content <u>in</u> your presence. *R/*

Text: Refrain, *Lectionary for Mass,* © 1969, 1981, 1997, ICEL; verses, *Lectionary for Mass*/New American Bible, © 1970, 1986, 1991, 1997, 2001, 2010, CCD. All rights reserved.
Music: *The Collegeville Chant Psalter,* © 2019, Order of Saint Benedict, Collegeville, MN. Published and administered by Liturgical Press, Collegeville, MN 56321. All rights reserved.

Psalm 18

30th Sunday in Ordinary Time, Year A • 31st Sunday in Ordinary Time, Year B

Psalm Tone

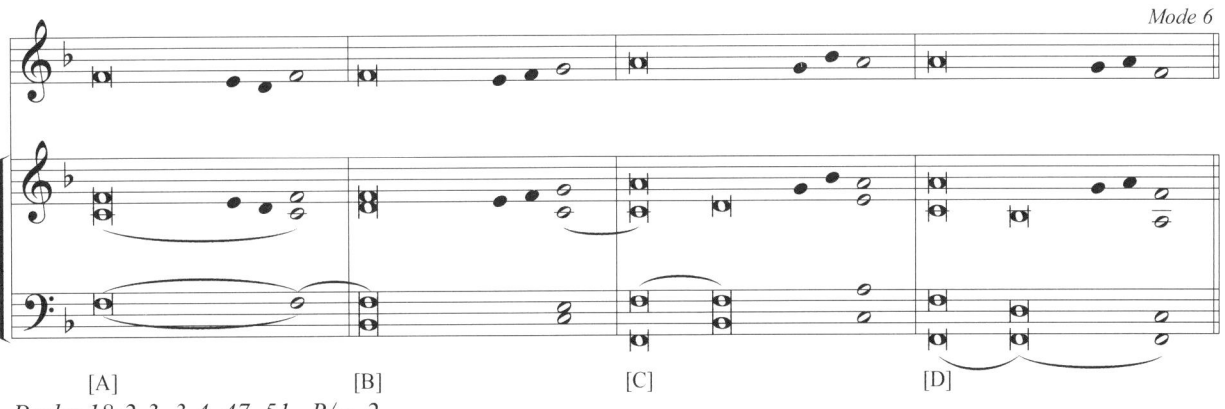

Psalm 18:2-3, 3-4, 47, 51. R/ v. 2

1. I love you, O L<small>ORD</small>, my strength,
   [omit B, C]
   O L<small>ORD</small>, my rock, my fortress, my deliverer. *R/*

2. My God, my rock of refuge,
   my shield, the horn of my salvation, my stronghold!
   Praised be the L<small>ORD</small>, I exclaim,
   and I am safe from my enemies. *R/*

3. The L<small>ORD</small> lives and blessed be my rock!
   Extolled be God my savior.
   You who gave great victories to your king
   and showed kindness to your anointed. *R/*

(In the Lectionary, verse 3 has minor differences of punctuation on the two Sundays, but the wording is identical.)

Text: Refrain, *Lectionary for Mass*, © 1969, 1981, 1997, ICEL; verses, *Lectionary for Mass*/New American Bible, © 1970, 1986, 1991, 1997, 2001, 2010, CCD. All rights reserved.
Music: *The Collegeville Chant Psalter*, © 2019, Order of Saint Benedict, Collegeville, MN. Published and administered by Liturgical Press, Collegeville, MN 56321. All rights reserved.

Psalm 19

3rd Sunday of Lent, Year B • Easter Vigil 6 • Pentecost Vigil 2, *alternate psalm* • Common Ordinary Time 1

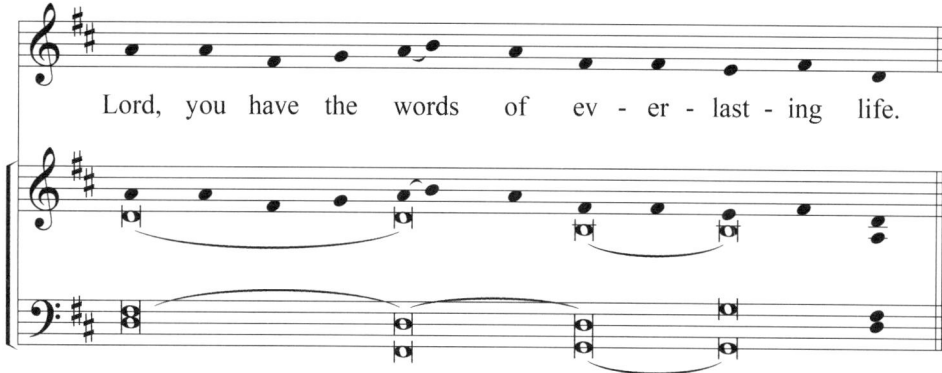

3rd Sunday in Ordinary Time, Year C • 15th Sunday in Ordinary Time Year C, *alternate psalm* • Common Ordinary Time 1, *alternate response*

26th Sunday in Ordinary Time, Year B

Psalm Tone

Mode 5

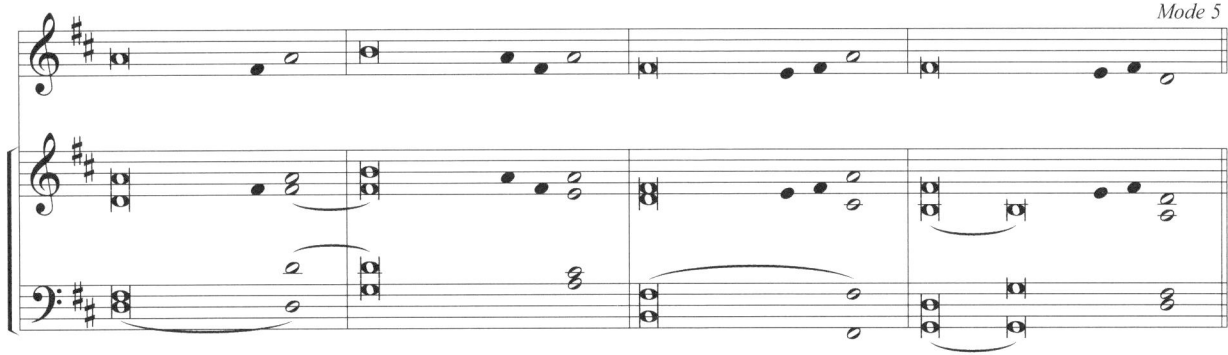

Psalm 19:8, 9, 10, 11. R/ John 6:68c; John 6:63c; Ps 19:9a.

1. The law of the L<small>ORD</small> <u>is</u> perfect,
   refresh<u>ing</u> the soul;
   the decree of the L<small>ORD</small> is trustworthy,
   giving wisdom <u>to</u> the simple. *R/*

2. The precepts of the L<small>ORD</small> <u>are</u> right,
   rejoic<u>ing</u> the heart;
   the command of the L<small>ORD</small> is clear,
   enlighten<u>ing</u> the eye. *R/*

3. The fear of the L<small>ORD</small> <u>is</u> pure,
   endur<u>ing</u> forever;
   the ordinances of the L<small>ORD</small> are true,
   all <u>of</u> them just. *R/*

4. They are more precious <u>than</u> gold,
   than a heap of <u>purest</u> gold;
   sweeter al<u>so</u> than syrup
   or honey <u>from</u> the comb. *R/*

(In the Lectionary, there are minor differences of punctuation in verses 1 and 2, but the wording is identical.)

26 OT B Verses 1 and 3 opposite, then:

3a. Though your servant is careful <u>of</u> them,
   very dili<u>gent</u> in keeping them,
   yet who can <u>detect</u> failings?
   Cleanse me from my <u>un</u>known faults! *R/*

4a. From wanton sin especially, restrain <u>your</u> servant;
   let it <u>not</u> rule over me.
   Then shall I be blame<u>less</u> and innocent
   of <u>serious</u> sin. *R/*

3 OT C Verses 1-2 opposite, then:

3b. Let the words of <u>my</u> mouth
   and the thought <u>of</u> my heart
   find fa<u>vor</u> before you,
   O L<small>ORD</small>, my rock and <u>my</u> redeemer. *R/*

---

3 Lent B, Easter Vigil 6, Pentecost Vigil 2 alt., 15 OT C alt., Common OT 1
    1. - 2. - 3. - 4.
26 OT B
    1 - 3. - 3a. - 4a.
3 OT C
    1. - 2. - 3b.

Text: Refrain, *Lectionary for Mass,* © 1969, 1981, 1997, ICEL; verses, *Lectionary for Mass*/New American Bible, © 1970, 1986, 1991, 1997, 2001, 2010, CCD. All rights reserved.
Music: *The Collegeville Chant Psalter,* © 2019, Order of Saint Benedict, Collegeville, MN. Published and administered by Liturgical Press, Collegeville, MN 56321. All rights reserved.

Saints Peter and Paul Vigil

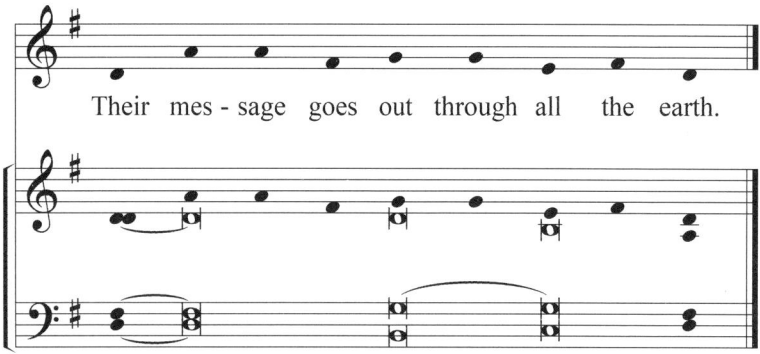

Psalm Tone

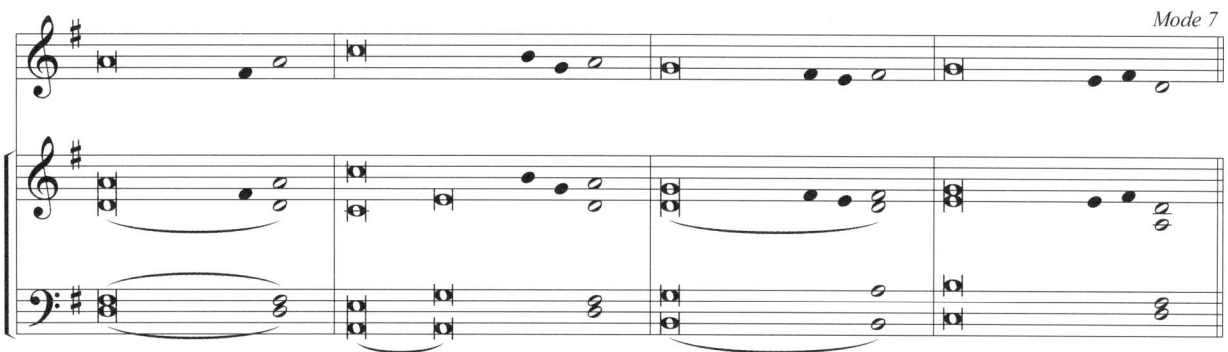

Psalm 19:2-3, 4-5. R/ v. 5

1. The heavens declare the glory <u>of</u> God,
   and the firmament pro<u>claims</u> his handiwork.
   Day pours out the <u>word</u> to day,
   and night to night <u>im</u>parts knowledge. *R/*

2. Not a word nor <u>a</u> discourse
   whose voice <u>is</u> not heard;
   through all the earth their <u>voice</u> resounds,
   and to the ends of the <u>world</u>, their message. *R/*

Text: Refrain, *Lectionary for Mass,* © 1969, 1981, 1997, ICEL; verses, *Lectionary for Mass*/New American Bible, © 1970, 1986, 1991, 1997, 2001, 2010, CCD. All rights reserved.
Music: *The Collegeville Chant Psalter,* © 2019, Order of Saint Benedict, Collegeville, MN. Published and administered by Liturgical Press, Collegeville, MN 56321. All rights reserved.

Psalm 22

Palm Sunday • Common Holy Week

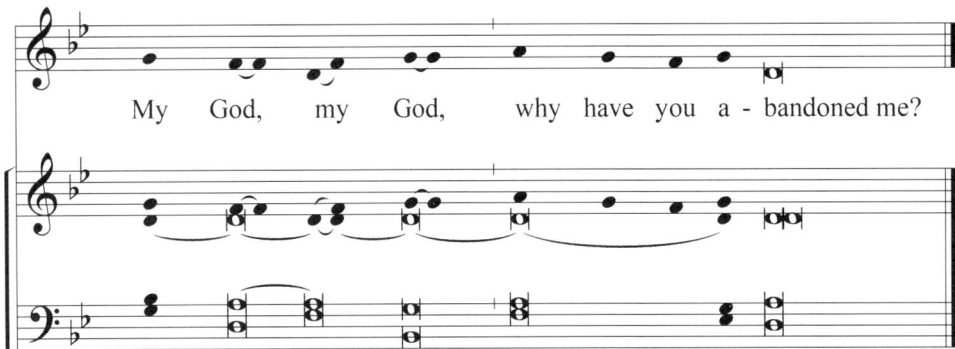

Psalm Tone

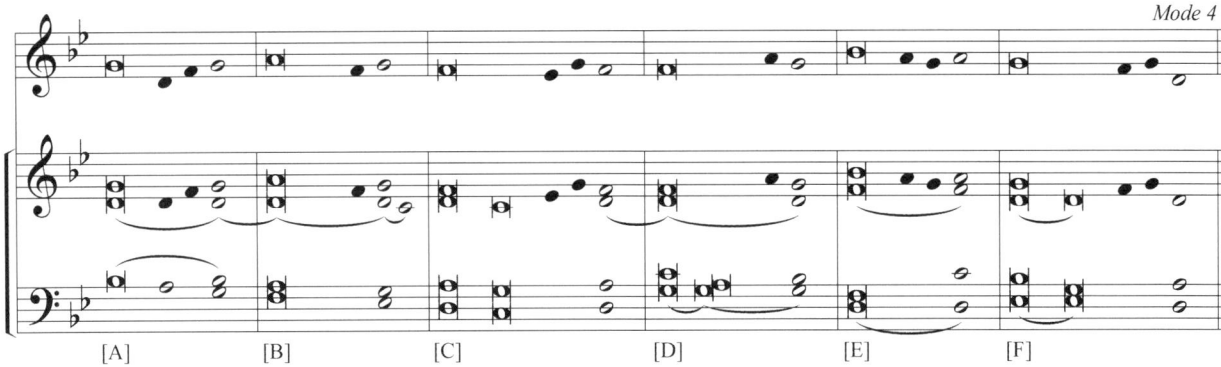

Psalm 22:8-9, 17-18, 19-20, 23-24. R./ v. 2a

1. All who <u>see</u> me scoff at me;
   they mock me with parted lips, they wag <u>their</u> heads:
   [omit C, D]
   "He relied on the Lord; let <u>him</u> deliver him,
   let him rescue him, <u>if</u> he loves him." *R/*

2. Indeed, many <u>dogs</u> surround me,
   a pack of evildoers closes in up<u>on</u> me;
   [omit C, D]
   they have pierced my hands <u>and</u> my feet;
   I can count <u>all</u> my bones. *R/*

3. They divide my <u>gar</u>ments among them,
   and for my vesture they <u>cast</u> lots.
   [omit C, D]
   But you, O Lord, be not <u>far</u> from me;
   O my help, has<u>ten</u> to aid me. *R/*

4. I will proclaim your name <u>to</u> my brethren;
   in the midst of the assembly I <u>will</u> praise you:
   "You who fear <u>the</u> Lord, praise him;
   all you descendants of Jacob, give glory <u>to</u> him;
   [omit E]
   revere him, all you descen<u>dants</u> of Israel!" *R/*

Text: Refrain, *Lectionary for Mass*, © 1969, 1981, 1997, ICEL; verses, *Lectionary for Mass*/New American Bible, © 1970, 1986, 1991, 1997, 2001, 2010, CCD. All rights reserved.
Music: *The Collegeville Chant Psalter*, © 2019, Order of Saint Benedict, Collegeville, MN. Published and administered by Liturgical Press, Collegeville, MN 56321. All rights reserved.

5th Sunday of Easter, Year B

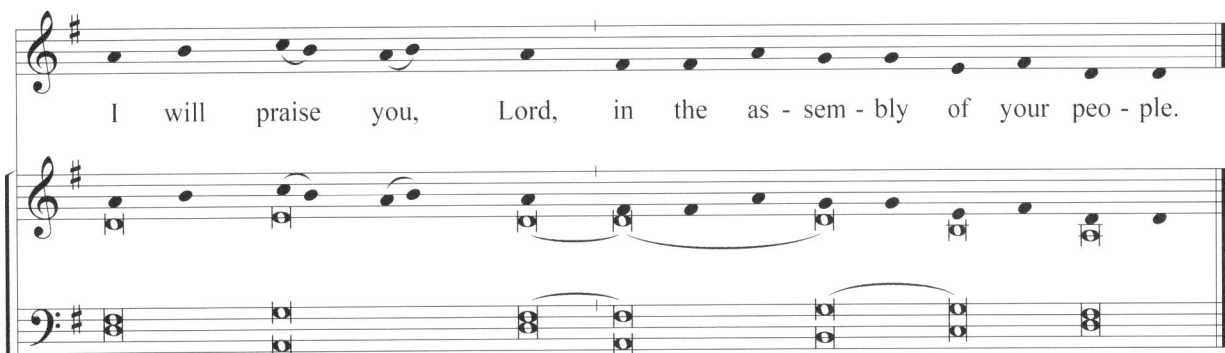

I will praise you, Lord, in the as-sem-bly of your peo-ple.

5th Sunday of Easter, *alternate response*

Al-le-lu-ia.

Psalm Tone

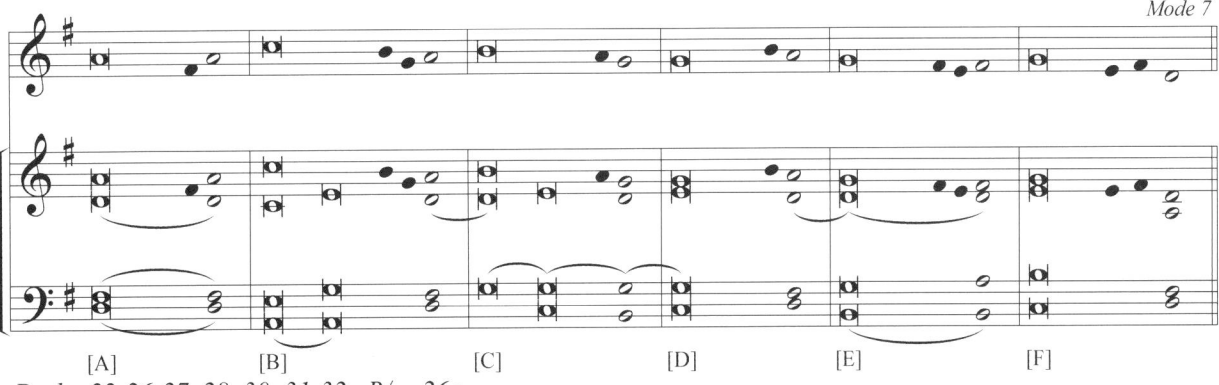

Mode 7

[A] [B] [C] [D] [E] [F]

Psalm 22:26-27, 28, 30, 31-32. R/ v. 26a

1. I will fulfill my vows before those who fear
    the LORD.
   The lowly shall eat their fill;
   [omit C, D]
   they who seek the LORD shall praise him:
   "May your hearts live forever!" *R/*

2. All the ends of the earth
   shall remember and turn to the LORD;
   [omit C, D]
   all the families of the nations
   shall bow down before him. *R/*

3. To him alone shall bow down
   all who sleep in the earth;
   [omit C, D]
   before him shall bend
   all who go down into the dust. *R/*

4. And to him my soul shall live;
   my descendants shall serve him.
   Let the coming generation be told of the LORD
   that they may proclaim to a people yet to be born
   [omit E]
   the justice he has shown. *R/*

Text: Refrain, *Lectionary for Mass,* © 1969, 1981, 1997, ICEL; verses, *Lectionary for Mass*/New American Bible, © 1970, 1986, 1991, 1997, 2001, 2010, CCD. All rights reserved.
Music: *The Collegeville Chant Psalter,* © 2019, Order of Saint Benedict, Collegeville, MN. Published and administered by Liturgical Press, Collegeville, MN 56321. All rights reserved.

Psalm 23

4th Sunday of Lent, Year A • 4th Sunday of Easter, Year A • Christ the King, Year A • 16th Sunday in Ordinary Time, Year B • Sacred Heart, Year C • All Souls, 1st Mass *(for alternate response, turn the page)*

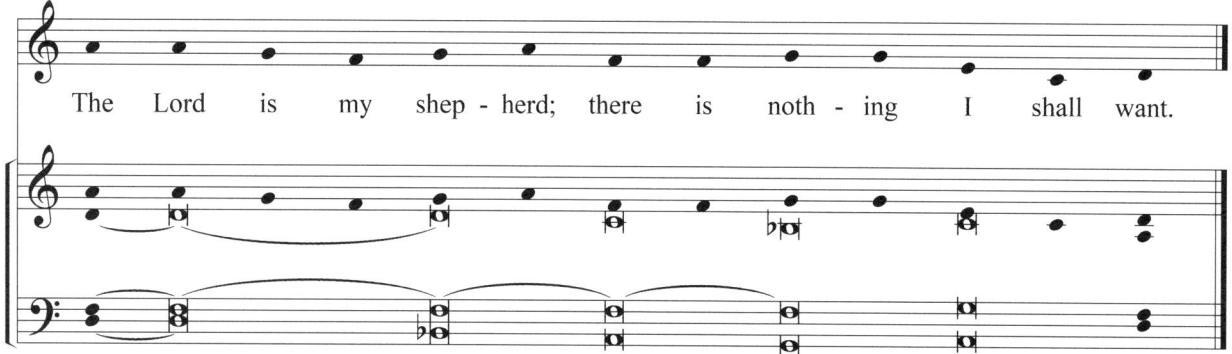

4th Sunday of Easter, Year A, *alternate response*

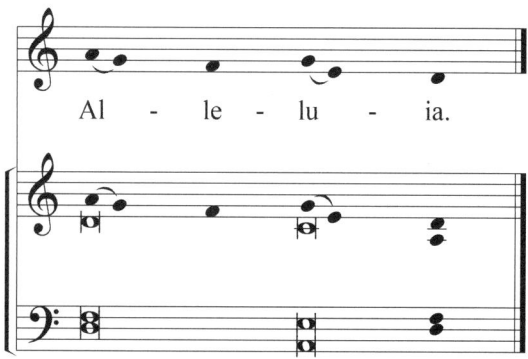

Psalm Tone

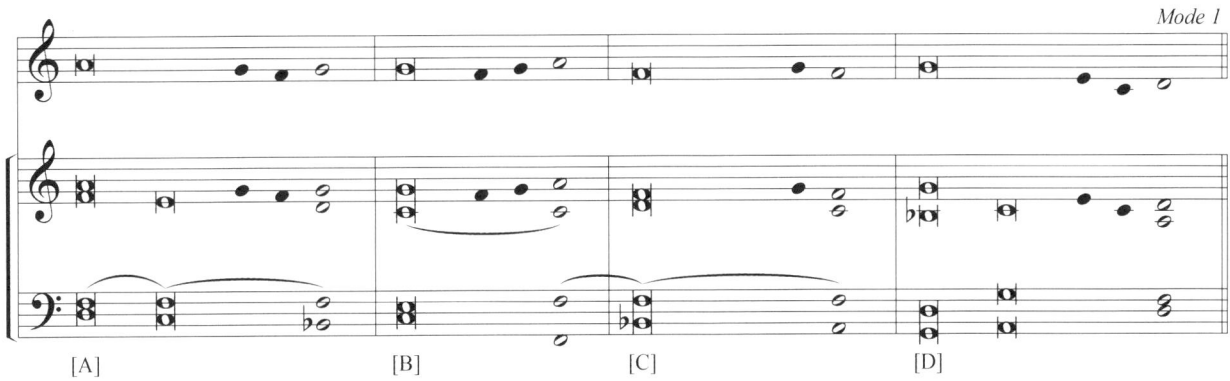

Mode 1

[A] [B] [C] [D]

All except Christ the King A
Psalm 23:1-3a, 3b-4, 5, 6. R/ v. 1

1. The Lord is my shepherd; I <u>shall</u> not want.
   In verdant pastures he gives <u>me</u> repose;
   beside restful waters <u>he</u> leads me;
   he refresh<u>es</u> my soul. *R/*

2. He guides me in right paths <u>for</u> his name's sake.
   Even though I walk in <u>the</u> dark valley
   I fear no evil; for you are at <u>my</u> side
   with your rod and your staff that <u>give</u> me courage. *R/*

3. You spread the ta<u>ble</u> before me
   in the sight <u>of</u> my foes;
   you anoint my head <u>with</u> oil;
   my cup <u>over</u>flows. *R/*

4. Only goodness and kindness <u>follow</u> me
   all the days <u>of</u> my life;
   and I shall dwell in the house of <u>the</u> Lord
   for <u>years</u> to come. *R/*

Christ the King A only
Psalm 23:1-2, 2-3, 5-6. R/ v. 1

1. The Lord is my shepherd; I <u>shall</u> not want.
   [omit B, C]
   In verdant pastures he gives <u>me</u> repose. *R/*

2. Beside restful wa<u>ters</u> he leads me;
   he refresh<u>es</u> my soul.
   He guides me in <u>right</u> paths
   for <u>his</u> name's sake. *R/*

3. You spread the ta<u>ble</u> before me
   in the sight <u>of</u> my foes;
   you anoint my head <u>with</u> oil;
   my cup <u>over</u>flows. *R/*

4. Only goodness and kindness <u>follow</u> me
   all the days <u>of</u> my life;
   and I shall dwell in the house of <u>the</u> Lord
   for <u>years</u> to come. *R/*

Text: Refrain, *Lectionary for Mass,* © 1969, 1981, 1997, ICEL; verses, *Lectionary for Mass*/New American Bible, © 1970, 1986, 1991, 1997, 2001, 2010, CCD. All rights reserved.
Music: *The Collegeville Chant Psalter,* © 2019, Order of Saint Benedict, Collegeville, MN. Published and administered by Liturgical Press, Collegeville, MN 56321. All rights reserved.

28th Sunday in Ordinary Time, Year A

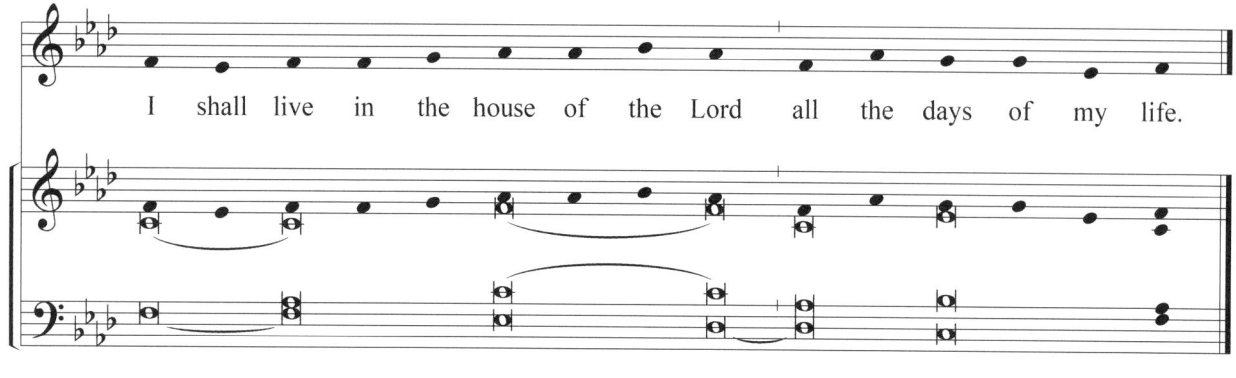

I shall live in the house of the Lord all the days of my life.

Psalm Tone

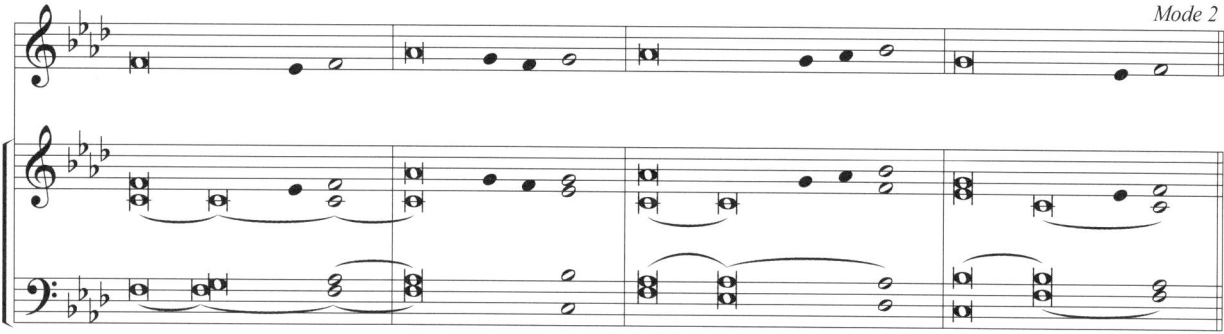

Mode 2

Psalm 23:1-3a, 3b-4, 5, 6. R/ v. 4ab

1. The Lord is my shepherd; I shall <u>not</u> want.
   In verdant pastures he gives <u>me</u> repose;
   beside restful wa<u>ters</u> he leads me;
   he refreshes <u>my</u> soul. *R/*

2. He guides me in right paths for <u>his</u> name's sake.
   Even though I walk in <u>the</u> dark valley
   I fear no evil; for you are <u>at</u> my side
   with your rod and your staff that give <u>me</u> courage. *R/*

3. You spread the table <u>before</u> me
   in the sight <u>of</u> my foes;
   you anoint my <u>head</u> with oil;
   my cup o<u>ver</u>flows. *R/*

4. Only goodness and kindness fol<u>low</u> me
   all the days <u>of</u> my life;
   and I shall dwell in the house <u>of</u> the Lord
   for years <u>to</u> come. *R/*

Text: Refrain, *Lectionary for Mass*, © 1969, 1981, 1997, ICEL; verses, *Lectionary for Mass*/New American Bible, © 1970, 1986, 1991, 1997, 2001, 2010, CCD. All rights reserved.
Music: *The Collegeville Chant Psalter*, © 2019, Order of Saint Benedict, Collegeville, MN. Published and administered by Liturgical Press, Collegeville, MN 56321. All rights reserved.

All Souls, 1st Mass, *alternate response*

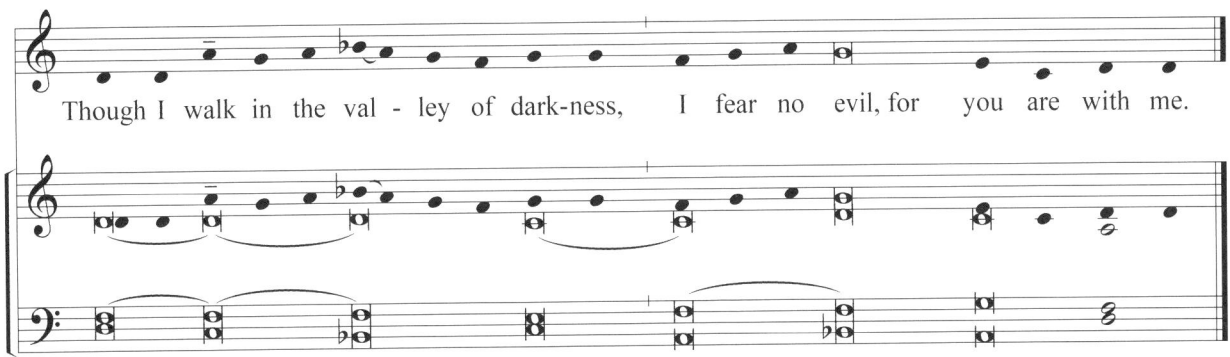

Though I walk in the val-ley of dark-ness, I fear no evil, for you are with me.

Psalm Tone *Mode 1*

Psalm 23:1-3a, 3b-4, 5, 6. R/ v. 4ab

1. The Lord is my shepherd; I <u>shall</u> not want.
   In verdant pastures he gives <u>me</u> repose;
   beside restful waters <u>he</u> leads me;
   he refresh<u>es</u> my soul. *R/*

2. He guides me in right paths <u>for</u> his name's sake.
   Even though I walk in <u>the</u> dark valley
   I fear no evil; for you are at <u>my</u> side
   with your rod and your staff that <u>give</u> me courage. *R/*

3. You spread the ta<u>ble</u> before me
   in the sight <u>of</u> my foes;
   you anoint my head <u>with</u> oil;
   my cup <u>over</u>flows. *R/*

4. Only goodness and kindness <u>follow</u> me
   all the days <u>of</u> my life;
   and I shall dwell in the house of <u>the</u> Lord
   for <u>years</u> to come. *R/*

Text: Refrain, *Lectionary for Mass,* © 1969, 1981, 1997, ICEL; verses, *Lectionary for Mass*/New American Bible, © 1970, 1986, 1991, 1997, 2001, 2010, CCD. All rights reserved.
Music: *The Collegeville Chant Psalter,* © 2019, Order of Saint Benedict, Collegeville, MN. Published and administered by Liturgical Press, Collegeville, MN 56321. All rights reserved.

Psalm 24

4th Sunday of Advent, Year A

Psalm Tone

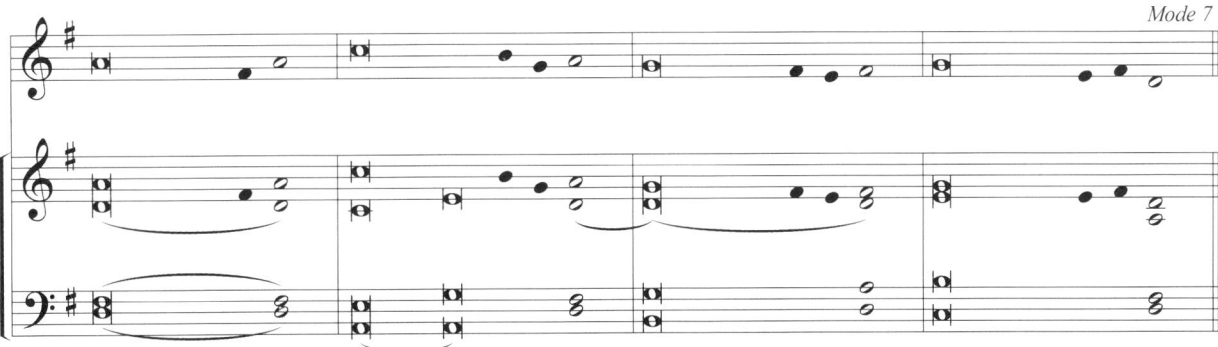

4 Advent A
Psalm 24:1-2, 3-4, 5-6. R/ vv. 7c and 10b; see v. 6

1. The Lord's are the earth and <u>its</u> fullness;
   the world and <u>those</u> who dwell in it.
   For he founded it up<u>on</u> the seas
   and established it up<u>on</u> the rivers. *R/*

2. Who can ascend the mountain of <u>the</u> Lord?
   or who may stand in his <u>holy</u> place?
   One whose hands are sinless, whose <u>heart</u> is clean,
   who desires not <u>what</u> is vain. *R/*

3. He shall receive a blessing from <u>the</u> Lord,
   a reward from <u>God</u> his savior.
   Such is the <u>race</u> that seeks for him,
   that seeks the face of the <u>God</u> of Jacob. *R/*

Text: Refrain, *Lectionary for Mass,* © 1969, 1981, 1997, ICEL; verses, *Lectionary for Mass*/New American Bible, © 1970, 1986, 1991, 1997, 2001, 2010, CCD. All rights reserved.
Music: *The Collegeville Chant Psalter,* © 2019, Order of Saint Benedict, Collegeville, MN. Published and administered by Liturgical Press, Collegeville, MN 56321. All rights reserved.

Presentation of the Lord

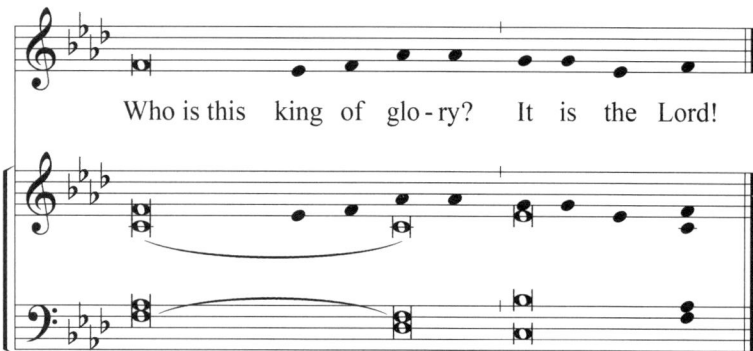

All Saints

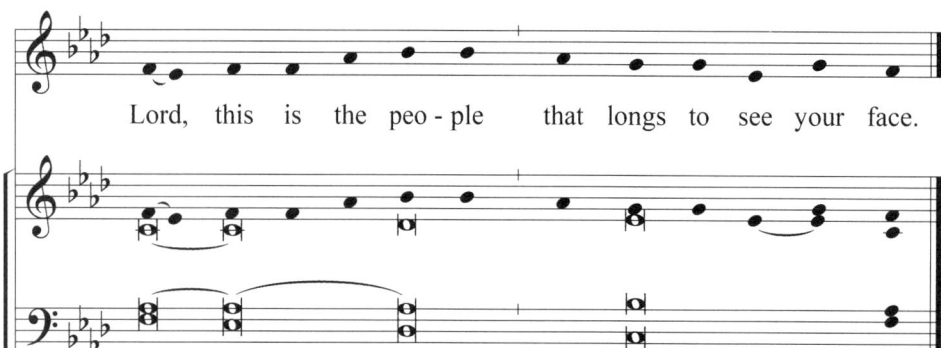

Psalm Tone

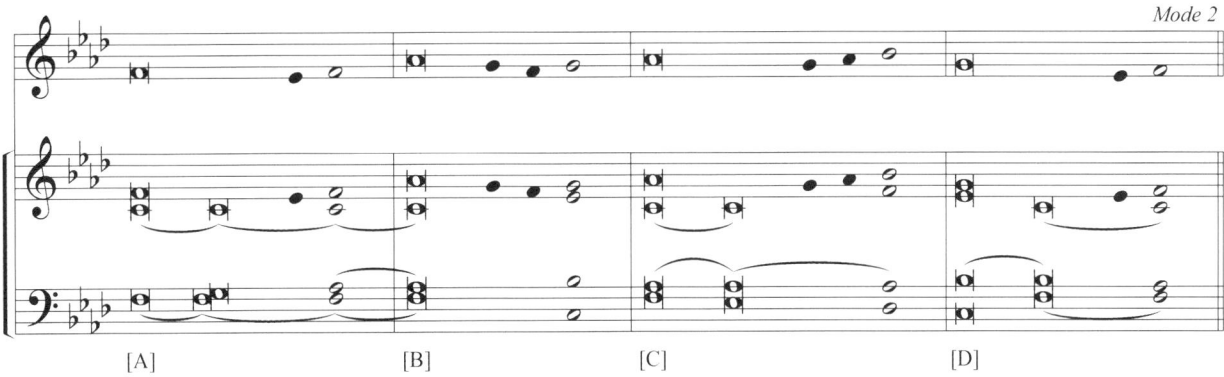

Mode 2

[A]   [B]   [C]   [D]

Presentation
Psalm 24:7, 8, 9, 10. R/ v. 8

1. Lift up, O gates, your lintels;
   reach up, you ancient portals,
   [omit C]
   that the king of glory may come in!   R/

2. Who is this king of glory?
   The Lord, strong and mighty,
   [omit C]
   the Lord, mighty in battle.   R/

3. Lift up, O gates, your lintels;
   reach up, you ancient portals,
   [omit C]
   that the king of glory may come in!   R/

4. Who is this king of glory?
   The Lord of hosts;
   [omit C]
   * he is the king of glory.   R/

All Saints
Psalm 24:1-2, 3-4, 5-6. R/ vv. 7c and 10b; see v. 6

1. The Lord's are the earth and its fullness;
   the world and those who dwell in it.
   For he founded it upon the seas
   and established it upon the rivers.   R/

2. Who can ascend the mountain of the Lord?
   or who may stand in his holy place?
   One whose hands are sinless, whose heart is clean,
   who desires not what is vain.   R/

3. He shall receive a blessing from the Lord,
   a reward from God his savior.
   Such is the race that seeks for him,
   that seeks the face of the God of Jacob.   R/

Text: Refrain, *Lectionary for Mass*, © 1969, 1981, 1997, ICEL; verses, *Lectionary for Mass*/New American Bible, © 1970, 1986, 1991, 1997, 2001, 2010, CCD. All rights reserved.
Music: *The Collegeville Chant Psalter*, © 2019, Order of Saint Benedict, Collegeville, MN. Published and administered by Liturgical Press, Collegeville, MN 56321. All rights reserved.

Psalm 25

26th Sunday in Ordinary Time, Year A

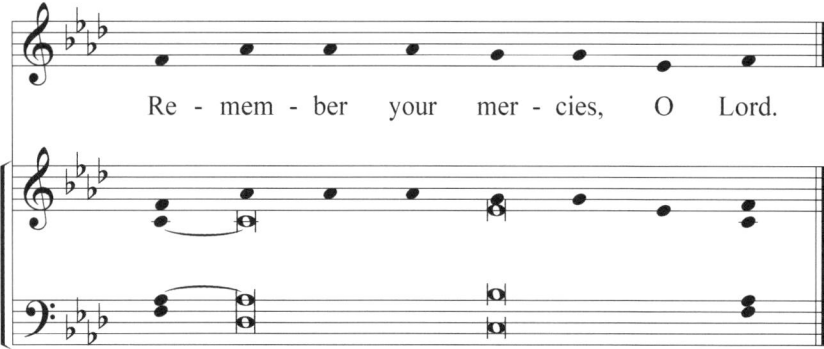

All Souls, 2nd Mass • 1st Sunday of Advent, Year C • Common Advent 1

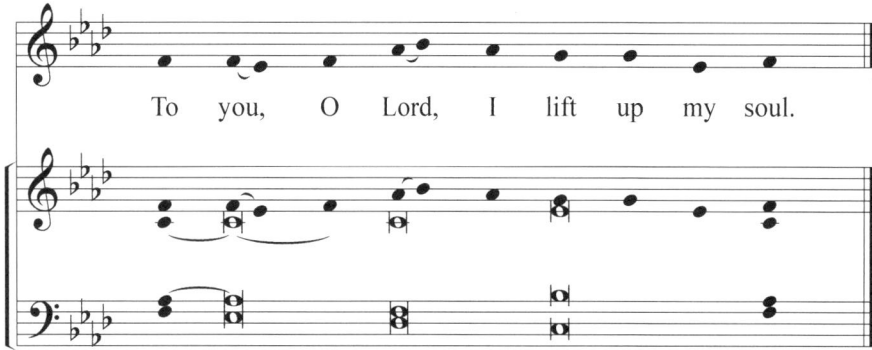

All Souls, 2nd Mass, *alternate response*

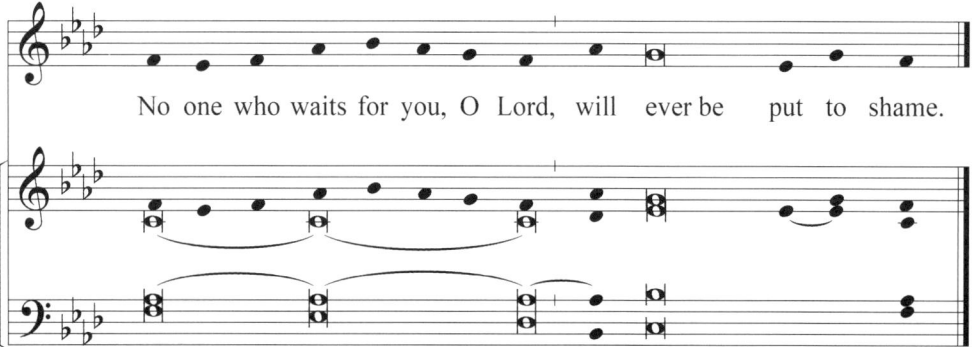

1st Sunday of Lent, Year B

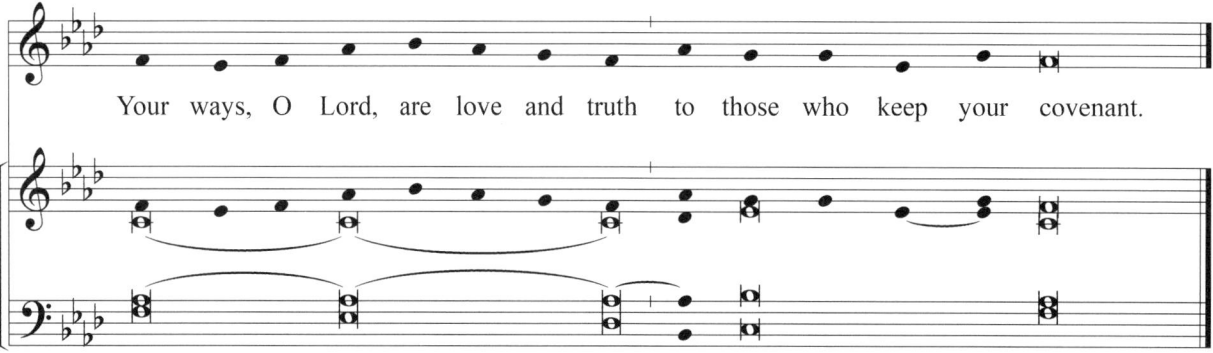

3rd Sunday in Ordinary Time, Year B

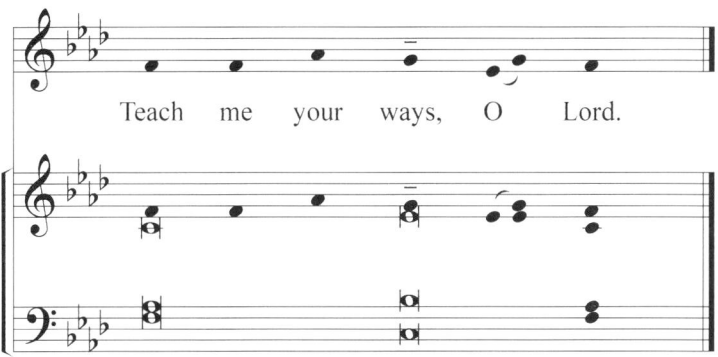

Teach me your ways, O Lord.

Psalm Tone

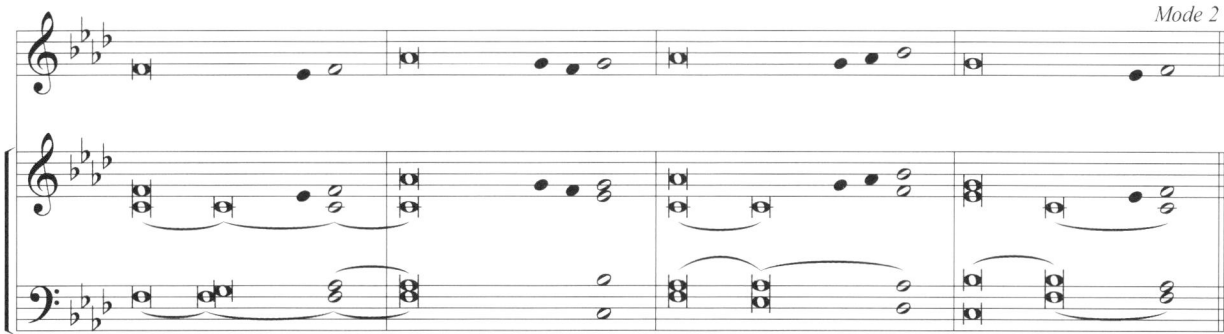

Mode 2

1 Lent B, 3 OT B
Psalm 25:4-5, 6-7, 8-9. R/ cf. v. 10; v. 4a

1. Your ways, O Lord, make known to me;
   teach me your paths,
      guide me in your truth and teach me,
   for you are God my savior. R/

2. Remember that your compassion, O Lord,
   and your love are from of old.
      In your kindness remember me,
   because of your goodness, O Lord. R/

3. Good and upright is the Lord;
   thus he shows sinners the way.
      He guides the humble to justice
   and teaches the humble his way. R/

All Souls 2
Psalm 25:6 and 7b, 17-18, 20-21. R/ v. 1a or v. 3a

*v. 1 = same as **v. 2** above*

2. Relieve the troubles of my heart;
   and bring me out of my distress.
      Put an end to my affliction and my suffering;
   and take away all my sins. R/

26 OT A [1. - 2a. - 3.]

*As at left, with R/ v. 6a, and **v. 2a** instead of **v. 2***

2a. Remember that your compassion, O Lord,
    and your love are from of old.
       The sins of my youth and my frailties remember not;
    in your kindness remember me,
       because of your goodness, O Lord. R/

1 Adv C, Common Advent 1 [1. - 3. - 4.]
Psalm 25:4-5, 8-9, 10, 14. R/ v. 1b

1 Adv C only, *v. 1, as at left, but with line 4*
for you are God my savior, and for you I wait all the day.

v. 3 as at left (omit v. 2)

4. All the paths of the Lord are kindness and constancy
   toward those who keep his covenant and his decrees.
      The friendship of the Lord is with those who fear him,
   and his covenant, for their instruction. R/

3. Preserve my life and rescue me;
   let me not be put to shame, for I take refuge in you.
      Let integrity and uprightness preserve me,
   because I wait for you, O Lord. R/

Text: Refrain, *Lectionary for Mass*, © 1969, 1981, 1997, ICEL; verses, *Lectionary for Mass*/New American Bible, © 1970, 1986, 1991, 1997, 2001, 2010, CCD. All rights reserved.
Music: *The Collegeville Chant Psalter*, © 2019, Order of Saint Benedict, Collegeville, MN. Published and administered by Liturgical Press, Collegeville, MN 56321. All rights reserved.

Psalm 27

3rd Sunday in Ordinary Time, Year A • 2nd Sunday of Lent, Year C • All Souls, 3rd Mass • Common Ordinary Time 2

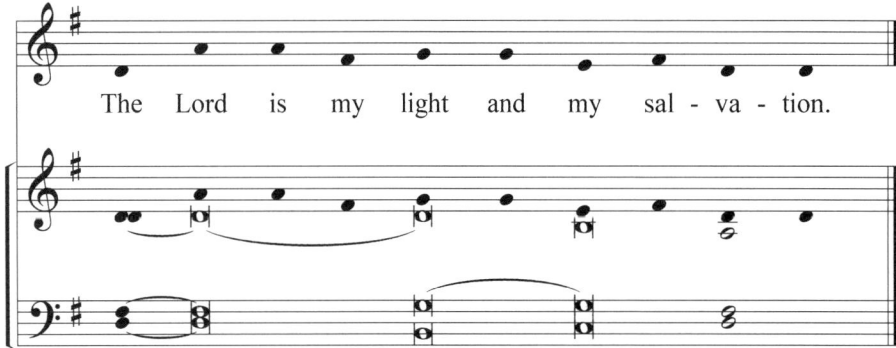

7th Sunday of Easter, Year A • All Souls, 3rd Mass, *alternate response*

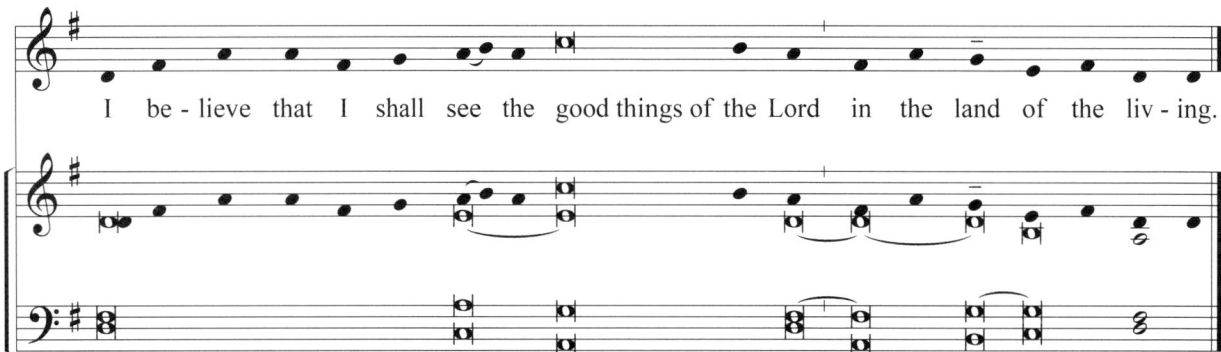

Psalm Tone

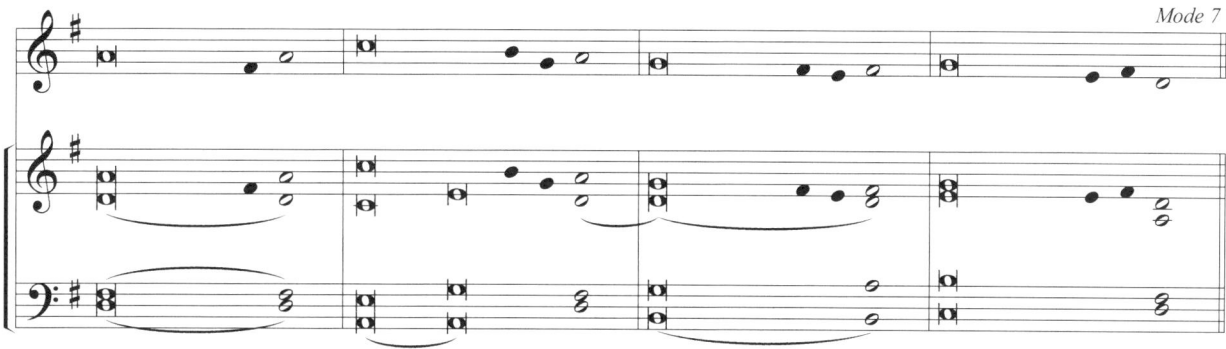

Mode 7

Psalm 27:1, 7-8, 8-9, 13-14. R/ v. 1a; 13

1. The LORD is my light and my <u>sal</u>vation;
   whom <u>should</u> I fear?
   The LORD is <u>my</u> life's refuge;
   of whom should I <u>be</u> afraid? *R/*

Omit on 2 Lent C

2. One thing I ask of the LORD; this <u>I</u> seek:
   to dwell in the house of the LORD all the days <u>of</u> my life,
   that I may gaze on the loveliness <u>of</u> the LORD
   and contem<u>plate</u> his temple. *R/*

7 Easter A and 2 Lent C only

3. Hear, O LORD, the sound of <u>my</u> call;
   have pity on me, and <u>answer</u> me.
   Of you <u>my</u> heart speaks;
            you <u>my</u> glance seeks. *R/*

2 Lent C only

4. Your presence, O LORD, <u>I</u> seek.
   Hide not your <u>face</u> from me;
   do not in anger re<u>pel</u> your servant.
   You are my helper: cast <u>me</u> not off. *R/*

Omit on 7 Easter A

5. I believe that I shall see the bounty of <u>the</u> LORD
   in the land <u>of</u> the living.
   Wait for the <u>LORD</u>, with courage;
   be stouthearted, and wait <u>for</u> the LORD. *R/*

> **7 Easter A**
> 1. - 2. - 3.
> **3 OT A, Common OT 2**
> 1. - 2. - 5.
> **2 Lent C**
> 1. - 3. - 4. - 5.
> **All Souls 3**
> 1. - 2. - 3a. - 5.

All Souls 3 only

3a. Hear, O LORD, the sound of <u>my</u> call;
   have pity on me, and <u>answer</u> me.
   Your presence, O <u>LORD</u>, I seek.
   Hide not your <u>face</u> from me. *R/*

Text: Refrain, *Lectionary for Mass,* © 1969, 1981, 1997, ICEL; verses, *Lectionary for Mass*/New American Bible, © 1970, 1986, 1991, 1997, 2001, 2010, CCD. All rights reserved.
Music: *The Collegeville Chant Psalter,* © 2019, Order of Saint Benedict, Collegeville, MN. Published and administered by Liturgical Press, Collegeville, MN 56321. All rights reserved.

Psalm 29

Baptism of the Lord, Year A

The Lord will bless his peo-ple with peace.

Psalm Tone

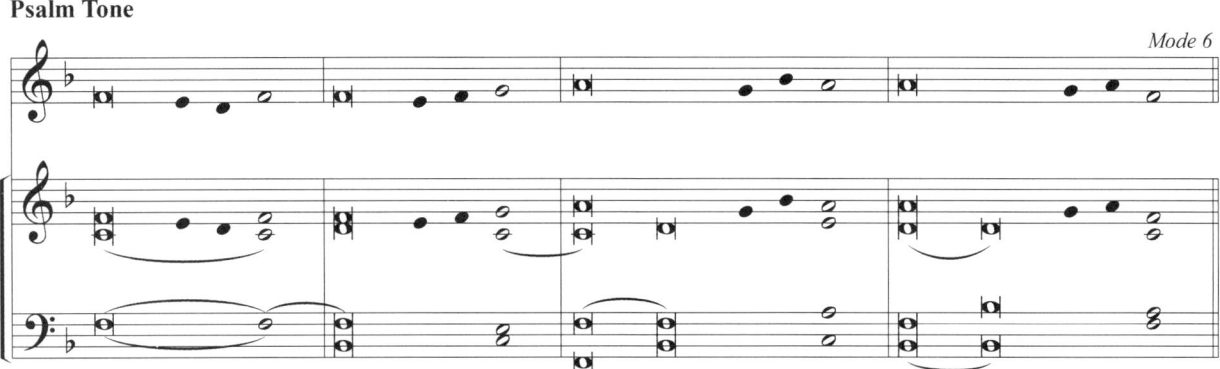

Mode 6

Psalm 29:1-2, 3-4, 3, 9-10. R/ v. 11

1. Give to the LORD, you <u>sons</u> of God,
   give to the LORD glo<u>ry</u> and praise,
   give to the LORD the glory <u>due</u> his name;
   adore the LORD in ho<u>ly</u> attire. *R/*

2. The voice of the LORD is o<u>ver</u> the waters,
   the LORD, o<u>ver</u> vast waters.
   The voice of the <u>LORD</u> is mighty;
   the voice of the LORD <u>is</u> majestic. *R/*

3. The God of <u>glory</u> thunders,
   and in his temple <u>all</u> say, "Glory!"
   The LORD is enthroned a<u>bove</u> the flood;
   the LORD is enthroned as <u>king</u> forever. *R/*

Text: Refrain, *Lectionary for Mass,* © 1969, 1981, 1997, ICEL; verses, *Lectionary for Mass*/New American Bible, © 1970, 1986, 1991, 1997, 2001, 2010, CCD. All rights reserved.
Music: *The Collegeville Chant Psalter,* © 2019, Order of Saint Benedict, Collegeville, MN. Published and administered by Liturgical Press, Collegeville, MN 56321. All rights reserved.

Psalm 30

Easter Vigil 4 • 13th Sunday in Ordinary Time, Year B • 3rd Sunday of Easter, Year C • 10th Sunday in Ordinary Time, Year C

3rd Sunday of Easter, Year C, *alternate response*

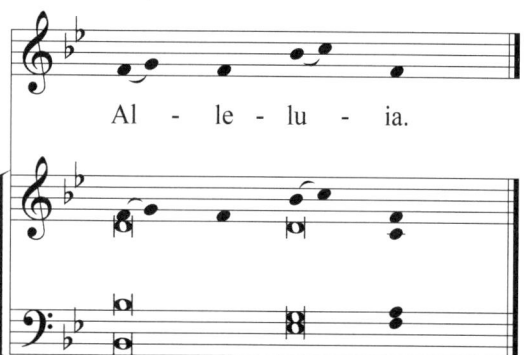

Psalm Tone

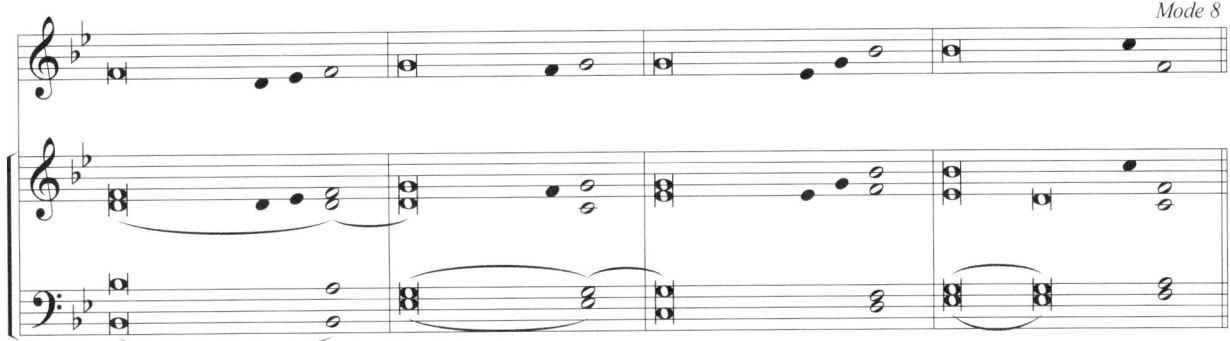

Psalm 30:2, 4, 5-6, 11-12, 13. R/ v. 2a

1. I will extol you, O Lord, for you <u>drew</u> me clear
    and did not let my enemies rejoice o<u>ver</u> me.
    O Lord, you brought me up <u>from</u> the netherworld;
    you preserved me from among those
              going down into <u>the</u> pit. *R/*

2. Sing praise to the Lord, <u>you</u> his faithful ones,
    and give thanks to his ho<u>ly</u> name.
    For his anger lasts but a moment;
    a lifetime, <u>his</u> good will.
    At nightfall, weeping enters in,
    but with the dawn, re<u>joic</u>ing. *R/*

3. Hear, O Lord, and have pi<u>ty</u> on me;
    O Lord, be <u>my</u> helper.
    You changed my mourning <u>in</u>to dancing;
    O Lord, my God, forever will I give <u>you</u> thanks. *R/*

Text: Refrain, *Lectionary for Mass*, © 1969, 1981, 1997, ICEL; verses, *Lectionary for Mass*/New American Bible, © 1970, 1986, 1991, 1997, 2001, 2010, CCD. All rights reserved.
Music: *The Collegeville Chant Psalter*, © 2019, Order of Saint Benedict, Collegeville, MN. Published and administered by Liturgical Press, Collegeville, MN 56321. All rights reserved.

Psalm 31

Good Friday

Psalm Tone

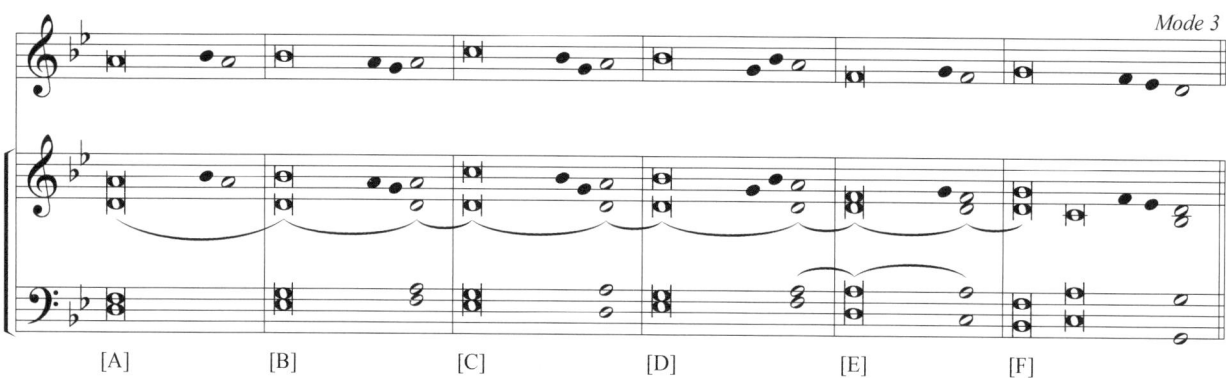

Mode 3

[A] [B] [C] [D] [E] [F]

Psalm 31:2, 6, 12-13, 15-16, 17, 25. R/ Lk 23:46

1. In you, O Lord, I <u>take</u> refuge;
   let me never be <u>put</u> to shame.
   In your justice <u>res</u>cue me.
   Into your hands I com<u>mend</u> my spirit;
   [omit E]
   you will redeem me, O Lord, O <u>faith</u>ful God. *R/*

2. For all my foes I am an object of <u>re</u>proach,
   a laughingstock to my neighbors, and a dread
                                    <u>to</u> my friends;
   they who see me abroad <u>flee</u> from me.
   I am forgotten like the unre<u>mem</u>bered dead;
   [omit E]
   I am like a dish <u>that</u> is broken. *R/*

3. But my trust is in you, <u>O</u> Lord;
   I say, "You <u>are</u> my God.
   [omit C, D]
   In your hands is my destiny; res<u>cue</u> me
   from the clutches of my enemies
                                    <u>and</u> my persecutors." *R/*

4. Let your face shine upon <u>your</u> servant;
   save me <u>in</u> your kindness.
   [omit C, D]
   Take courage and be <u>stout</u>hearted,
   all you who hope <u>in</u> the Lord. *R/*

Text: Refrain, *Lectionary for Mass,* © 1969, 1981, 1997, ICEL; verses, *Lectionary for Mass*/New American Bible, © 1970, 1986, 1991, 1997, 2001, 2010, CCD. All rights reserved.
Music: *The Collegeville Chant Psalter,* © 2019, Order of Saint Benedict, Collegeville, MN. Published and administered by Liturgical Press, Collegeville, MN 56321. All rights reserved.

9th Sunday in Ordinary Time, Year A

Psalm Tone

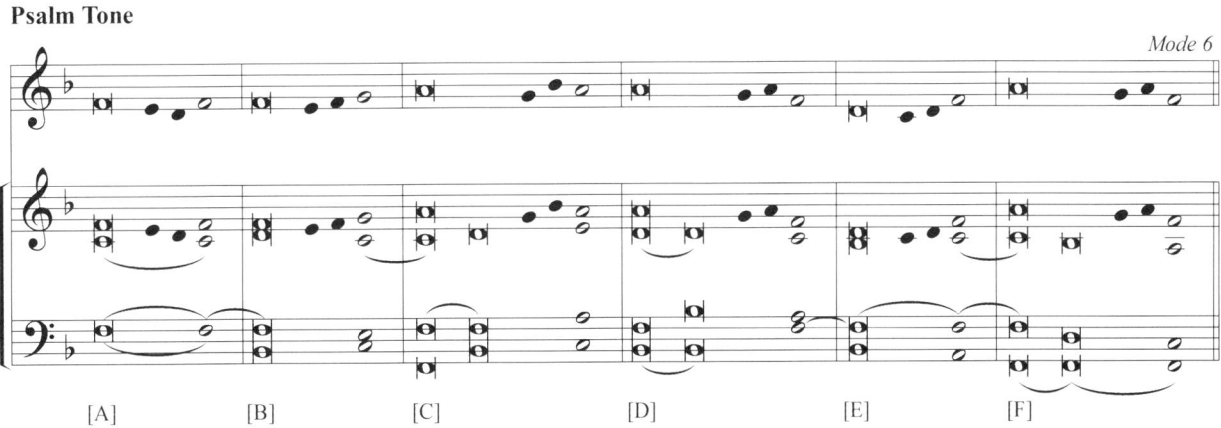

Psalm 31:2-3, 3-4, 17, 25. R/ v. 3b

1. In you, O Lord, I take refuge;
   let me never be put to shame.
   [omit C]
   In your justice rescue me,
   incline your ear to me,
   make haste to deliver me! R/

2. Be my rock of refuge,
   a stronghold to give me safety.
   You are my rock and my fortress;
   [omit D, E]
   for your name's sake you will lead and guide me. R/

3. Let your face shine upon your servant;
   save me in your kindness.
   Take courage and be stouthearted,
   [omit D, E]
   all you who hope in the Lord. R/

Text: Refrain, *Lectionary for Mass*, © 1969, 1981, 1997, ICEL; verses, *Lectionary for Mass*/New American Bible, © 1970, 1986, 1991, 1997, 2001, 2010, CCD. All rights reserved.
Music: *The Collegeville Chant Psalter*, © 2019, Order of Saint Benedict, Collegeville, MN. Published and administered by Liturgical Press, Collegeville, MN 56321. All rights reserved.

Psalm 32

6th Sunday in Ordinary Time, Year B

I turn to you, Lord, in time of trou-ble, and you fill me with the joy of sal-va-tion.

Psalm Tone   Mode 7

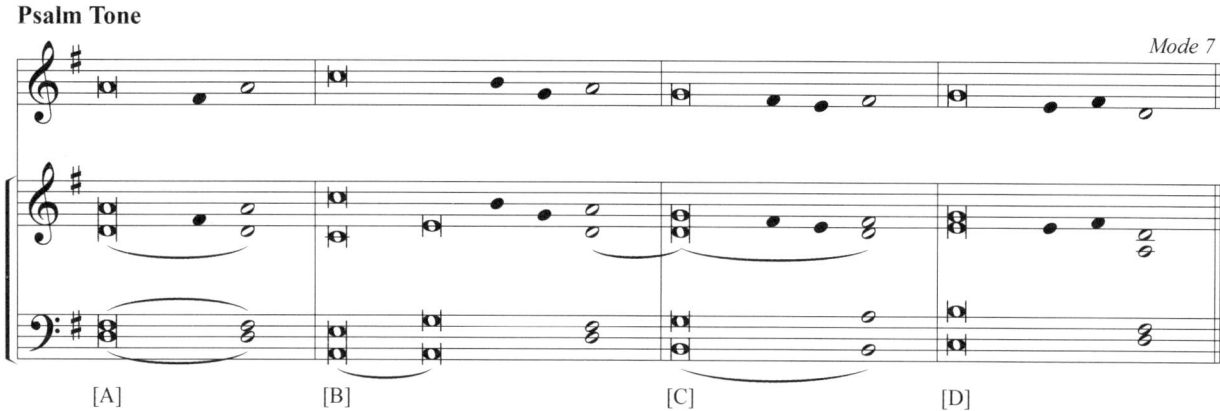

[A]   [B]   [C]   [D]

Psalm 32:1-2, 5, 11. R/ v. 7

6 OT B

1. Blessed is he whose fault is taken <u>a</u>way,
   whose <u>sin</u> is covered.
   Blessed the man to whom the L<small>ORD</small> im<u>putes</u> not guilt,
   in whose spirit there <u>is</u> no guile. *R/*

2. I acknowledged my sin <u>to</u> you,
   my guilt I <u>covered</u> not.
   I said, "I confess my faults <u>to</u> the L<small>ORD</small>,"
   and you took away the guilt <u>of</u> my sin. *R/*

3. Be glad in the L<small>ORD</small> and rejoice, <u>you</u> just;
   [omit B, C]
   exult, all you up<u>right</u> of heart. *R/*

Text: Refrain, *Lectionary for Mass,* © 1969, 1981, 1997, ICEL; verses, *Lectionary for Mass*/New American Bible, © 1970, 1986, 1991, 1997, 2001, 2010, CCD. All rights reserved.
Music: *The Collegeville Chant Psalter,* © 2019, Order of Saint Benedict, Collegeville, MN. Published and administered by Liturgical Press, Collegeville, MN 56321. All rights reserved.

11th Sunday in Ordinary Time, Year C

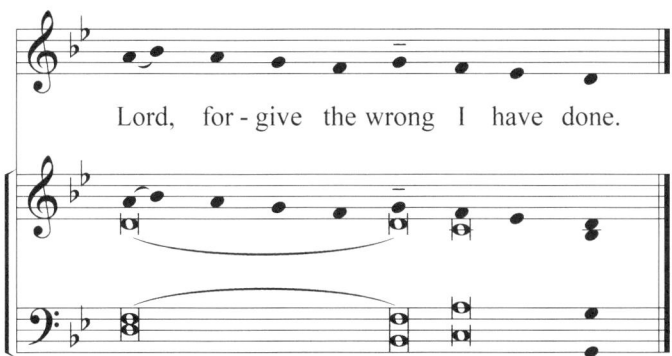

Lord, forgive the wrong I have done.

Psalm Tone

Mode 3

[A] [B] [C] [D]

Psalm 32:1-2, 5, 7, 11. R/ cf. v. 5c

11 OT C

1. Blessed is the one whose fault is taken <u>a</u>way,
    whose <u>sin</u> is covered.
       Blessed the man to whom the L<small>ORD</small> imputes <u>not</u> guilt,
    in whose spirit there <u>is</u> no guile. *R/*

2. I acknowledged my sin <u>to</u> you,
    my guilt I <u>covered</u> not.
       I said, "I confess my faults to <u>the</u> L<small>ORD</small>,"
    and you took away the guilt <u>of</u> my sin. *R/*

3. You are <u>my</u> shelter;
           from distress you <u>will</u> preserve me;
    with glad cries <u>of</u> freedom
              you will <u>ring</u> me round. *R/*

4. Be glad in the L<small>ORD</small> and rejoice, <u>you</u> just;
    [omit B, C]
    exult, all you up<u>right</u> of heart. *R/*

Text: Refrain, *Lectionary for Mass,* © 1969, 1981, 1997, ICEL; verses, *Lectionary for Mass*/New American Bible, © 1970, 1986, 1991, 1997, 2001, 2010, CCD. All rights reserved.
Music: *The Collegeville Chant Psalter,* © 2019, Order of Saint Benedict, Collegeville, MN. Published and administered by Liturgical Press, Collegeville, MN 56321. All rights reserved.

Psalm 33

2nd Sunday of Lent, Year A • 5th Sunday of Easter, Year A •
29th Sunday in Ordinary Time, Year B

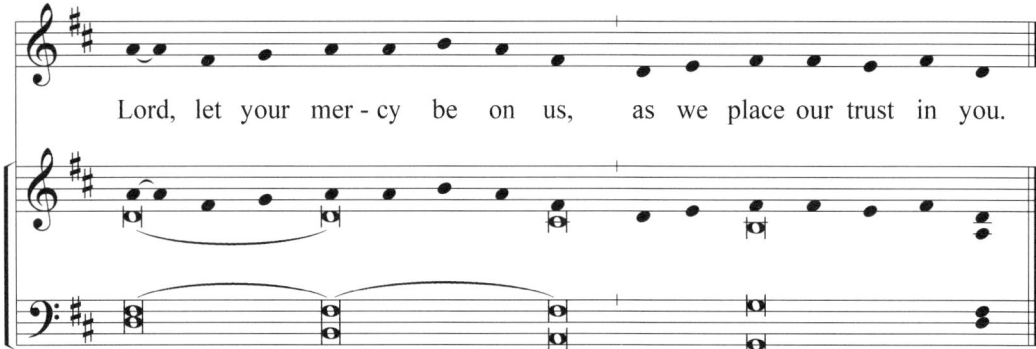

Lord, let your mercy be on us, as we place our trust in you.

Pentecost Vigil 1 • Trinity Sunday, Year B • 19th Sunday in Ordinary Time, Year C

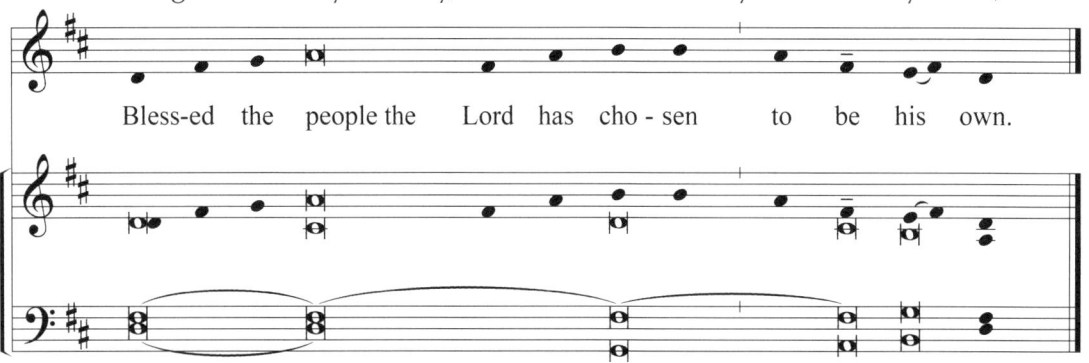

Blessed the people the Lord has chosen to be his own.

Easter Vigil 1, *alternate psalm*

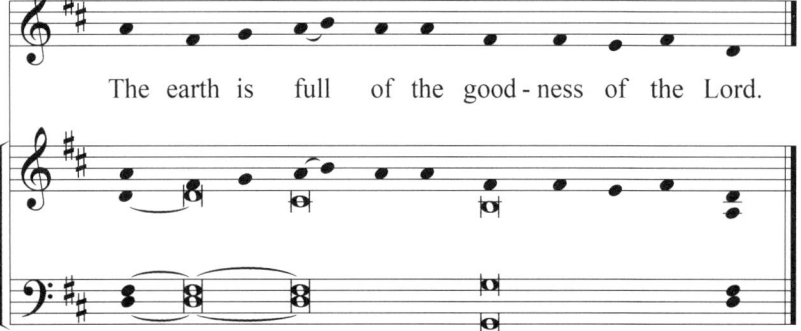

The earth is full of the goodness of the Lord.

5th Sunday of Easter, Year A, *alternate response*

Alleluia.

Psalm Tone

Mode 5

Psalm 33:1-2, 4-5, 6, 7, 8-9, 10-11, 12-13, 14-15, 18-19, 20, 22. R/ v. 22; 12b; 5b

5 Easter A, 19 OT C
1. Exult, you just, in <u>the</u> L<small>ORD</small>;
    praise from the up<u>right</u> is fitting.
    Give thanks to the L<small>ORD</small> <u>on</u> the harp;
    with the ten-stringed lyre <u>chant</u> his praises. *R/*

Easter Vigil 1, alt., 2 Lent A, 5 Easter A, Trinity B, 29 OT B
2. Upright is the word of <u>the</u> L<small>ORD</small>,
    and all his <u>works</u> are trustworthy.
    He loves <u>jus</u>tice and right;
    of the kindness of the L<small>ORD</small> the <u>earth</u> is full. *R/*

Easter Vigil 1, alt.
3. By the word of the L<small>ORD</small> the heavens <u>were</u> made;
    by the breath of his mouth <u>all</u> their host.
    He gathers the waters of the sea as <u>in</u> a flask;
    in cellars he con<u>fines</u> the deep. *R/*

2 Lent A, 5 Easter A, Trinity B, 29 OT B, 19 OT C
4. See, the eyes of the L<small>ORD</small> are upon those <u>who</u> fear him,
    upon those who hope <u>for</u> his kindness,
    to deliver <u>them</u> from death
    and preserve them in <u>spite</u> of famine. *R/*

Easter Vigil 1, alt., 2 Lent A, Trinity B, 29 OT B, 19 OT C
5. Our soul waits for <u>the</u> L<small>ORD</small>,
    who is our help <u>and</u> our shield.
    May your kindness, O L<small>ORD</small>, <u>be</u> upon us
    who have put our <u>hope</u> in you. *R/*

Pentecost Vigil
1a. The L<small>ORD</small> brings to nought the plans
                            <u>of</u> nations;
    he foils the de<u>signs</u> of peoples.
    But the plan of the L<small>ORD</small> <u>stands</u> forever;
    the design of his heart, through all
                            gene<u>ra</u>tions. *R/*

Trinity B
3a. By the word of the L<small>ORD</small> the heavens
                            <u>were</u> made;
    by the breath of his mouth <u>all</u> their host.
    For he spoke, and <u>it</u> was made;
    he commanded, and <u>it</u> stood forth. *R/*

Easter Vigil 1, alt., Pentecost Vigil
4a. Blessed the nation whose God is <u>the</u> L<small>ORD</small>,
    the people he has chosen for his
                            <u>own</u> inheritance.
    From heaven the L<small>ORD</small> looks down;
    he sees <u>all</u> mankind. *R/*

Pentecost Vigil
5a. From his fixed throne he be<u>holds</u>
    all who dwell <u>on</u> the earth,
    He who fashioned the <u>heart</u> of each,
    he who knows <u>all</u> their works. *R/*

Text: Refrain, *Lectionary for Mass*, © 1969, 1981, 1997, ICEL; verses, *Lectionary for Mass/New American Bible*, © 1970, 1986, 1991, 1997, 2001, 2010, CCD. All rights reserved.
Music: *The Collegeville Chant Psalter*, © 2019, Order of Saint Benedict, Collegeville, MN. Published and administered by Liturgical Press, Collegeville, MN 56321. All rights reserved.

2 Lent A, 29 OT B	**Pentecost Vigil**
2. - 4. - 5.	1a. - 4a. - 5a.
Easter Vigil 1, alt.	**Trinity B**
2. - 3. - 4a. - 5.	2. - 3a. - 4. - 5.
5 Easter A	**19 OT C**
1. - 2. - 4. - 5.	1. - 4. - 5.

Psalm 34

19th, 20th, and 21st Sundays in Ordinary Time, Year B • 4th Sunday of Lent, Year C • Common Ordinary Time 3, *alternate response*

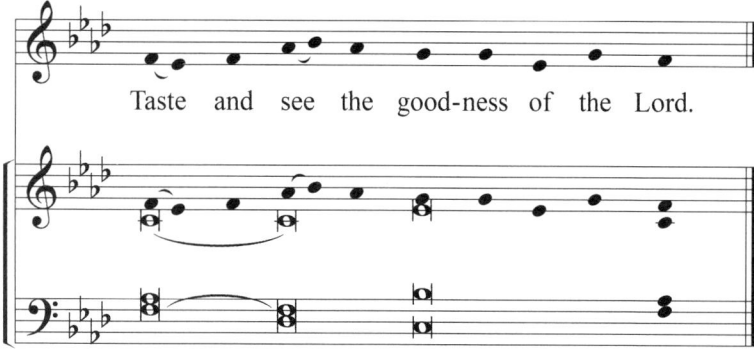

Taste and see the good-ness of the Lord.

Common Ordinary Time 3

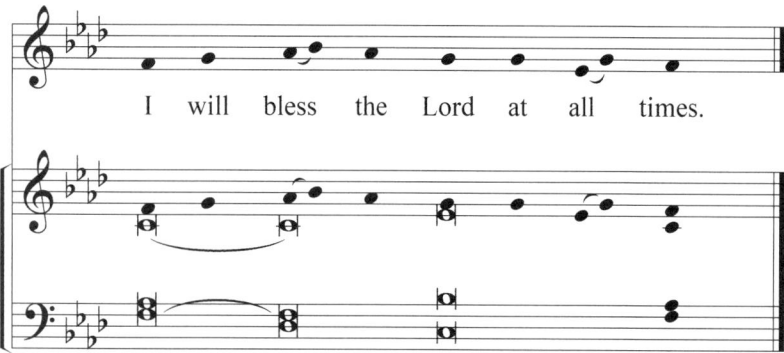

I will bless the Lord at all times.

Saints Peter and Paul Day

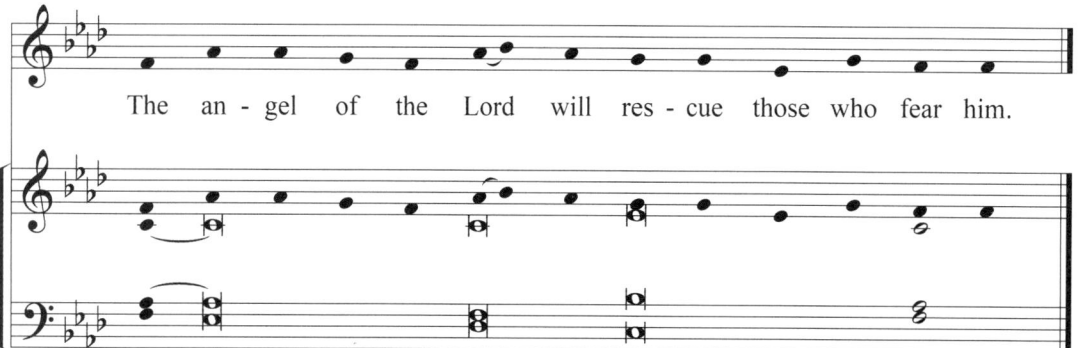

The an-gel of the Lord will res-cue those who fear him.

30th Sunday in Ordinary Time, Year C

The Lord hears the cry of the poor.

Psalm Tone

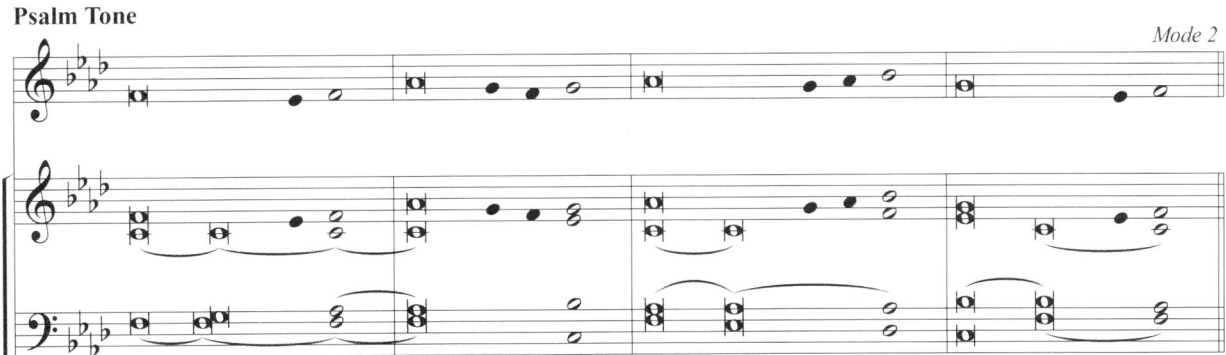

Mode 2

Psalm 34:2-3, 4-5, 6-7, 8-9, 16-17, 18-19, 20-21, 23. R/ vv. 9a; 2; 8b; 7a

1. I will bless the LORD at <u>all</u> times;
   his praise shall be ever <u>in</u> my mouth.
   Let my soul glory <u>in</u> the LORD;
   the lowly will hear me and <u>be</u> glad. *R/*

2. Glorify the LORD <u>with</u> me,
   let us together ex<u>tol</u> his name.
   I sought the LORD, <u>and</u> he answered me
   and delivered me from all <u>my</u> fears. *R/*

3. Look to him that you may be radiant <u>with</u> joy,
   and your faces may not <u>blush</u> with shame.
   When the afflicted man called out, <u>the</u> LORD heard,
   and from all his distress <u>he</u> saved him. *R/*

Omit on 4 Lent C, 20 OT B

4. The angel of the LORD <u>en</u>camps
   around those who fear him <u>and</u> delivers them.
   Taste and see how good <u>the</u> LORD is;
   blessed the man who takes refuge <u>in</u> him. *R/*

Peter and Paul Day, 19 OT B, Common OT 3
   1. - 2. - 3. - 4.
20 OT B
   1. - 2. - 3a.
21 OT B
   1. - 2b. - 3b. - 4b.
30 OT C
   1. - 2c. - 3c.
4 Lent C
   1. - 2. - 3.

---

20 OT B only

3a. Look to him that you may be radiant <u>with</u> joy,
   and your faces may not <u>blush</u> with shame.
   When the poor one called out, <u>the</u> LORD heard,
   and from all his distress <u>he</u> saved him. *R/*

21 OT B only

2b. The LORD has eyes for <u>the</u> just,
   and ears <u>for</u> their cry.
   The LORD con<u>fronts</u> the evildoers,
   to destroy remembrance of them from
                                   <u>the</u> earth. *R/*

3b. When the just cry out, the <u>LORD</u> hears them,
   and from all their dis<u>tress</u> he rescues them.
   The LORD is close to the <u>broken</u>hearted;
   and those who are crushed in spirit <u>he</u> saves. *R/*

4b. Many are the troubles of <u>the</u> just one,
   but out of them all the <u>LORD</u> delivers him;
   he watches over <u>all</u> his bones;
   not one of them shall <u>be</u> broken. *R/*

30 OT C only

2c. The LORD confronts the e<u>vil</u>doers,
   to destroy remembrance of them <u>from</u> the earth.
   When the just cry out, <u>the</u> LORD hears them,
   and from all their distress <u>he</u> rescues them. *R/*

3c. The LORD is close to the broken<u>heart</u>ed;
   and those who are crushed in <u>spir</u>it he saves.
   The LORD redeems the lives <u>of</u> his servants;
   no one incurs guilt who takes refuge <u>in</u> him. *R/*

Text: Refrain, *Lectionary for Mass,* © 1969, 1981, 1997, ICEL; verses, *Lectionary for Mass*/New American Bible, © 1970, 1986, 1991, 1997, 2001, 2010, CCD. All rights reserved.
Music: *The Collegeville Chant Psalter,* © 2019, Order of Saint Benedict, Collegeville, MN. Published and administered by Liturgical Press, Collegeville, MN 56321. All rights reserved.

Psalm 40

2nd Sunday in Ordinary Time, Year A • 2nd Sunday in Ordinary Time, Year B • Annunciation

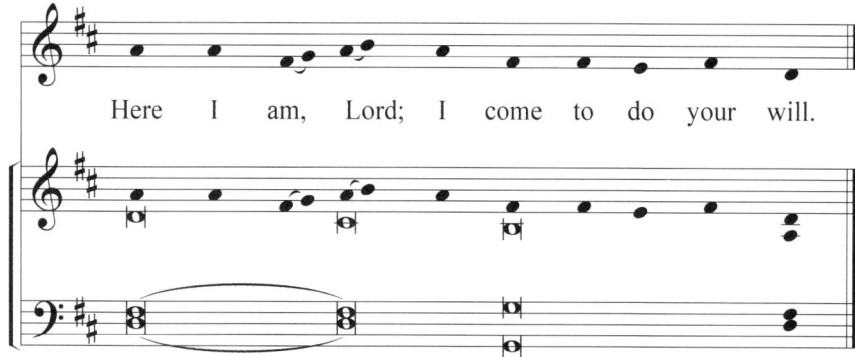

Psalm Tone

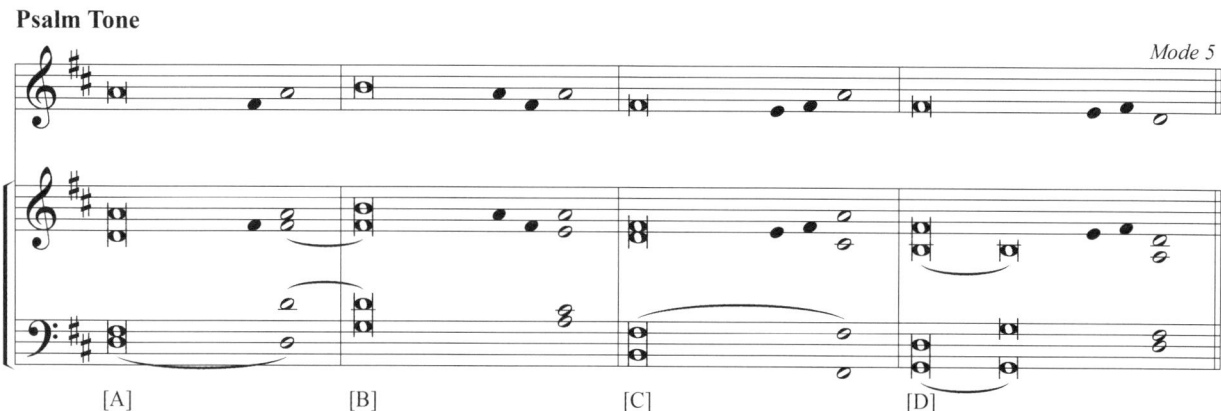

[A]   [B]   [C]   [D]

Psalm 40:2, 4, 7-8, 8-9, 10. R/ vv. 8a and 9a

2 OT A and 2 OT B only

1. I have waited, waited for <u>the</u> L<small>ORD</small>,
   and he stooped toward me and <u>heard</u> my cry.
   And he put a new song in<u>to</u> my mouth,
   a hymn <u>to</u> our God. *R/*

2. Sacrifice or offering <u>you</u> wished not,
   but ears open to obedi<u>ence</u> you gave me.
   Holocausts or sin-offer<u>ings</u> you sought not;
   then said I, "Be<u>hold</u> I come." *R/*

3. "In the written scroll it is prescribed <u>for</u> me,
   to do your will, O my God, is <u>my</u> delight,
   [omit C]
   and your law is with<u>in</u> my heart!" *R/*

4. I announced your justice in the vast <u>as</u>sembly;
   [omit B, C]
   I did not restrain my lips, as you, <u>O</u> L<small>ORD</small>, know. *R/*

| 2 OT A, 2 OT B |
| 1. - 2. - 3. - 4. |
| **Annunciation** |
| 2. - 3. - 4. - 5. |

Annunciation only

5. Your justice I kept not hid within <u>my</u> heart;
   your faithfulness and your salvation <u>I</u> have spoken of;
   I have made no secret of your kindness <u>and</u> your truth
   in the <u>vast</u> assembly. *R/*

Text: Refrain, *Lectionary for Mass*, © 1969, 1981, 1997, ICEL; verses, *Lectionary for Mass/New American Bible*, © 1970, 1986, 1991, 1997, 2001, 2010, CCD. All rights reserved.
Music: *The Collegeville Chant Psalter*, © 2019, Order of Saint Benedict, Collegeville, MN. Published and administered by Liturgical Press, Collegeville, MN 56321. All rights reserved.

20th Sunday in Ordinary Time, Year C

Lord, come to my aid!

Psalm Tone

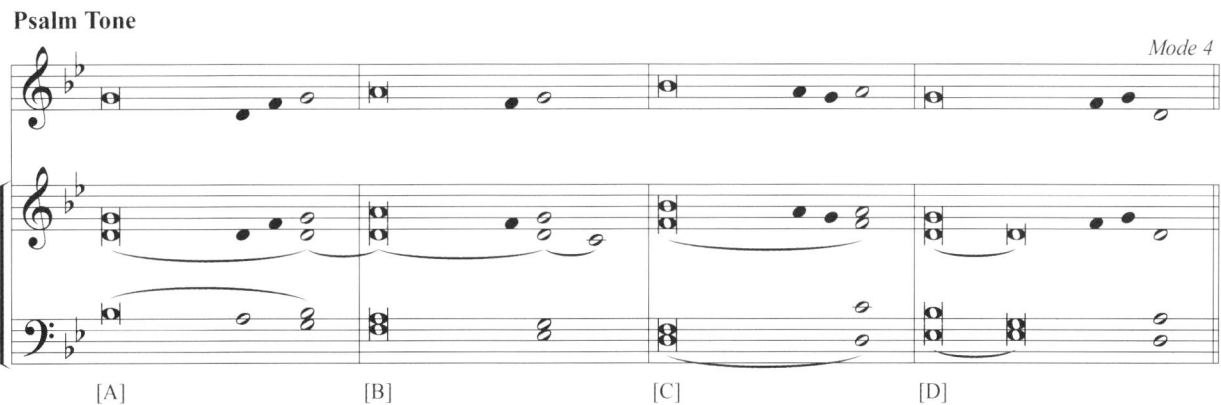

Mode 4

[A]   [B]   [C]   [D]

Psalm 40:2, 3, 4, 18. R/ v. 14b

1. I have waited, waited <u>for</u> the Lord,
   [omit B, C]
   and he <u>stooped</u> toward me. *R/*

2. The Lord <u>heard</u> my cry.
   He drew me out of the pit of destruction, out of the mud of <u>the</u> swamp;
   he set my feet up<u>on</u> a crag;
   he made <u>firm</u> my steps. *R/*

3. And he put a new song in<u>to</u> my mouth,
   a hymn to <u>our</u> God.
   Many shall look <u>on</u> in awe
   and trust <u>in</u> the Lord. *R/*

4. Though I am afflic<u>ted</u> and poor,
   yet the Lord thinks <u>of</u> me.
   You are my help and <u>my</u> deliverer;
   O my God, <u>hold</u> not back! *R/*

Text: Refrain, *Lectionary for Mass,* © 1969, 1981, 1997, ICEL; verses, *Lectionary for Mass*/New American Bible, © 1970, 1986, 1991, 1997, 2001, 2010, CCD. All rights reserved.
Music: *The Collegeville Chant Psalter,* © 2019, Order of Saint Benedict, Collegeville, MN. Published and administered by Liturgical Press, Collegeville, MN 56321. All rights reserved.

Psalm 41

7th Sunday in Ordinary Time, Year B

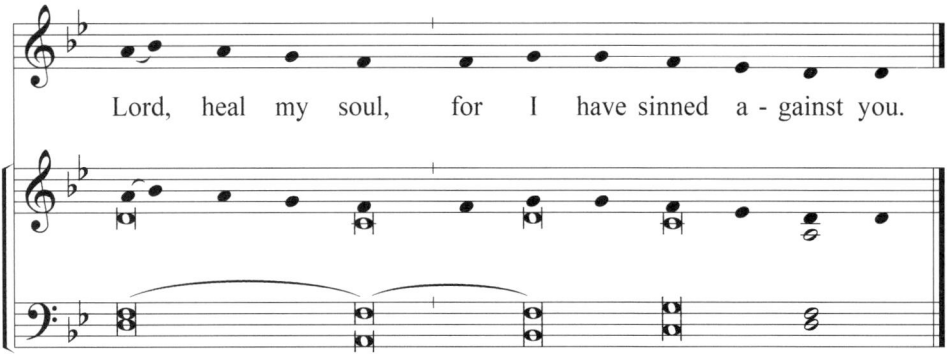

Lord, heal my soul, for I have sinned a-gainst you.

Psalm Tone

Mode 3

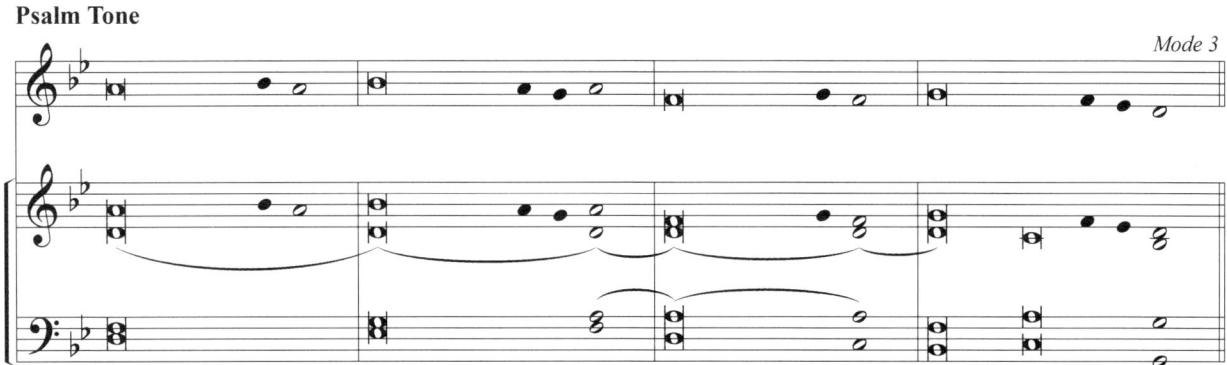

Psalm 41:2-3, 4-5, 13-14. R/ v. 5b

1. Blessed is the one who has regard for the lowly and <u>the</u> poor;
   in the day of misfortune the Lord will de<u>liv</u>er him.
   The Lord will keep and preserve him; and make him blessed <u>on</u> earth,
   and not give him over to the will <u>of</u> his enemies. *R/*

2. The Lord will help him on <u>his</u> sickbed,
   he will take away all his ailment when <u>he</u> is ill.
   Once I said, "O Lord, have pity <u>on</u> me;
   heal me, though I have <u>sinned</u> against you." *R/*

3. But because of my integrity you <u>sustain</u> me
   and let me stand before <u>you</u> forever.
   Blessed be the Lord, the God <u>of</u> Israel,
   from all eternity. A<u>men</u>. Amen. *R/*

Text: Refrain, *Lectionary for Mass*, © 1969, 1981, 1997, ICEL; verses, *Lectionary for Mass*/New American Bible, © 1970, 1986, 1991, 1997, 2001, 2010, CCD. All rights reserved.
Music: *The Collegeville Chant Psalter*, © 2019, Order of Saint Benedict, Collegeville, MN. Published and administered by Liturgical Press, Collegeville, MN 56321. All rights reserved.

Psalm 42–43

Easter Vigil 7

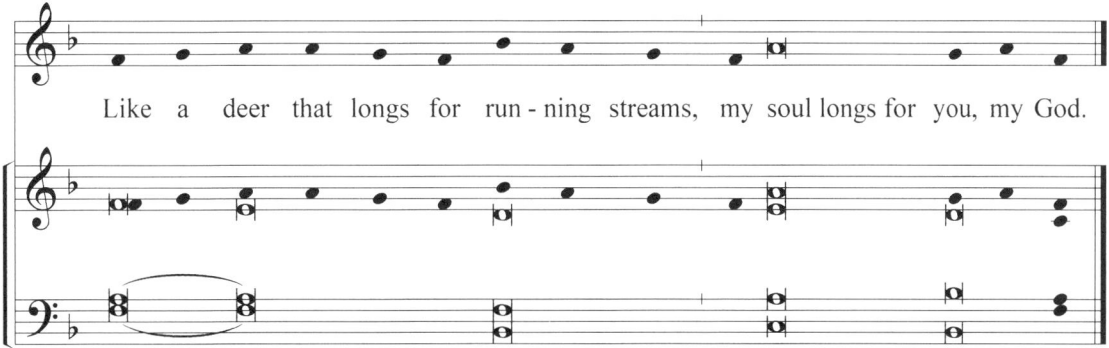

Like a deer that longs for running streams, my soul longs for you, my God.

Psalm Tone

Mode 6

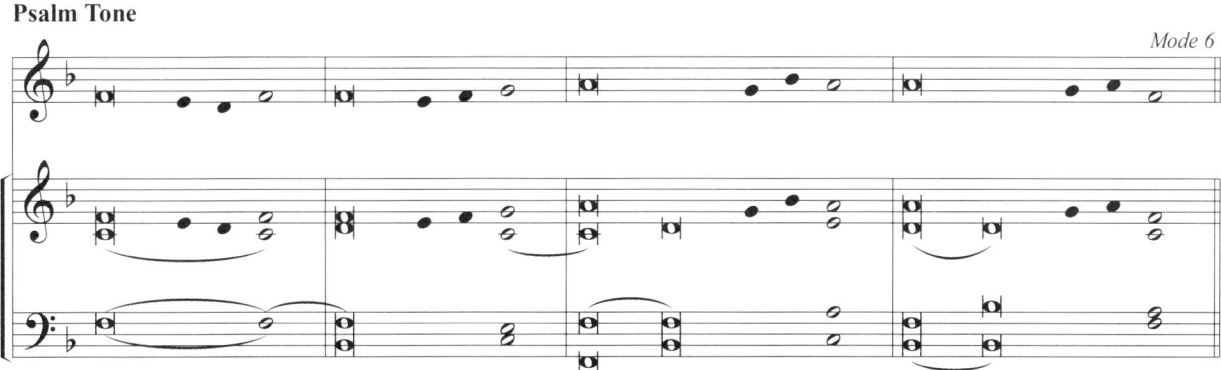

Psalm 42:3, 5; 43:3, 4. R/ 42:2

1. Athirst is my soul
        for God, the living God.
    When shall I go
        and behold the face of God? *R/*

2. I went with the throng
    and led them in procession to the house of God,
    amid loud cries of joy and thanksgiving,
    with the multitude keeping festival. *R/*

3. Send forth your light and your fidelity;
    they shall lead me on
    and bring me to your holy mountain,
    to your dwelling-place. *R/*

4. Then will I go in to the altar of God,
    the God of my gladness and joy;
    then will I give you thanks upon the harp,
    O God, my God! *R/*

Text: Refrain, *Lectionary for Mass*, © 1969, 1981, 1997, ICEL; verses, *Lectionary for Mass*/New American Bible, © 1970, 1986, 1991, 1997, 2001, 2010, CCD. All rights reserved.
Music: *The Collegeville Chant Psalter*, © 2019, Order of Saint Benedict, Collegeville, MN. Published and administered by Liturgical Press, Collegeville, MN 56321. All rights reserved.

Psalm 45

Assumption Day

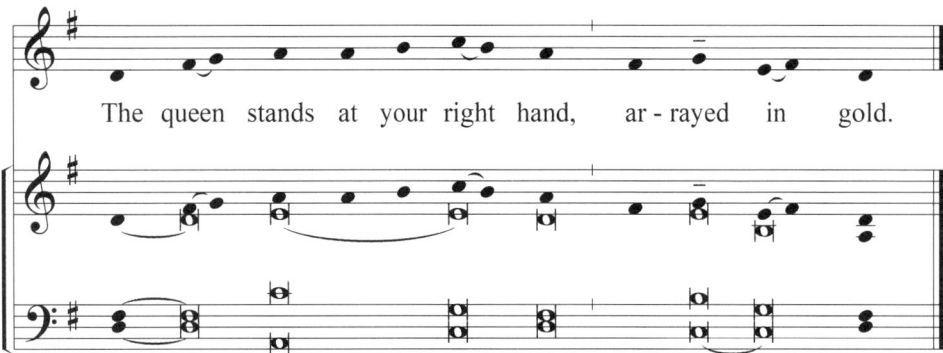

Psalm Tone

Psalm 45:10bc, 11, 12ab, 16. R/ v. 10bc

1. The queen takes her place at <u>your</u> right hand
   in <u>gold</u> of Ophir. *R/*

2. Hear, O daughter, and see; turn <u>your</u> ear,
   forget your people and your <u>father</u>'s house. *R/*

3. So shall the king desire <u>your</u> beauty;
   for he <u>is</u> your lord. *R/*

4. They are borne in with gladness <u>and</u> joy;
   they enter the palace <u>of</u> the king. *R/*

Text: Refrain, *Lectionary for Mass,* © 1969, 1981, 1997, ICEL; verses, *Lectionary for Mass*/New American Bible, © 1970, 1986, 1991, 1997, 2001, 2010, CCD. All rights reserved.
Music: *The Collegeville Chant Psalter,* © 2019, Order of Saint Benedict, Collegeville, MN. Published and administered by Liturgical Press, Collegeville, MN 56321. All rights reserved.

Psalm 46

49

Dedication of the Lateran Basilica • Anniversary of the Dedication of a Church, 2nd option

The waters of the river gladden the city of God,
* There is a stream whose runlets
the holy dwelling of the Most High!

Psalm Tone

Mode 8

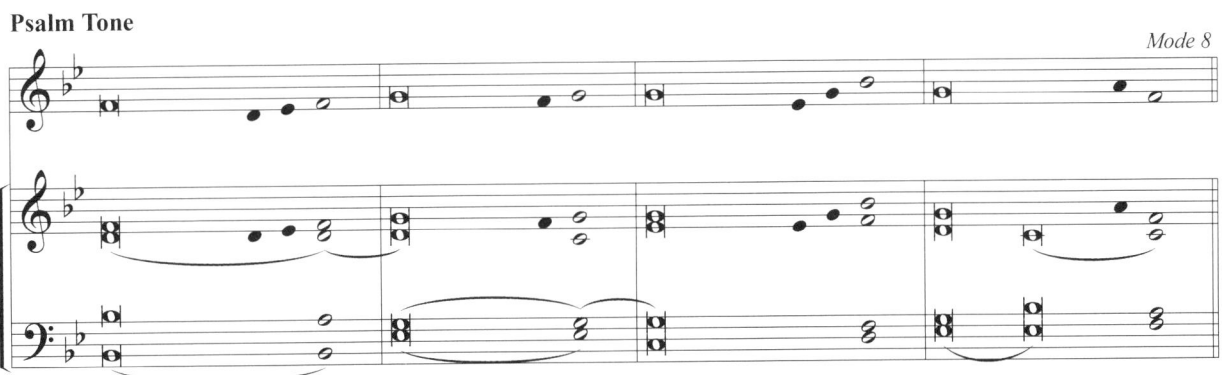

Psalm 46:2-3, 5-6, 8-9. R/ v. 5

1. God is our refuge <u>and</u> our strength,
    an ever-present help in <u>distress</u>.
      Therefore, we fear not, though the <u>earth</u> be shaken
      and mountains plunge into the depths of <u>the</u> sea. R/

2. There is a stream whose runlets gladden
                                the ci<u>ty</u> of God,
    the holy dwelling of the <u>Most</u> High.
    God is in its midst; it shall not <u>be</u> disturbed;
    God will help it at the break <u>of</u> dawn. R/

3. The Lord of <u>hosts</u> is with us;
    our stronghold is the God of Jacob.
      Come! behold the deeds <u>of</u> the Lord,
      the astounding things he has wrought <u>on</u> earth. R/

<sub>Text: Refrain, *Lectionary for Mass*, © 1969, 1981, 1997, ICEL; verses, *Lectionary for Mass*/New American Bible, © 1970, 1986, 1991, 1997, 2001, 2010, CCD. All rights reserved.
Music: *The Collegeville Chant Psalter*, © 2019, Order of Saint Benedict, Collegeville, MN. Published and administered by Liturgical Press, Collegeville, MN 56321. All rights reserved.</sub>

* *Lectionary wording of the response for the Anniversary of Dedication.*
The wording for the Lateran Basilica seems preferable.

Psalm 47

Ascension Vigil and Day • Common Ascension

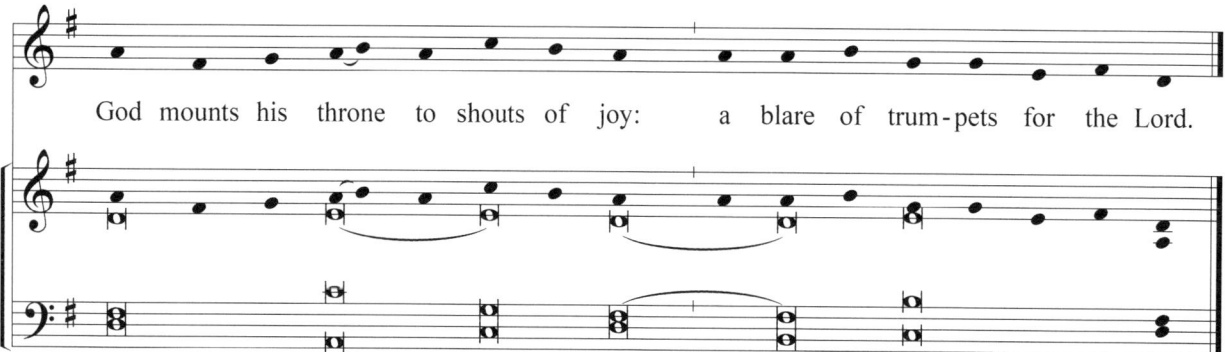

God mounts his throne to shouts of joy: a blare of trumpets for the Lord.

Ascension Vigil and Day, *alternate response*

Alleluia.

Psalm Tone

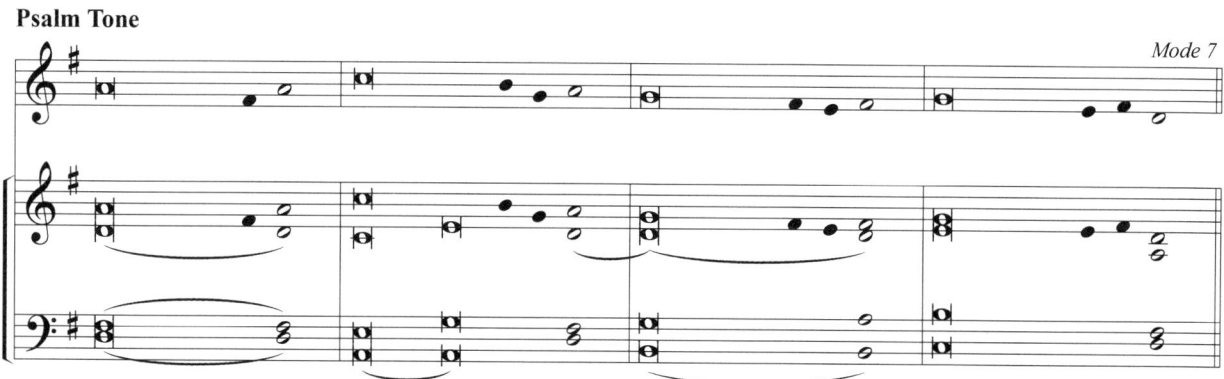

Mode 7

Psalm 47:2-3, 6-7, 8-9. R/ v. 6

1. All you peoples, clap <u>your</u> hands,
   shout to God with <u>cries</u> of gladness,
   for the Lord, the Most <u>High</u>, the awesome,
   is the great king over <u>all</u> the earth. *R/*

2. God mounts his throne amid shouts <u>of</u> joy;
   the Lord, amid <u>trumpet</u> blasts.
   Sing praise to <u>God</u>, sing praise;
   sing praise to our <u>king</u>, sing praise. *R/*

3. For king of all the earth <u>is</u> God;
   sing <u>hymns</u> of praise.
   God reigns o<u>ver</u> the nations,
   God sits upon his <u>holy</u> throne. *R/*

Text: Refrain, *Lectionary for Mass*, © 1969, 1981, 1997, ICEL; verses, *Lectionary for Mass*/New American Bible, © 1970, 1986, 1991, 1997, 2001, 2010, CCD. All rights reserved.
Music: *The Collegeville Chant Psalter*, © 2019, Order of Saint Benedict, Collegeville, MN. Published and administered by Liturgical Press, Collegeville, MN 56321. All rights reserved.

Psalm 50

10th Sunday in Ordinary Time, Year A

Psalm Tone Mode 3

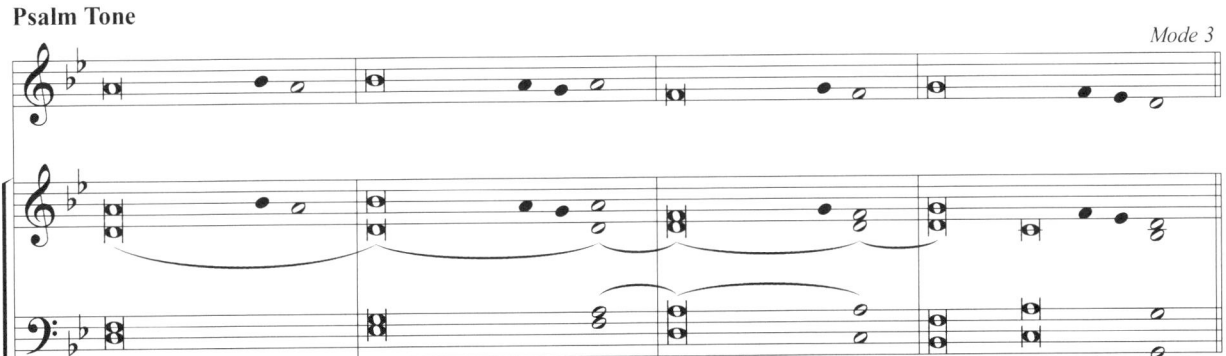

Psalm 50:1, 8, 12-13, 14-15. R/ v. 23b

1. God the LORD has spoken and summoned <u>the</u> earth,
   from the rising of the sun <u>to</u> its setting.
   "Not for your sacrifices do I <u>re</u>buke you,
   for your holocausts are be<u>fore</u> me always." *R/*

2. "If I were hungry, I would <u>not</u> tell you,
   for mine are the world <u>and</u> its fullness.
   Do I eat the flesh <u>of</u> strong bulls,
   or is the blood of <u>goats</u> my drink?" *R/*

3. "Offer to God praise as <u>your</u> sacrifice
   and fulfill your vows to <u>the</u> Most High;
   then call upon me in time of <u>dis</u>tress;
   I will rescue you, and you shall glo<u>ri</u>fy me." *R/*

Text: Refrain, *Lectionary for Mass*, © 1969, 1981, 1997, ICEL; verses, *Lectionary for Mass*/New American Bible, © 1970, 1986, 1991, 1997, 2001, 2010, CCD. All rights reserved.
Music: *The Collegeville Chant Psalter*, © 2019, Order of Saint Benedict, Collegeville, MN. Published and administered by Liturgical Press, Collegeville, MN 56321. All rights reserved.

Psalm 51

Ash Wednesday • 1st Sunday of Lent, Year A • Common Lent 1

Be merciful, O Lord, for we have sinned.

5th Sunday of Lent, Year B • Easter Vigil 7, *alternate psalm*

Create a clean heart in me, O God.

24th Sunday in Ordinary Time, Year C

I will rise and go to my father.

Psalm Tone

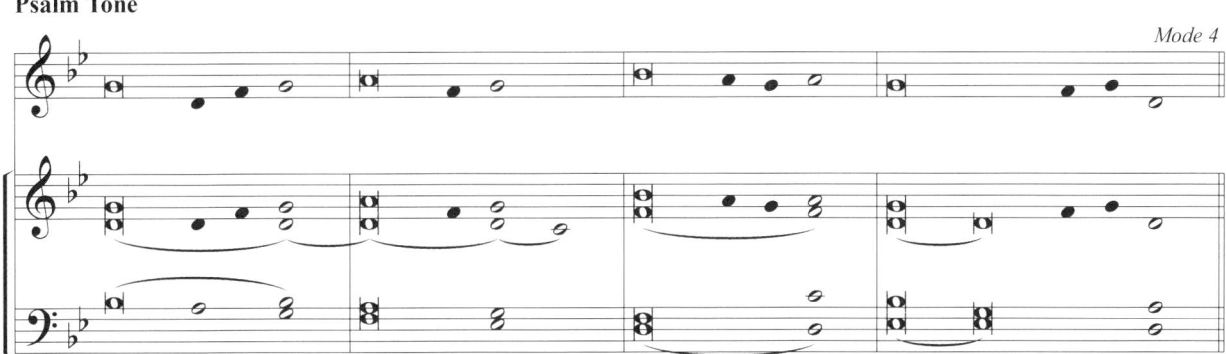

Psalm 51:3-4, 5-6ab, 12-13, 14, 17, 18-19. R/ see v. 3a; 12a; Lk 15:18

Omit on Easter Vigil 7, alt.
1. Have mercy on me, O God, in your goodness;
   in the greatness of your compassion wipe out my offense.
   Thoroughly wash me from my guilt;
   and of my sin cleanse me. *R/*

Omit on Easter Vigil 7, alt., 5 Lent B, 24 OT C
2. For I acknowledge my offense,
   and my sin is before me always.
   "Against you only have I sinned,
   and done what is evil in your sight." *R/*

3. A clean heart create for me, O God,
   and a steadfast spirit renew within me.
   Cast me not out from your presence,
   and your Holy Spirit take not from me. *R/*

| **Ash Wednesday, 1 Lent A, Common Lent 1** |
| 1. - 2. - 3. - 4. |
| **Easter Vigil 7, alt.** |
| 3. - 4a. - 5. |
| **5 Lent B** |
| 1. - 3. - 4a. |
| **24 OT C** |
| 1. - 3. - 5a. |

Omit on 24 OT C
4. Give me back the joy of your salvation,
   and a willing spirit sustain in me.
   O Lord, open my lips,
   and my mouth shall proclaim your praise. *R/*

Easter Vigil 7, alt., 5 Lent B only
4a. Give me back the joy of your salvation,
    and a willing spirit sustain in me.
    I will teach transgressors your ways,
    and sinners shall return to you. *R/*

Easter Vigil 7, alt., only
5. For you are not pleased with sacrifices;
   should I offer a holocaust, you would not accept it.
   My sacrifice, O God, is a contrite spirit;
   a heart contrite and humbled, O God, you will not spurn. *R/*

24 OT C only
5a. O Lord, open my lips,
    and my mouth shall proclaim your praise.
    My sacrifice, O God, is a contrite spirit;
    a heart contrite and humbled, O God, you will not spurn. *R/*

Text: Refrain, *Lectionary for Mass*, © 1969, 1981, 1997, ICEL; verses, *Lectionary for Mass*/New American Bible, © 1970, 1986, 1991, 1997, 2001, 2010, CCD. All rights reserved.
Music: *The Collegeville Chant Psalter*, © 2019, Order of Saint Benedict, Collegeville, MN. Published and administered by Liturgical Press, Collegeville, MN 56321. All rights reserved.

Psalm 54

25th Sunday in Ordinary Time, Year B

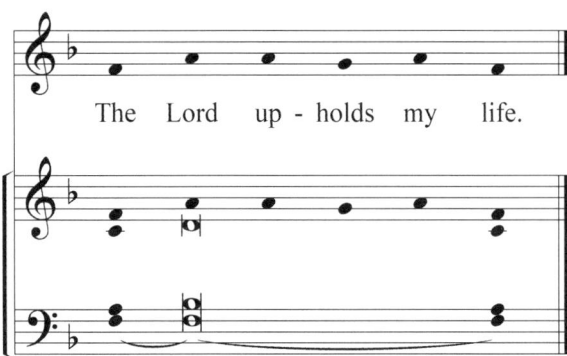

The Lord up-holds my life.

Psalm Tone　　　　　　　　　　　　　　　　　　　　　　　　　　　　　　　　　　Mode 6

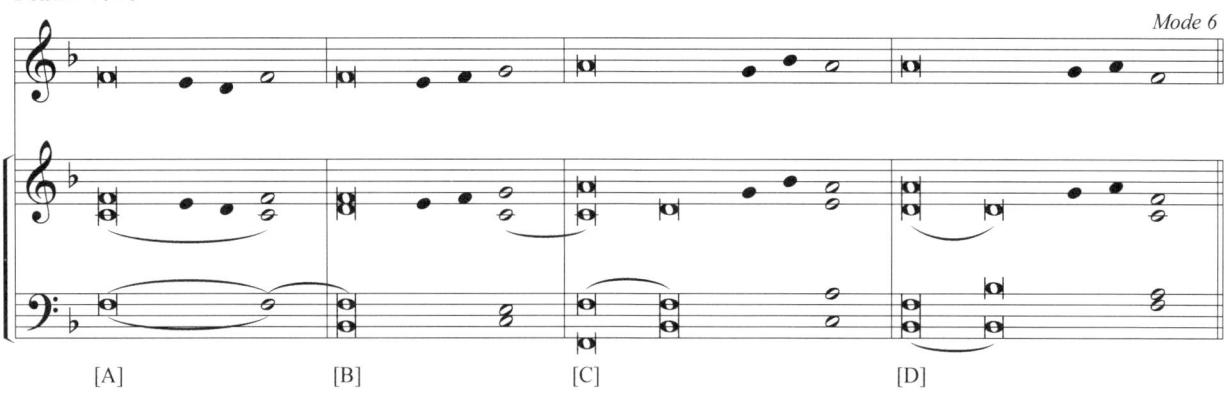

[A]　　　[B]　　　[C]　　　[D]

Psalm 54:3-4, 5, 6-8. R/ v. 6b

1. O God, by <u>your</u> name save me,
   and by your might de<u>fend</u> my cause.
   O God, <u>hear</u> my prayer;
   hearken to the words <u>of</u> my mouth.　*R/*

2. For the haughty men have risen <u>up</u> against me,
   the ruthless <u>seek</u> my life;
   [omit C]
   they set not God be<u>fore</u> their eyes.　*R/*

3. Behold, God <u>is</u> my helper;
   the Lord sus<u>tains</u> my life.
   Freely will I of<u>fer</u> you sacrifice;
   I will praise your name, O L<small>ORD</small>, <u>for</u> its goodness.　*R/*

Text: Refrain, *Lectionary for Mass,* © 1969, 1981, 1997, ICEL; verses, *Lectionary for Mass*/New American Bible, © 1970, 1986, 1991, 1997, 2001, 2010, CCD. All rights reserved.
Music: *The Collegeville Chant Psalter,* © 2019, Order of Saint Benedict, Collegeville, MN. Published and administered by Liturgical Press, Collegeville, MN 56321. All rights reserved.

Psalm 62

55

8th Sunday in Ordinary Time, Year A

Psalm Tone

Mode 6

Psalm 62:2-3, 6-7, 8-9. R/ v. 6a

1. Only in God is my <u>soul</u> at rest;
   from him comes <u>my</u> salvation.
   He only is my rock and <u>my</u> salvation,
   my stronghold; I shall not be dis<u>turbed</u> at all.   *R/*

2. Only in God be at <u>rest</u>, my soul,
   for from him <u>comes</u> my hope.
   He only is my rock and <u>my</u> salvation,
   my stronghold; I shall not <u>be</u> disturbed.   *R/*

3. With God is my safety <u>and</u> my glory,
   he is the rock of my strength; my refuge <u>is</u> in God.
   Trust in him at all times, <u>O</u> my people!
   Pour out your <u>hearts</u> before him.   *R/*

Text: Refrain, *Lectionary for Mass,* © 1969, 1981, 1997, ICEL; verses, *Lectionary for Mass*/New American Bible, © 1970, 1986, 1991, 1997, 2001, 2010, CCD. All rights reserved.
Music: *The Collegeville Chant Psalter,* © 2019, Order of Saint Benedict, Collegeville, MN. Published and administered by Liturgical Press, Collegeville, MN 56321. All rights reserved.

Psalm 63

22nd Sunday in Ordinary Time, Year A • 32nd Sunday in Ordinary Time, Year A •
12th Sunday in Ordinary Time, Year C • Common Ordinary Time 4

Psalm Tone

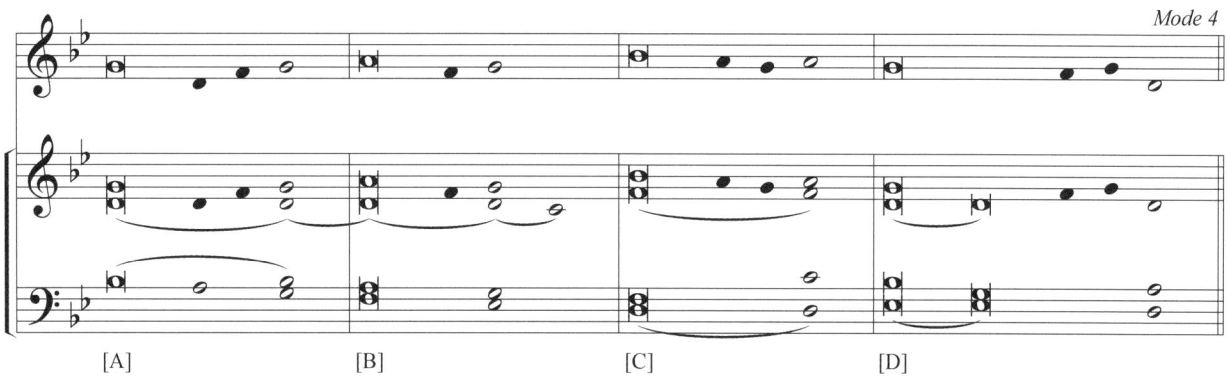

Psalm 63:2, 3-4, 5-6, 7, 8-9. R/ v. 2b

1. O God, you are my God <u>whom</u> I seek;
   for you my flesh pines and my <u>soul</u> thirsts
   [omit C]
   like the earth, parched, lifeless and <u>without</u> water. *R/*

2. Thus have I gazed toward you <u>in</u> the sanctuary
   to see your power and <u>your</u> glory,
   for your kindness is a greater <u>good</u> than life;
   my lips shall glo<u>ri</u>fy you. *R/*

3. Thus will I bless you <u>while</u> I live;
   lifting up my hands, I will call upon <u>your</u> name.
   As with the riches of a banquet shall my <u>soul</u> be satisfied,
   and with exultant lips my <u>mouth</u> shall praise you. *R/*

22 OT A, 12 OT C, Common OT 4 only

4. You <u>are</u> my help,
   and in the shadow of your wings I shout <u>for</u> joy.
   My soul clings <u>fast</u> to you;
   your right <u>hand</u> upholds me. *R/*

32 OT A only

4a. I will remember you up<u>on</u> my couch,
    and through the night-watches I will
                    meditate <u>on</u> you:
    you <u>are</u> my help,
    and in the shadow of your wings I
                    <u>shout</u> for joy. *R/*

Text: Refrain, *Lectionary for Mass*, © 1969, 1981, 1997, ICEL; verses, *Lectionary for Mass*/New American Bible, © 1970, 1986, 1991, 1997, 2001, 2010, CCD. All rights reserved.
Music: *The Collegeville Chant Psalter*, © 2019, Order of Saint Benedict, Collegeville, MN. Published and administered by Liturgical Press, Collegeville, MN 56321. All rights reserved.

Psalm 65

15th Sunday in Ordinary Time, Year A

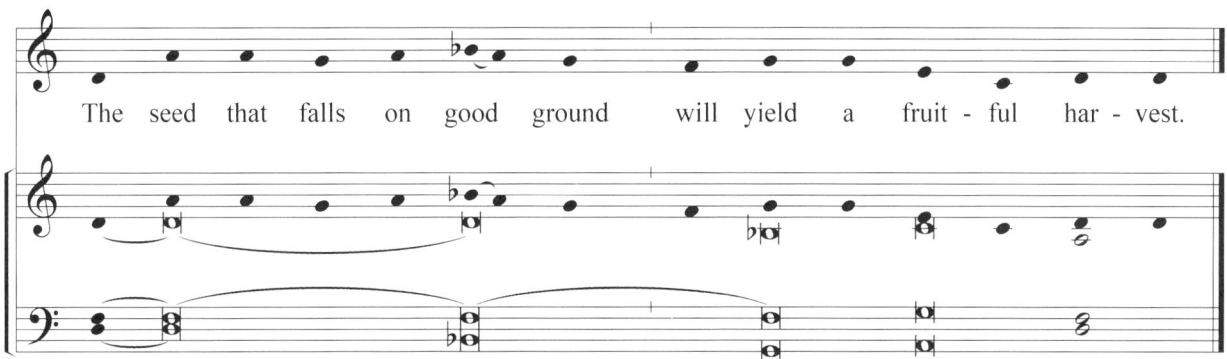

Psalm Tone

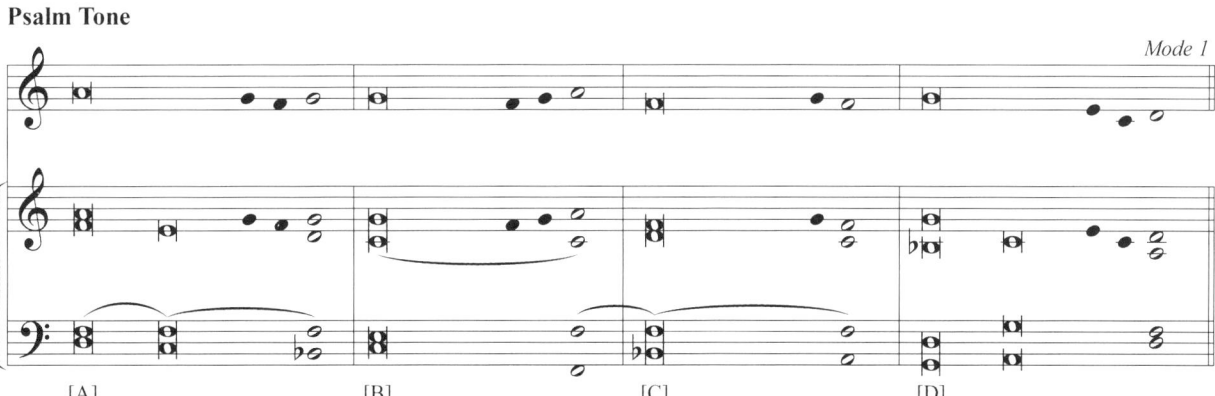

[A]   [B]   [C]   [D]

Psalm 65:10, 11, 12-13, 14. R/ Lk 8:8

1. You have visited the <u>land</u> and watered it;
   greatly have <u>you</u> enriched it.
   God's watercourses <u>are</u> filled;
   you have pre<u>pared</u> the grain.   *R/*

2. Thus have you prepared the land: drench<u>ing</u> its furrows,
   breaking <u>up</u> its clods,
   softening it <u>with</u> showers,
   bless<u>ing</u> its yield.   *R/*

3. You have crowned the year <u>with</u> your bounty,
   and your paths overflow with <u>a</u> rich harvest;
   the untilled meadows o<u>ver</u>flow with it,
   and rejoicing <u>clothes</u> the hills.   *R/*

4. The fields are gar<u>mented</u> with flocks
   and the valleys blanket<u>ed</u> with grain.
   [omit C]
   They shout and <u>sing</u> for joy.   *R/*

Text: Refrain, *Lectionary for Mass,* © 1969, 1981, 1997, ICEL; verses, *Lectionary for Mass*/New American Bible, © 1970, 1986, 1991, 1997, 2001, 2010, CCD. All rights reserved.
Music: *The Collegeville Chant Psalter,* © 2019, Order of Saint Benedict, Collegeville, MN. Published and administered by Liturgical Press, Collegeville, MN 56321. All rights reserved.

Psalm 66

6th Sunday of Easter, Year A • 14th Sunday in Ordinary Time, Year C

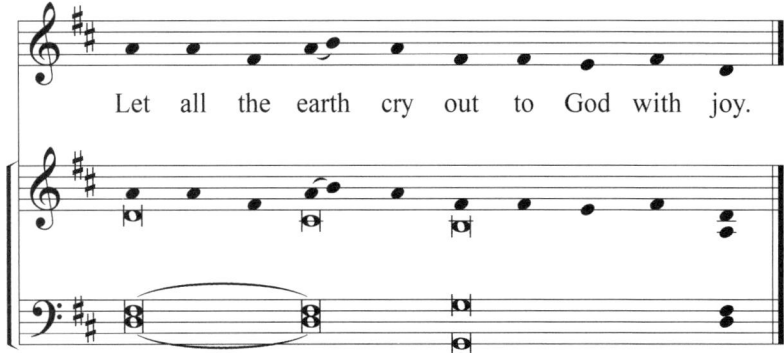

6th Sunday of Easter, *alternate response*

Common Eastertide 2

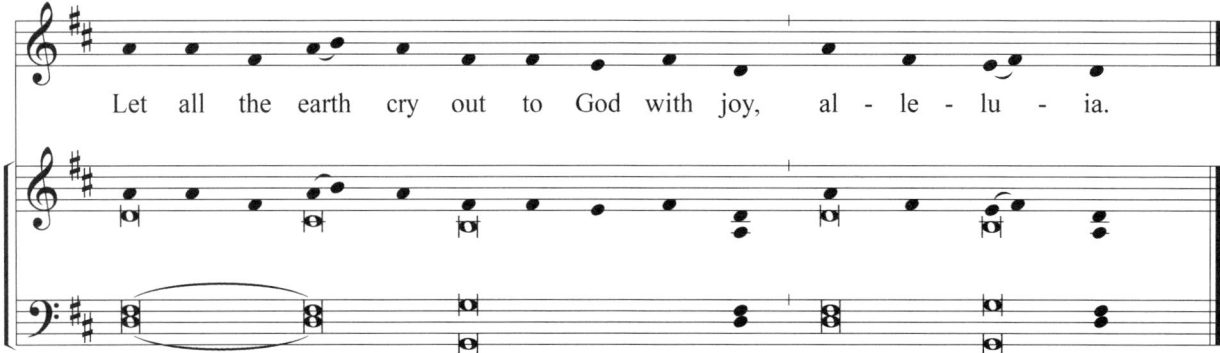

Psalm Tone

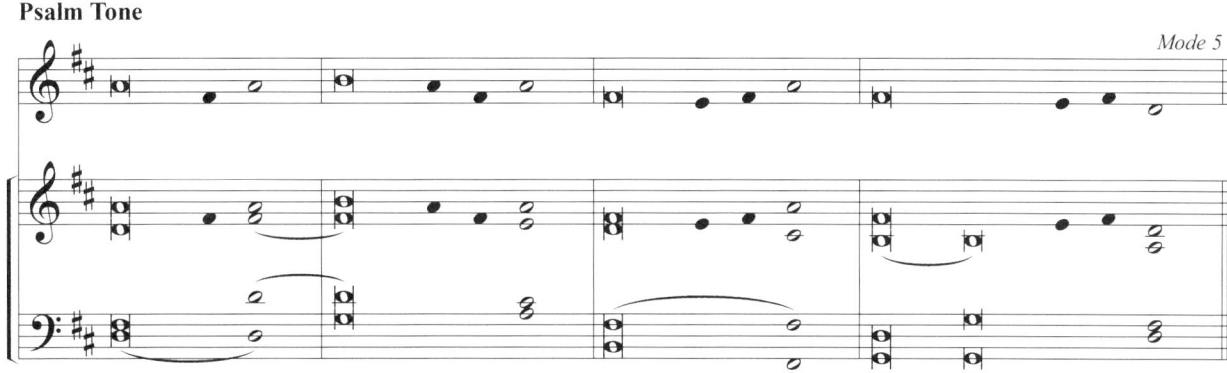

Psalm 66:1-3, 4-5, 6-7, 16, 20. R/ v. 1

1. Shout joyfully to God, all <u>the</u> earth,
   sing praise to the glory <u>of</u> his name;
   proclaim his <u>glo</u>rious praise.
   Say to God, "How tremendous <u>are</u> your deeds!"   *R/*

2. "Let all on earth worship and sing praise <u>to</u> you,
   sing praise <u>to</u> your name!"
   Come and see the <u>works</u> of God,
   his tremendous deeds among the chil<u>dren</u> of Adam.   *R/*

3. He has changed the sea into <u>dry</u> land;
   through the river they <u>passed</u> on foot.
   Therefore let us re<u>joice</u> in him.
   He rules by his <u>might</u> forever.   *R/*

4. Hear now, all you who <u>fear</u> God,
   while I declare what he has <u>done</u> for me.
   Blessed be God who re<u>fused</u> me not
   my prayer <u>or</u> his kindness!   *R/*

Text: Refrain, *Lectionary for Mass,* © 1969, 1981, 1997, ICEL; verses, *Lectionary for Mass*/New American Bible, © 1970, 1986, 1991, 1997, 2001, 2010, CCD. All rights reserved.
Music: *The Collegeville Chant Psalter,* © 2019, Order of Saint Benedict, Collegeville, MN. Published and administered by Liturgical Press, Collegeville, MN 56321. All rights reserved.

Psalm 67

Mary, the Mother of God (January 1)

May God bless us in his mercy.

20th Sunday in Ordinary Time, Year A • 6th Sunday of Easter, Year C • Thanksgiving Day, *C.E. alternate psalm, alternate response*

O God, let all the nations praise you.

Thanksgiving Day, *C.E. alternate psalm*

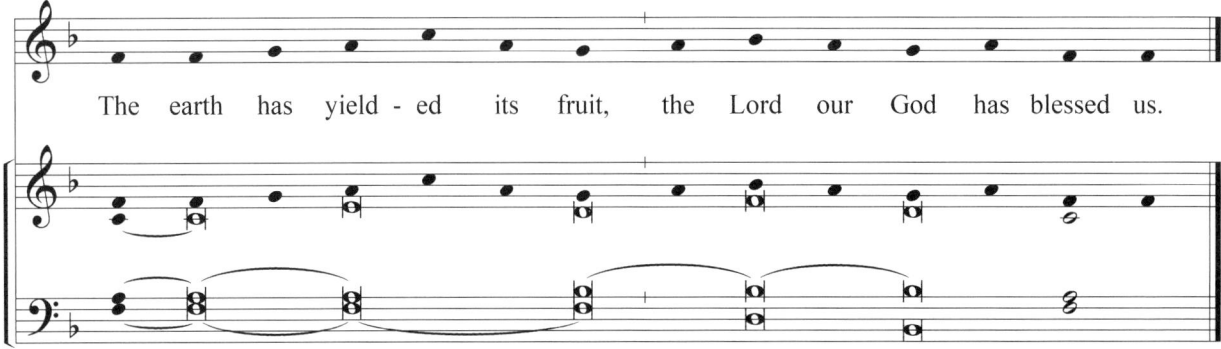

The earth has yielded its fruit, the Lord our God has blessed us.

Psalm Tone

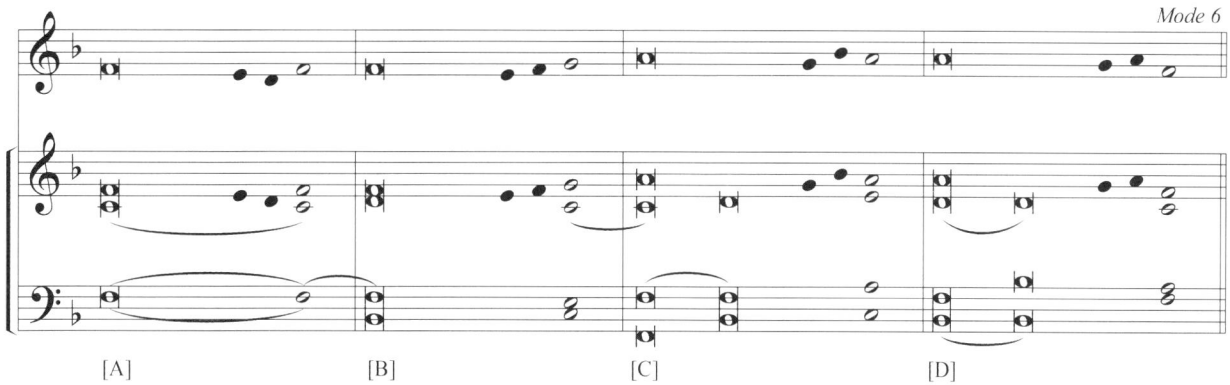

Psalm 67:2-3, 5, 6, 8. R/ v. 2a; v. 4; v. 7

1. May God have pity on us and bless us;
   may he let his face shine upon us.
   So may your way be known upon earth;
   among all nations, your salvation. *R/*

2. May the nations be glad and exult
   because you rule the peoples in equity;
   [omit C]
   the nations on the earth you guide. *R/*

3. May the peoples praise you, O God;
   may all the peoples praise you!
   May God bless us,
   and may all the ends of the earth fear him! *R/*

Text: Refrain, *Lectionary for Mass*, © 1969, 1981, 1997, ICEL; verses, *Lectionary for Mass*/New American Bible, © 1970, 1986, 1991, 1997, 2001, 2010, CCD. All rights reserved.
Music: *The Collegeville Chant Psalter*, © 2019, Order of Saint Benedict, Collegeville, MN. Published and administered by Liturgical Press, Collegeville, MN 56321. All rights reserved.

Psalm 68

22nd Sunday in Ordinary Time, Year C

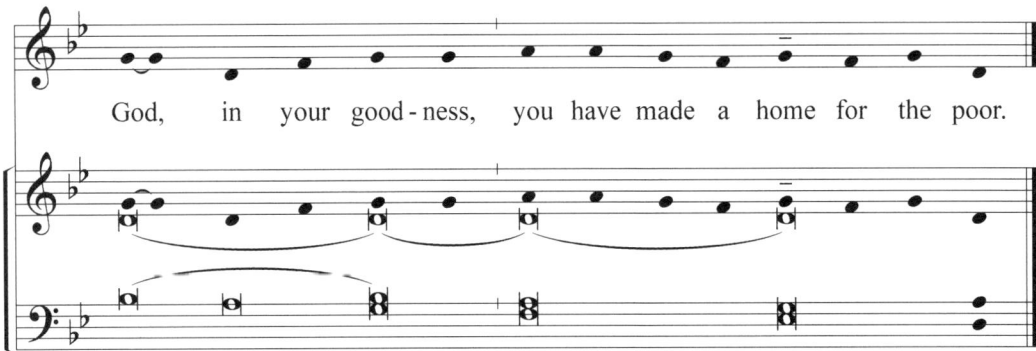

Psalm Tone

Psalm 68:4-5, 6-7, 10-11. R/ see v. 11b

1. The just rejoice and exult <u>be</u>fore God;
   they are glad and re<u>joice</u>.
   Sing to God, chant praise <u>to</u> his name;
   whose name <u>is</u> the Lord. *R/*

2. The father of orphans and the defend<u>er</u> of widows
   is God in his ho<u>ly</u> dwelling.
   God gives a home to <u>the</u> forsaken;
   he leads forth prisoners <u>to</u> prosperity. *R/*

3. A bountiful rain you showered down, O God, upon <u>your</u> inheritance;
   you restored the land when <u>it</u> languished;
   your flock <u>set</u>tled in it;
   in your goodness, O God, you provided it <u>for</u> the needy. *R/*

Text: Refrain, *Lectionary for Mass,* © 1969, 1981, 1997, ICEL; verses, *Lectionary for Mass*/New American Bible, © 1970, 1986, 1991, 1997, 2001, 2010, CCD. All rights reserved.
Music: *The Collegeville Chant Psalter,* © 2019, Order of Saint Benedict, Collegeville, MN. Published and administered by Liturgical Press, Collegeville, MN 56321. All rights reserved.

Psalm 69

12th Sunday in Ordinary Time, Year A

Psalm Tone

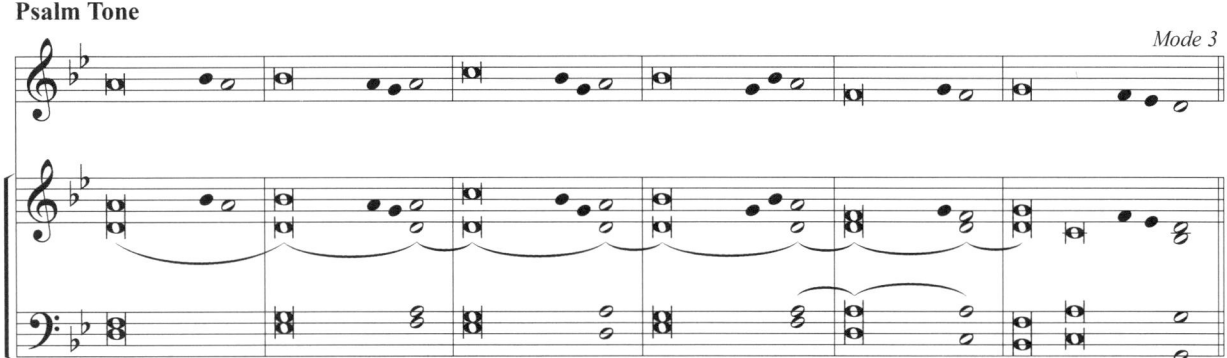

Psalm 69:8-10, 14, 17, 33-35. R/ v. 14c

1. For your sake I <u>bear</u> insult,
   and shame cov<u>ers</u> my face.
   I have become an outcast <u>to</u> my brothers,
   a stranger <u>to</u> my children,
   because zeal for your house <u>con</u>sumes me,
   and the insults of those who blaspheme you <u>fall</u> upon me. *R/*

2. I pray to you, <u>O</u> Lord,
   for the time of your fa<u>vor</u>, O God!
   In your great kindness <u>answer</u> me
   with your <u>con</u>stant help.
   Answer me, O Lord, for bounteous is <u>your</u> kindness;
   in your great mercy <u>turn</u> toward me. *R/*

3. "See, you lowly ones, and <u>be</u> glad;
   you who seek God, may your <u>hearts</u> revive!
   For the Lord <u>hears</u> the poor,
   and his own who are in bonds <u>he</u> spurns not.
   Let the heavens and the <u>earth</u> praise him,
   the seas and what<u>ever</u> moves in them!" *R/*

Text: Refrain, *Lectionary for Mass,* © 1969, 1981, 1997, ICEL; verses, *Lectionary for Mass*/New American Bible, © 1970, 1986, 1991, 1997, 2001, 2010, CCD. All rights reserved.
Music: *The Collegeville Chant Psalter,* © 2019, Order of Saint Benedict, Collegeville, MN. Published and administered by Liturgical Press, Collegeville, MN 56321. All rights reserved.

15th Sunday in Ordinary Time, Year C

Turn to the Lord in your need, and you will live.

Psalm Tone Mode 8

[A] [B] [C] [D] [E] [F]

Psalm 69:14, 17, 30-31, 33-34, 36, 37. R/ see v. 33

1. I pray to <u>you</u>, O L<small>ORD</small>,
   for the time of your favor, <u>O</u> God!
   In your great kindness <u>an</u>swer me
   with your con<u>stant</u> help.
   Answer me, O L<small>ORD</small>, for bounteous <u>is</u> your kindness:
   in your great mercy turn to<u>ward</u> me. *R/*

2. I am afflicted <u>and</u> in pain;
   let your saving help, O God, <u>pro</u>tect me.
   I will praise the name of <u>God</u> in song,
   [omit D, E]
   and I will glorify him with <u>thanks</u>giving. *R/*

3. "See, you lowly ones, <u>and</u> be glad;
   you who seek God, may your hearts <u>re</u>vive!
   For the L<small>ORD</small> <u>hears</u> the poor,
   [omit D, E]
   and his own who are in bonds he <u>spurns</u> not." *R/*

4. For God <u>will</u> save Zion
   and rebuild the cities <u>of</u> Judah.
   The descendants of his servants <u>shall</u> inherit it,
   [omit D, E]
   and those who love his name shall <u>in</u>habit it. *R/*

Text: Refrain, *Lectionary for Mass*, © 1969, 1981, 1997, ICEL; verses, *Lectionary for Mass*/New American Bible, © 1970, 1986, 1991, 1997, 2001, 2010, CCD. All rights reserved.
Music: *The Collegeville Chant Psalter*, © 2019, Order of Saint Benedict, Collegeville, MN. Published and administered by Liturgical Press, Collegeville, MN 56321. All rights reserved.

Psalm 71

4th Sunday in Ordinary Time, Year C

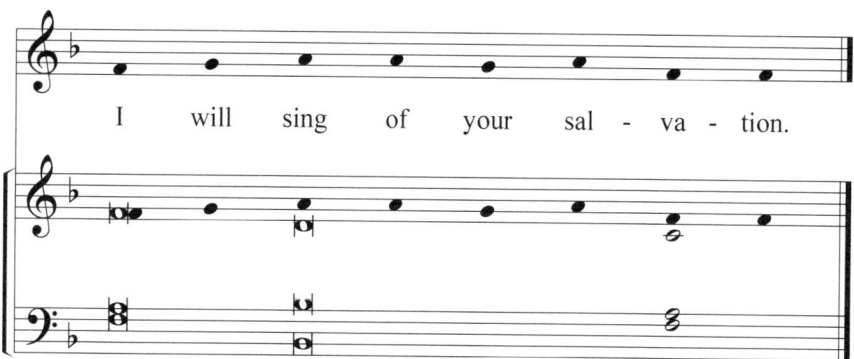

I will sing of your sal-va-tion.

St. John the Baptist Vigil

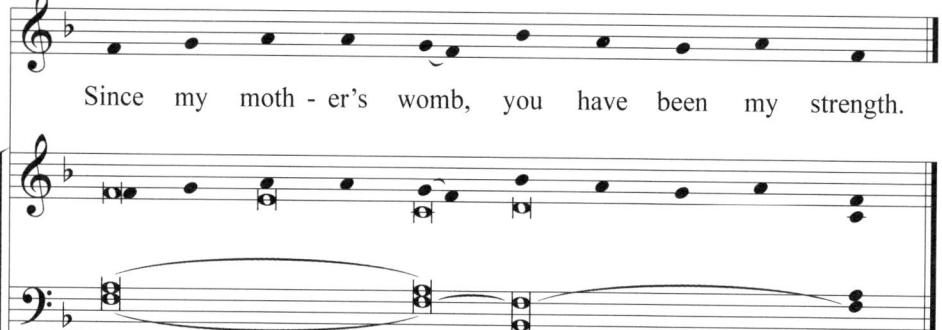

Since my moth-er's womb, you have been my strength.

Psalm Tone   *Mode 6*

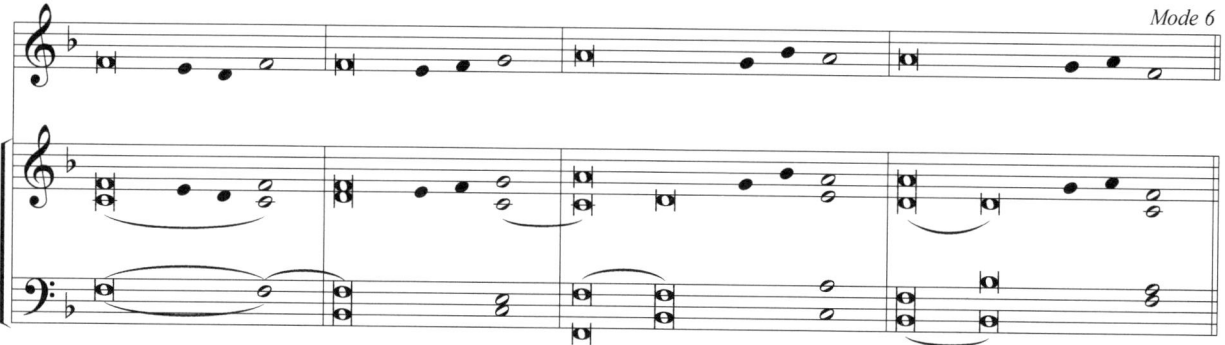

Psalm 71:1-2, 3-4, 5-6, 15, 17. R/ see v. 15ab; v. 6

1. In you, O LORD, <u>I</u> take refuge;
   let me never be <u>put</u> to shame.
   In your justice rescue me, <u>and</u> deliver me;
   incline your ear to <u>me</u>, and save me. *R/*

2. Be my <u>rock</u> of refuge,
   a stronghold to <u>give</u> me safety,
   for you are my rock <u>and</u> my fortress.
   O my God, rescue me from the hand <u>of</u> the wicked. *R/*

3. For you are my <u>hope</u>, O Lord;
   my trust, O God, <u>from</u> my youth.
   On you I <u>depend</u> from birth;
   from my mother's womb you
                   <u>are</u> my strength. *R/*

4. My mouth shall de<u>clare</u> your justice,
   day by day <u>your</u> salvation.
   O God, you have taught me <u>from</u> my youth,
   and till the present I proclaim your
                   <u>won</u>drous deeds. *R/*

Text: Refrain, *Lectionary for Mass*, © 1969, 1981, 1997, ICEL; verses, *Lectionary for Mass*/New American Bible, © 1970, 1986, 1991, 1997, 2001, 2010, CCD. All rights reserved.
Music: *The Collegeville Chant Psalter*, © 2019, Order of Saint Benedict, Collegeville, MN. Published and administered by Liturgical Press, Collegeville, MN 56321. All rights reserved.

Note:
St. John the Baptist, Vigil Mass, v. 3, ln 2 uses the word LORD instead of God.

Psalm 72

Epiphany of the Lord, Vigil and Day • Common Epiphany

Lord, ev-'ry nation on earth will a-dore you.

Psalm Tone

Mode 8

Psalm 72:1-2, 7-8, 10-11, 12-13. R/ cf. v. 11; cf. v. 7

1. O God, with your judgment en<u>dow</u> the king,
   and with your justice <u>the</u> king's son;
   he shall govern your peo<u>ple</u> with justice
   and your afflicted ones <u>with</u> judgment. *R/*

2. Justice shall flower <u>in</u> his days,
   and profound peace, till the moon be <u>no</u> more.
   May he rule from <u>sea</u> to sea,
   and from the River to the ends of <u>the</u> earth. *R/*

3. The kings of Tarshish and the Isles shall <u>offer</u> gifts;
   the kings of Arabia and Seba shall <u>bring</u> tribute.
   All kings shall <u>pay</u> him homage,
   all nations <u>shall</u> serve him. *R/*

4. For he shall rescue the poor when <u>he</u> cries out,
   and the afflicted when he has no one <u>to</u> help him.
   He shall have pity for the lowly <u>and</u> the poor;
   the lives of the poor he <u>shall</u> save. *R/*

Text: Refrain, *Lectionary for Mass*, © 1969, 1981, 1997, ICEL; verses, *Lectionary for Mass/New American Bible*, © 1970, 1986, 1991, 1997, 2001, 2010, CCD. All rights reserved.
Music: *The Collegeville Chant Psalter*, © 2019, Order of Saint Benedict, Collegeville, MN. Published and administered by Liturgical Press, Collegeville, MN 56321. All rights reserved.

2nd Sunday of Advent, Year A

Justice shall flourish in his time, and fullness of peace for ever.

Psalm Tone Mode 4

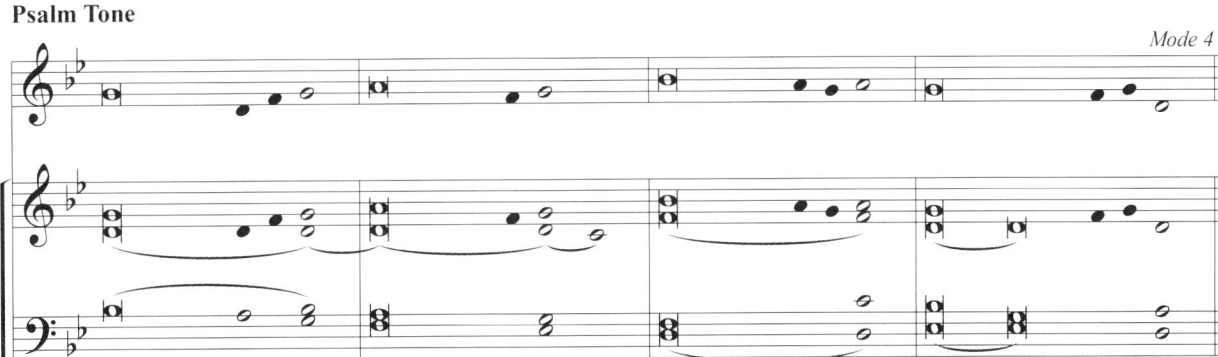

Psalm 72:1-2, 7-8, 12-13, 17. R/ cf. v. 11; cf. v. 7

1. O God, with your judgment en<u>dow</u> the king,
   and with your justice <u>the</u> king's son;
   he shall govern your peo<u>ple</u> with justice
   and your afflicted <u>ones</u> with judgment. *R/*

2. Justice shall flower <u>in</u> his days,
   and profound peace, till the moon be <u>no</u> more.
   May he rule from <u>sea</u> to sea,
   and from the River to the ends <u>of</u> the earth. *R/*

3. For he shall rescue the poor when <u>he</u> cries out,
   and the afflicted when he has no one <u>to</u> help him.
   He shall have pity for the lowly <u>and</u> the poor;
   the lives of the poor <u>he</u> shall save. *R/*

4. May his name be <u>blessed</u> forever;
   as long as the sun his name shall <u>remain</u>.
   In him shall all the tribes of the <u>earth</u> be blessed;
   all the nations shall pro<u>claim</u> his happiness. *R/*

Text: Refrain, *Lectionary for Mass*, © 1969, 1981, 1997, ICEL; verses, *Lectionary for Mass*/New American Bible, © 1970, 1986, 1991, 1997, 2001, 2010, CCD. All rights reserved.
Music: *The Collegeville Chant Psalter*, © 2019, Order of Saint Benedict, Collegeville, MN. Published and administered by Liturgical Press, Collegeville, MN 56321. All rights reserved.

Psalm 78

18th Sunday in Ordinary Time, Year B

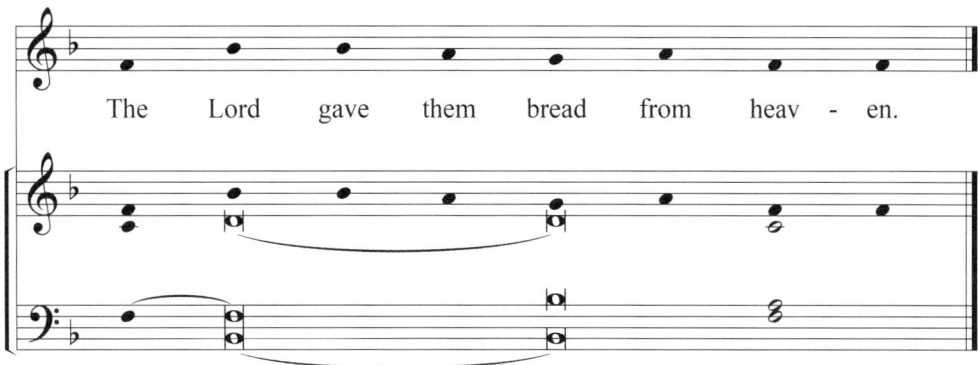

The Lord gave them bread from heav-en.

Psalm Tone

Mode 6

Psalm 78:3-4, 23-24, 25, 54. R/ v. 24b

1. What we have <u>heard</u> and know,
   and what our fathers have de<u>clared</u> to us,
   we will declare to the gener<u>a</u>tion to come
   the glorious deeds of the L<small>ORD</small> and his strength
          and the wonders <u>that</u> he wrought. *R/*

2. He commanded the <u>skies</u> above
   and opened the <u>doors</u> of heaven;
   he rained manna upon <u>them</u> for food
   and gave them heav<u>en</u>ly bread. *R/*

3. Man ate the <u>bread</u> of angels,
   food he sent them <u>in</u> abundance.
   And he brought them to his <u>holy</u> land,
   to the mountains his right <u>hand</u> had won. *R/*

Text: Refrain, *Lectionary for Mass,* © 1969, 1981, 1997, ICEL; verses, *Lectionary for Mass*/New American Bible, © 1970, 1986, 1991, 1997, 2001, 2010, CCD. All rights reserved.
Music: *The Collegeville Chant Psalter,* © 2019, Order of Saint Benedict, Collegeville, MN. Published and administered by Liturgical Press, Collegeville, MN 56321. All rights reserved.

Exaltation of the Holy Cross

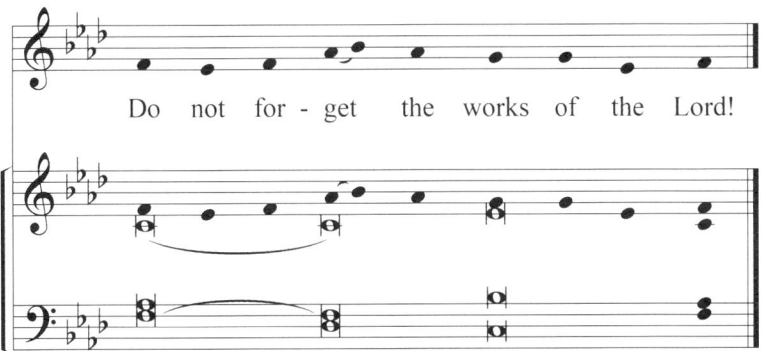

Psalm Tone

Mode 2

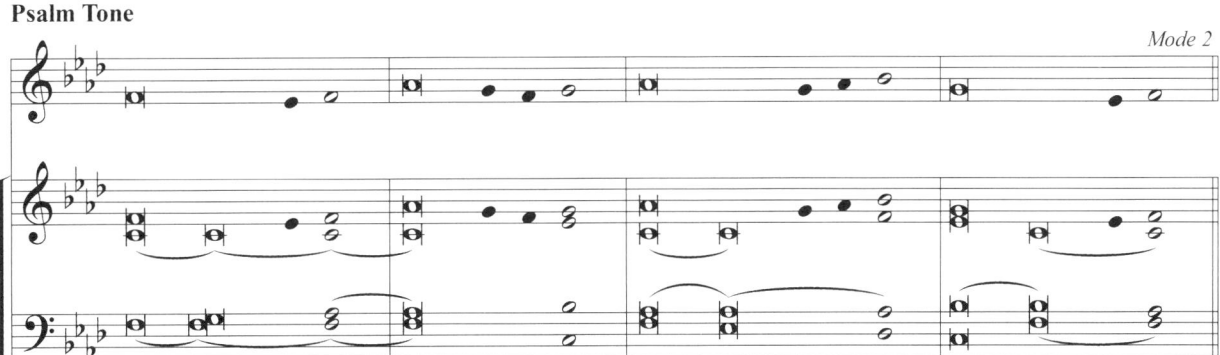

Psalm 78:1bc-2, 34-35, 36-37, 38. R/ see v. 7b

1. Hearken, my people, to my teaching;
   incline your ears to the words of my mouth.
   I will open my mouth in a parable,
   I will utter mysteries from of old. *R/*

2. While he slew them they sought him
   and inquired after God again,
   Remembering that God was their rock
   and the Most High God, their redeemer. *R/*

3. But they flattered him with their mouths
   and lied to him with their tongues,
   Though their hearts were not steadfast toward him,
   nor were they faithful to his covenant. *R/*

4. But he, being merciful, forgave their sin
   and destroyed them not;
   Often he turned back his anger
   and let none of his wrath be roused. *R/*

Text: Refrain, *Lectionary for Mass,* © 1969, 1981, 1997, ICEL; verses, *Lectionary for Mass*/New American Bible, © 1970, 1986, 1991, 1997, 2001, 2010, CCD. All rights reserved.
Music: *The Collegeville Chant Psalter,* © 2019, Order of Saint Benedict, Collegeville, MN. Published and administered by Liturgical Press, Collegeville, MN 56321. All rights reserved.

Psalm 80

1st Sunday of Advent, Year B • 4th Sunday of Advent, Year C

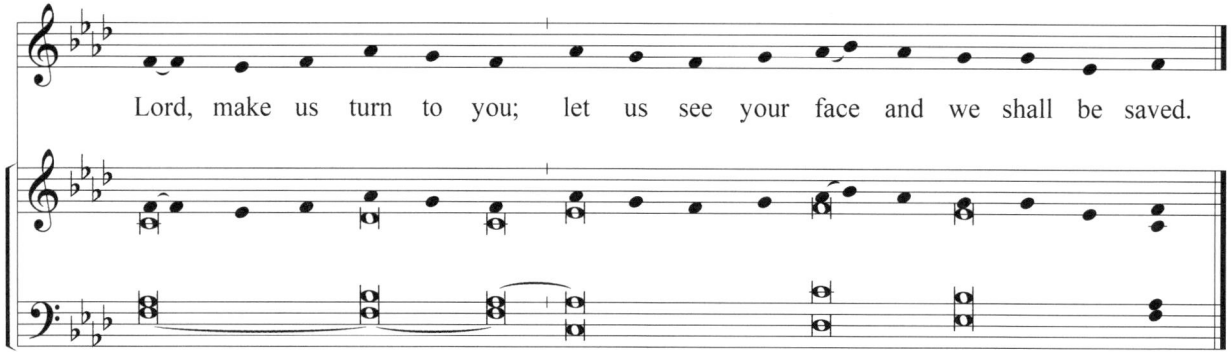

Lord, make us turn to you; let us see your face and we shall be saved.

Psalm Tone

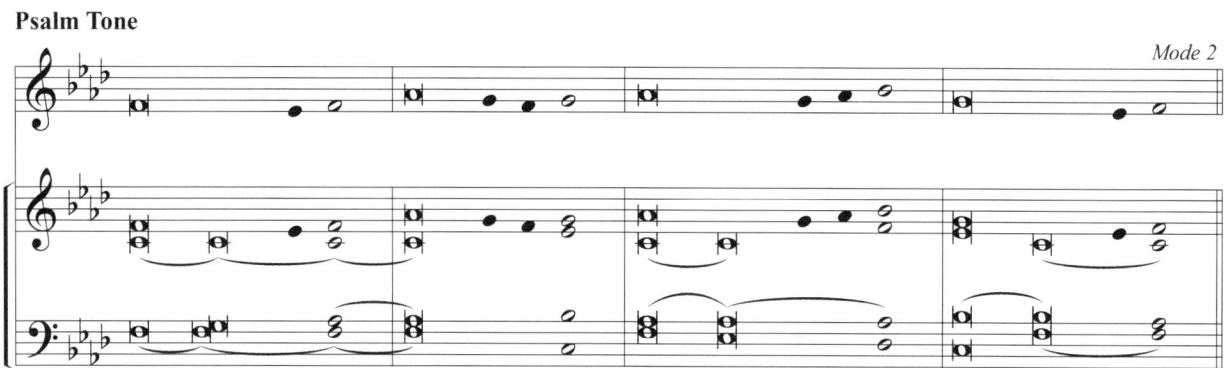

Mode 2

Psalm 80:2-3, 15-16, 18-19. R/ v. 4

1. O shepherd of Isr<u>ae</u>l, hearken,
   from your throne upon the cheru<u>bim</u>, shine forth.
   <u>Rouse</u> your power,
   and come <u>to</u> save us. *R/*

2. Once again, O L<small>ORD</small> <u>of</u> hosts,
   look down from heav<u>en</u>, and see;
   take care of this vine,
       and protect what your right <u>hand</u> has planted,
   the son of man whom you yourself <u>made</u> strong. *R/*

3. May your help be with the man of <u>your</u> right hand,
   with the son of man whom you your<u>self</u> made strong.
   Then we will no <u>more</u> withdraw from you;
   give us new life, and we will call upon <u>your</u> name. *R/*

Text: Refrain, *Lectionary for Mass,* © 1969, 1981, 1997, ICEL; verses, *Lectionary for Mass*/New American Bible, © 1970, 1986, 1991, 1997, 2001, 2010, CCD. All rights reserved.
Music: *The Collegeville Chant Psalter,* © 2019, Order of Saint Benedict, Collegeville, MN. Published and administered by Liturgical Press, Collegeville, MN 56321. All rights reserved.

27th Sunday in Ordinary Time, Year A

The vine-yard of the Lord is the house of Israel.

Psalm Tone　　　　　　　　　　　　　　　　　　　　　　　　　　　　　Mode 5

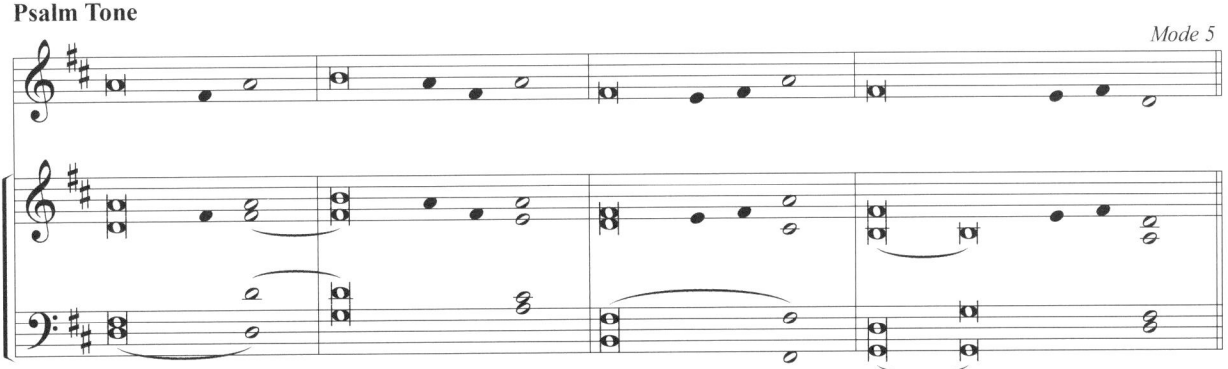

Psalm 80:9, 12, 13-14, 15-16, 19-20.　R/ Isaiah 5:7a

1. A vine from Egypt you <u>trans</u>planted;
   you drove away the na<u>tions</u> and planted it.
   It put forth its foliage <u>to</u> the Sea,
   its shoots as far <u>as</u> the River.　*R/*

2. Why have you broken down <u>its</u> walls,
   so that every passer-by <u>plucks</u> its fruit,
   the boar from the forest <u>lays</u> it waste,
   and the beasts of the field <u>feed</u> upon it?　*R/*

3. Once again, O Lord <u>of</u> hosts,
   look down from heav<u>en</u>, and see;
   take care of this vine,
       and protect what your right <u>hand</u> has planted
   the son of man whom you your<u>self</u> made strong.　*R/*

4. Then we will no more withdraw <u>from</u> you;
   give us new life, and we will call u<u>pon</u> your name.
   O Lord, God of <u>hosts</u>, restore us;
   if your face shine upon us, then we <u>shall</u> be saved.　*R/*

Text: Refrain, *Lectionary for Mass,* © 1969, 1981, 1997, ICEL; verses, *Lectionary for Mass*/New American Bible, © 1970, 1986, 1991, 1997, 2001, 2010, CCD. All rights reserved.
Music: *The Collegeville Chant Psalter,* © 2019, Order of Saint Benedict, Collegeville, MN. Published and administered by Liturgical Press, Collegeville, MN 56321. All rights reserved.

Psalm 81

9th Sunday in Ordinary Time, Year B

Psalm Tone

Psalm 81:3-4, 5-6, 7-8, 10-11. R/ v. 2a

1. Take up a melody, and sound <u>the</u> timbrel,
   the pleasant harp <u>and</u> the lyre.
   Blow the trumpet <u>at</u> the new moon,
   at the full moon, on our <u>sol</u>emn feast. *R/*

2. For it is a statute <u>in</u> Israel,
   an ordinance of the <u>God</u> of Jacob,
   who made it a de<u>cree</u> for Joseph
   when he came forth from the <u>land</u> of Egypt. *R/*

3. An unfamiliar speech <u>I</u> hear:
   "I relieved his shoulder <u>of</u> the burden;
   his hands were freed <u>from</u> the basket.
   In distress you called, <u>and</u> I rescued you." *R/*

4. "There shall be no strange god <u>among</u> you
   nor shall you worship any al<u>ien</u> god.
   I, the Lord, <u>am</u> your God
   who led you forth from the <u>land</u> of Egypt." *R/*

Text: Refrain, *Lectionary for Mass*, © 1969, 1981, 1997, ICEL; verses, *Lectionary for Mass*/New American Bible, © 1970, 1986, 1991, 1997, 2001, 2010, CCD. All rights reserved.
Music: *The Collegeville Chant Psalter*, © 2019, Order of Saint Benedict, Collegeville, MN. Published and administered by Liturgical Press, Collegeville, MN 56321. All rights reserved.

Psalm 84

Holy Family, Year C

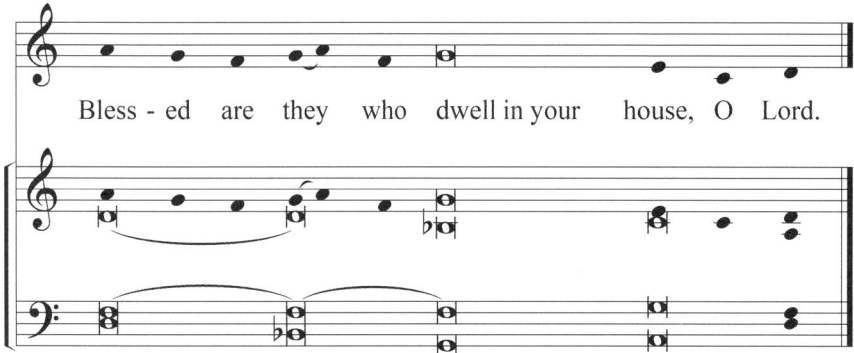

Psalm Tone

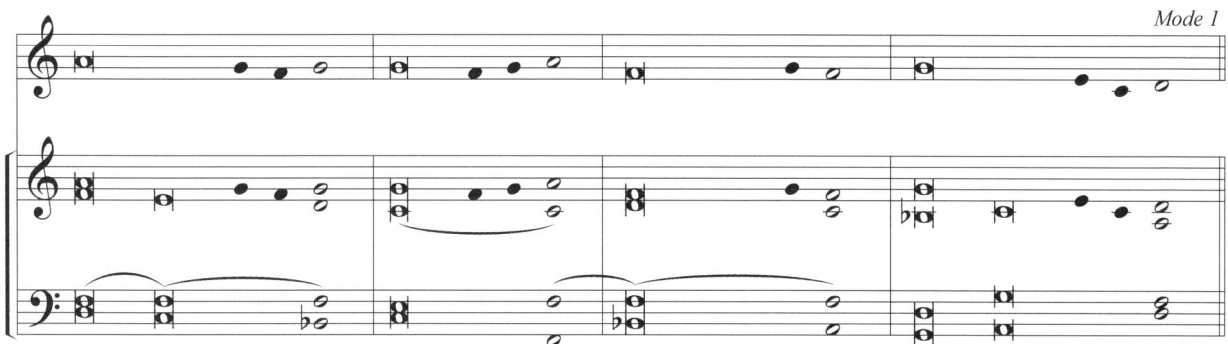

Psalm 84:2-3, 5-6, 9-10. R/ cf. v. 5a

1. How lovely is your dwelling place,
   O Lord of hosts!
   My soul yearns and pines
   for the courts of the Lord.
   My heart and my flesh
   cry out for the living God. *R/*

2. Happy they who dwell in your house!
   Continually they praise you.
   Happy the men whose strength you are!
   Their hearts are set upon the pilgrimage. *R/*

3. O Lord of hosts, hear our prayer;
   hearken, O God of Jacob!
   O God, behold our shield,
   and look upon the face of your anointed. *R/*

Text: Refrain, *Lectionary for Mass,* © 1969, 1981, 1997, ICEL; verses, *Lectionary for Mass*/New American Bible, © 1970, 1986, 1991, 1997, 2001, 2010, CCD. All rights reserved.
Music: *The Collegeville Chant Psalter,* © 2019, Order of Saint Benedict, Collegeville, MN. Published and administered by Liturgical Press, Collegeville, MN 56321. All rights reserved.

Anniversary of Dedication of a Church, option 3

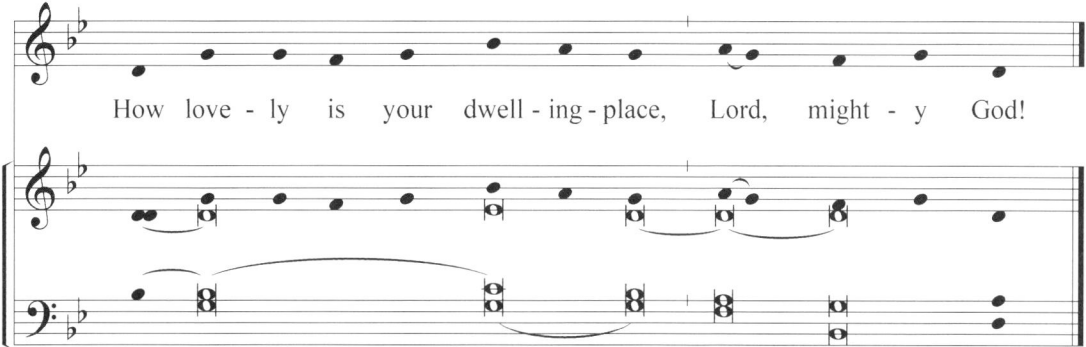

How love-ly is your dwell-ing-place, Lord, might-y God!

Anniversary of Dedication of a Church, option 3, *alternate response*

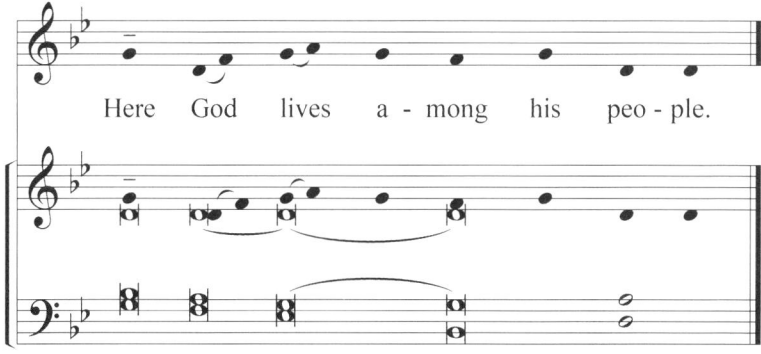

Here God lives a-mong his peo-ple.

Psalm Tone

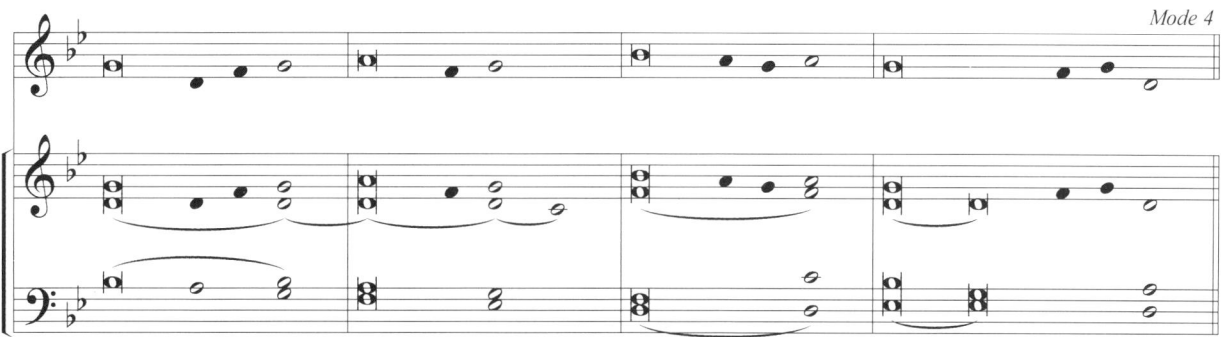

Mode 4

Psalm 84:3, 4, 5, 10, 11. R/ v. 2; Rev 21:3

1. My soul yearns and pines
    for the courts of the Lord.
   My heart and my flesh
    cry out for the living God. R/

2. Even the sparrow finds a home,
   and the swallow a nest
    in which she puts her young —
   Your altars, O Lord of hosts,
   my king and my God! R/

3. Blessed they who dwell in your house!
   continually they praise you.
   O God, behold our shield,
   and look upon the face of your anointed. R/

4. I had rather one day in your courts
   than a thousand elsewhere;
   I had rather lie at the threshold of the house
            of my God
   than dwell in the tents of the wicked. R/

Text: Refrain, *Lectionary for Mass*, © 1969, 1981, 1997, ICEL; verses, *Lectionary for Mass*/New American Bible, © 1970, 1986, 1991, 1997, 2001, 2010, CCD. All rights reserved.
Music: *The Collegeville Chant Psalter*, © 2019, Order of Saint Benedict, Collegeville, MN. Published and administered by Liturgical Press, Collegeville, MN 56321. All rights reserved.

Psalm 85

19th Sunday in Ordinary Time, Year A • 2nd Sunday of Advent, Year B • 15th Sunday in Ordinary Time, Year B

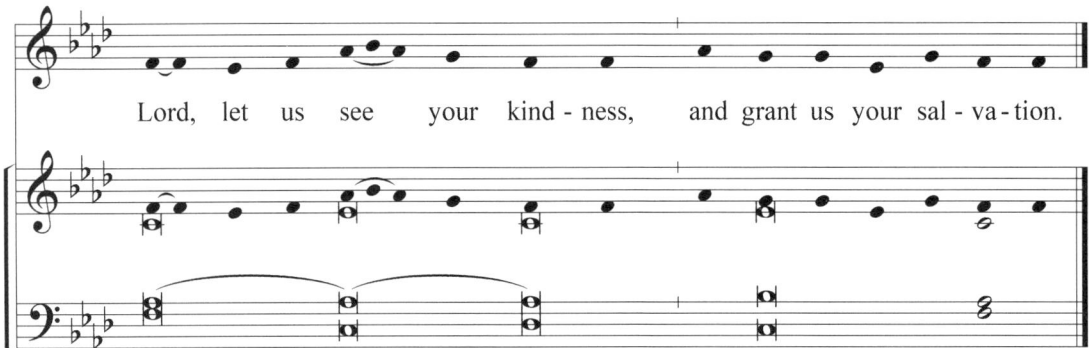

Common Advent 2

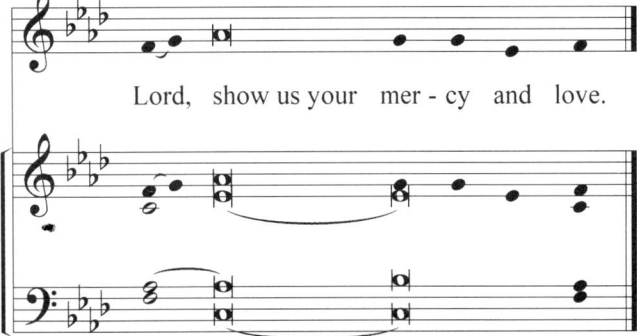

Psalm Tone

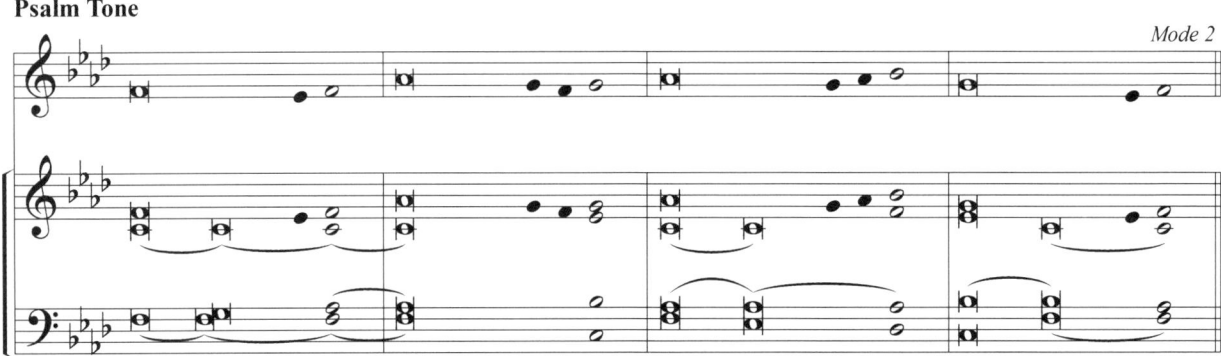

Psalm 85:9-10, 11-12, 13-14. R/ v. 8

1. I will hear what God pro<u>claims</u>;
   the L<small>ORD</small>—for he proclaims peace <u>to</u> his people.
   Near indeed is his salvation to <u>those</u> who fear him,
   glory dwelling in <u>our</u> land. *R/*

2. Kindness and truth <u>shall</u> meet;
   justice and <u>peace</u> shall kiss.
   Truth shall spring out <u>of</u> the earth,
   and justice shall look down <u>from</u> heaven. *R/*

3. The L<small>ORD</small> himself will give <u>his</u> benefits;
   our land shall <u>yield</u> its increase.
   Justice shall <u>walk</u> before him,
   and prepare the way of <u>his</u> steps. *R/*

Text: Refrain, *Lectionary for Mass*, © 1969, 1981, 1997, ICEL; verses, *Lectionary for Mass*/New American Bible, © 1970, 1986, 1991, 1997, 2001, 2010, CCD. All rights reserved.
Music: *The Collegeville Chant Psalter*, © 2019, Order of Saint Benedict, Collegeville, MN. Published and administered by Liturgical Press, Collegeville, MN 56321. All rights reserved.

Psalm 86

16th Sunday in Ordinary Time, Year A

Psalm Tone

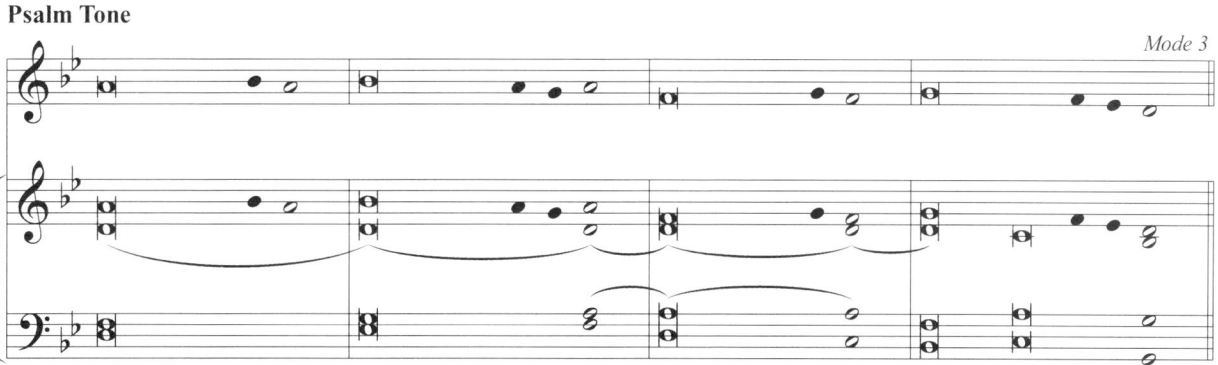

Psalm 86:5-6, 9-10, 15-16. R/ v. 5a

1. You, O Lord, are good and <u>for</u>giving,
   abounding in kindness to all who <u>call</u> upon you.
   Hearken, O Lord, to <u>my</u> prayer
   and attend to the sound <u>of</u> my pleading. *R/*

2. All the nations you have made shall come
       and worship you, <u>O</u> Lord,
   and g<u>lori</u>fy your name.
   For you are great, and you do wo<u>ndrous</u> deeds;
   you a<u>lone</u> are God. *R/*

3. You, O Lord, are a God merciful <u>and</u> gracious,
   slow to anger, abounding in kindness <u>and</u> fidelity.
   Turn toward me, and have pity <u>on</u> me;
   give your strength <u>to</u> your servant. *R/*

Text: Refrain, *Lectionary for Mass*, © 1969, 1981, 1997, ICEL.; verses, *Lectionary for Mass*/New American Bible, © 1970, 1986, 1991, 1997, 2001, 2010, CCD. All rights reserved.
Music: *The Collegeville Chant Psalter*, © 2019, Order of Saint Benedict, Collegeville, MN. Published and administered by Liturgical Press, Collegeville, MN 56321. All rights reserved.

Psalm 89

4th Sunday of Advent, Year B • Christmas Vigil • 13th Sunday in Ordinary Time, Year A

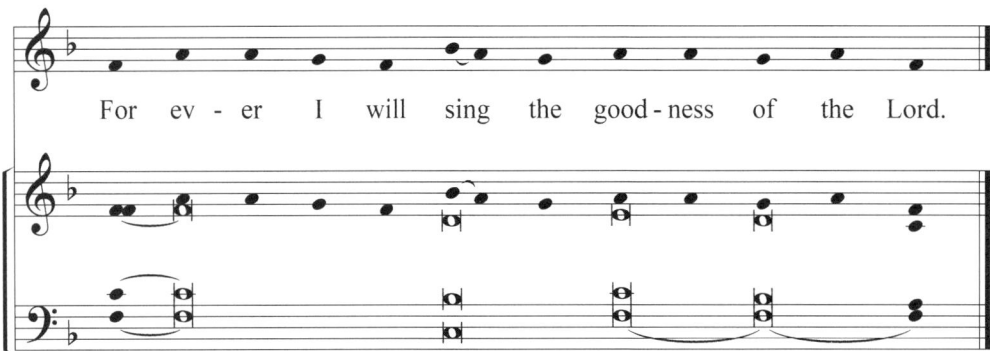

Psalm Tone

Mode 6

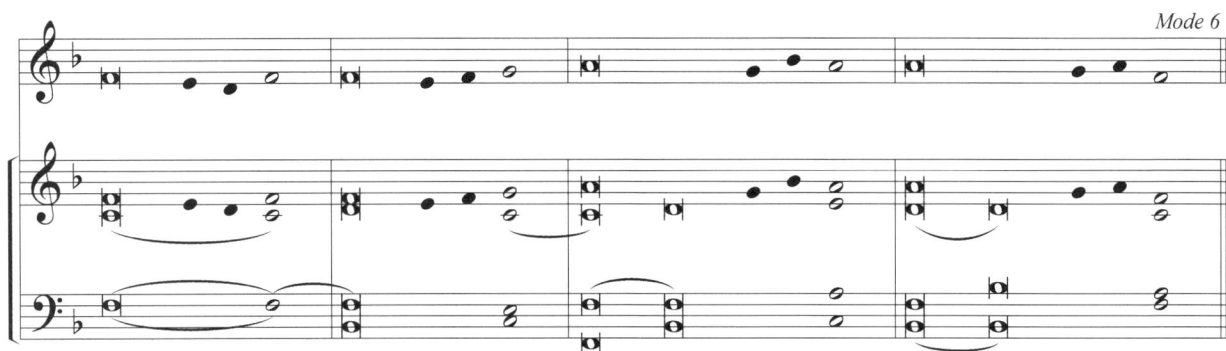

Psalm 89:2-3, 4-5, 16-17, 18-19, 27, 29. R/ v. 2a

4 Advent B and 13 OT A only   *[Christmas Vigil begins at v. 2]*
1. The promises of the Lord I will <u>sing</u> forever;
   through all generations my mouth shall pro<u>claim</u> your faithfulness.
   For you have said, "My kindness is estab<u>lished</u> forever";
   in heaven you have con<u>firmed</u> your faithfulness.   *R/*

   4 Advent B and Christmas Vigil only
2. "I have made a covenant <u>with</u> my chosen one,
   I have sworn to Da<u>vid</u> my servant:
   forever will I confirm <u>your</u> posterity
   and establish your throne for all <u>gen</u>erations."   *R/*

      Christmas Vigil and 13 OT A only
      2a. Blessed the people who know the <u>joy</u>ful shout;
         in the light of your countenance, O <u>Lord</u>, they walk.
         At your name they rejoice <u>all</u> the day,
         and through your justice they <u>are</u> exalted.   *R/*

4 Advent B and Christmas Vigil only
3. "He shall say of me, 'You <u>are</u> my father,
   my God, the <u>Rock</u>, my savior.'
   Forever I will maintain my <u>kind</u>ness toward him,
   and my covenant with <u>him</u> stands firm."   *R/*

13 OT A only
3a. You are the splendor <u>of</u> their strength,
   and by your favor our horn <u>is</u> exalted.
   For to the Lord be<u>longs</u> the shield,
   and to the Holy One of Isra<u>el</u>, our king.   *R/*

4 Advent B
  1. - 2. - 3.
Christmas Vigil
  2. - 2a. - 3.
13 OT A
  1. - 2a. - 3a.

Text: Refrain, *Lectionary for Mass*, © 1969, 1981, 1997, ICEL; verses, *Lectionary for Mass*/New American Bible, © 1970, 1986, 1991, 1997, 2001, 2010, CCD. All rights reserved.
Music: *The Collegeville Chant Psalter*, © 2019, Order of Saint Benedict, Collegeville, MN. Published and administered by Liturgical Press, Collegeville, MN 56321. All rights reserved.

Psalm 90

28th Sunday in Ordinary Time, Year B

18th Sunday in Ordinary Time, Year C *(Lectionary response)*

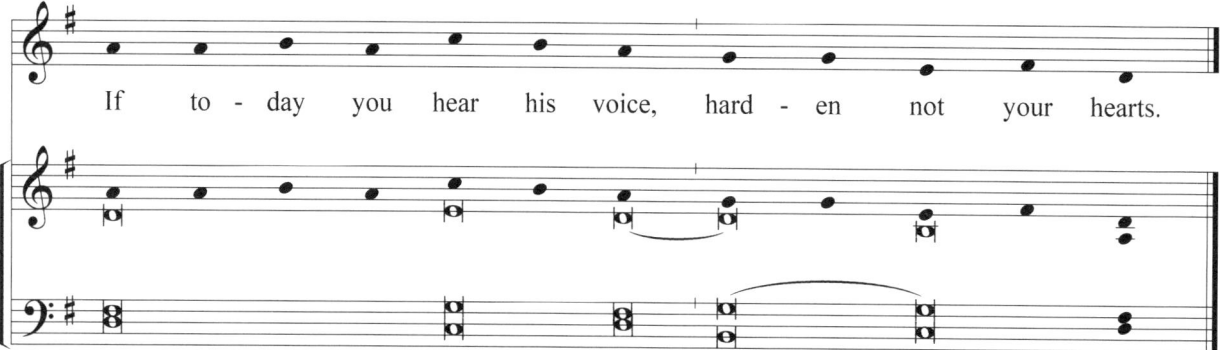

23rd Sunday in Ordinary Time, Year C •
18th Sunday in Ordinary Time, Year C

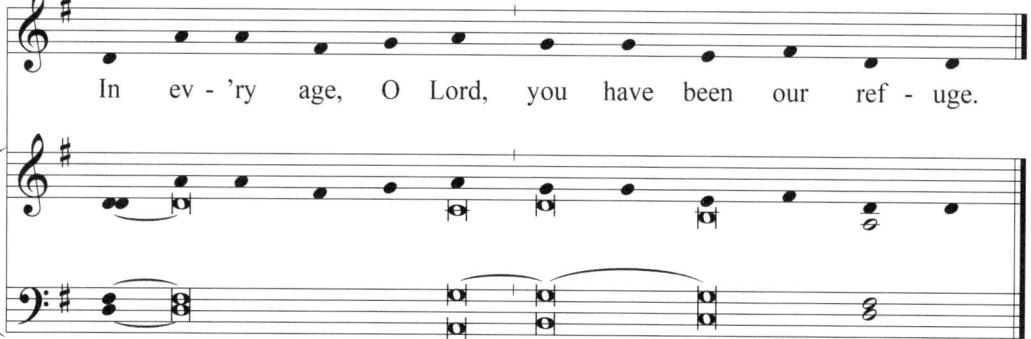

Psalm Tone

Mode 7

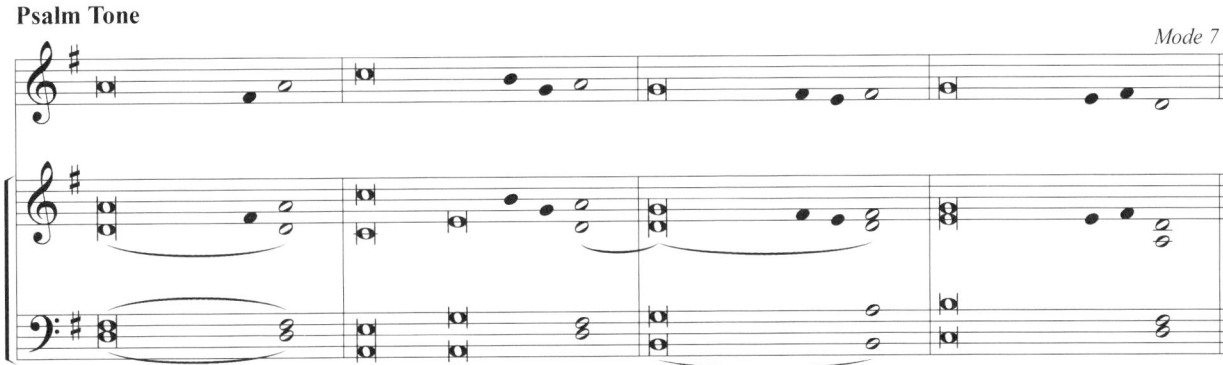

28 OT B
Psalm 90:12-13, 14-15, 16-17. R/ v. 14

1. Teach us to number our days a<u>right</u>,
   that we may gain wis<u>dom</u> of heart.
   Return, O L<u>ord</u>! How long?
   Have pity <u>on</u> your servants! *R/*

2. Fill us at daybreak with <u>your</u> kindness,
   that we may shout for joy and gladness <u>all</u> our days.
   Make us glad, for the days when <u>you</u> afflicted us,
   for the years when <u>we</u> saw evil. *R/*

3. Let your work be seen by <u>your</u> servants
   and your glory <u>by</u> their children;
   and may the gracious care of the Lord our
   God be ours;
   prosper the work of our hands for us!
   Prosper the work <u>of</u> our hands! *R/*

18 and 23 OT C
Psalm 90:3-4, 5-6, 12-13, 14, 17. R/ v. 1; Ps 95:8

1. You turn man back <u>to</u> dust,
   saying, "Return, O chil<u>dren</u> of men."
   For a thousand years in your sight
   are as yesterday, now that <u>it</u> is past,
   or as a watch <u>of</u> the night. *R/*

2. You make an end of them in <u>their</u> sleep;
   the next morning they are like the <u>changing</u> grass,
   which at dawn springs <u>up</u> anew,
   but by evening <u>wilts</u> and fades. *R/*

3. Teach us to number our days a<u>right</u>,
   that we may gain wis<u>dom</u> of heart.
   Return, O L<u>ord</u>! How long?
   Have pity <u>on</u> your servants! *R/*

4. Fill us at daybreak with <u>your</u> kindness,
   that we may shout for joy and gladness
   <u>all</u> our days.
   And may the gracious care of the Lord our
   God be ours;
   prosper the work of our hands for us!
   Prosper the work <u>of</u> our hands! *R/*

Text: Refrain, *Lectionary for Mass,* © 1969, 1981, 1997, ICEL; verses, *Lectionary for Mass*/New American Bible, © 1970, 1986, 1991, 1997, 2001, 2010, CCD. All rights reserved.
Music: *The Collegeville Chant Psalter,* © 2019, Order of Saint Benedict, Collegeville, MN. Published and administered by Liturgical Press, Collegeville, MN 56321. All rights reserved.

Psalm 91

1st Sunday of Lent, Year C • Common Lent 2

Psalm Tone

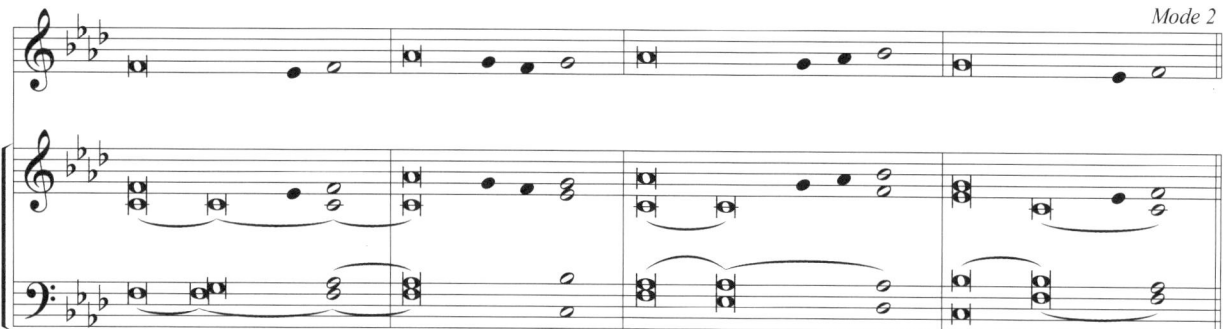

Psalm 91:1-2, 10-11, 12-13, 14-15. R/ cf. v. 15b

1. You who dwell in the shelter of the <u>Most</u> High,
   who abide in the shadow of <u>the</u> Almighty,
   say to the Lord, "My re<u>fuge</u> and fortress,
   my God in whom <u>I</u> trust." *R/*

2. No evil shall be<u>fall</u> you,
   nor shall affliction come <u>near</u> your tent,
   for to his angels he has given com<u>mand</u> about you,
   that they guard you in all <u>your</u> ways. *R/*

3. Upon their hands they shall bear <u>you</u> up,
   lest you dash your foot a<u>gainst</u> a stone.
   You shall tread upon the asp <u>and</u> the viper;
   you shall trample down the lion and <u>the</u> dragon. *R/*

4. Because he clings to me, I will <u>deliver</u> him;
   I will set him on high because he acknowled<u>ges</u> my name.
   He shall call upon me, and <u>I</u> will answer him;
   I will be with him in distress; I will deliver him and glo<u>rify</u> him. *R/*

Common Lent 2

2a. No evil shall be<u>fall</u> you,
   nor affliction come <u>near</u> your tent.
   For God com<u>mands</u> the angels
   to guard you in all <u>your</u> ways. *R/*

Text: Refrain, *Lectionary for Mass*, © 1969, 1981, 1997, ICEL; verses, *Lectionary for Mass*/New American Bible, © 1970, 1986, 1991, 1997, 2001, 2010, CCD. All rights reserved.
Music: *The Collegeville Chant Psalter*, © 2019, Order of Saint Benedict, Collegeville, MN. Published and administered by Liturgical Press, Collegeville, MN 56321. All rights reserved.

Psalm 92

85

11th Sunday in Ordinary Time, Year B • 8th Sunday in Ordinary Time, Year C

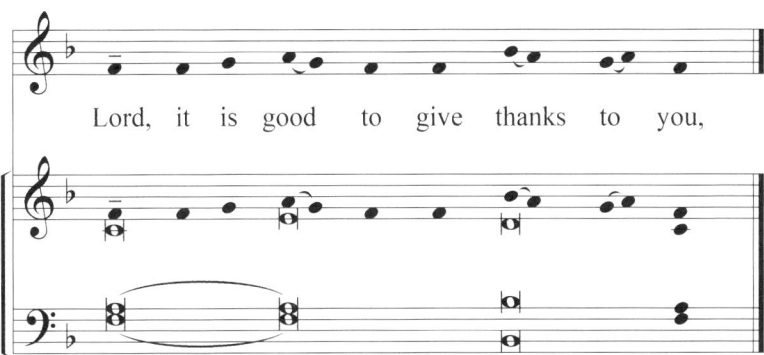

Psalm Tone

Mode 6

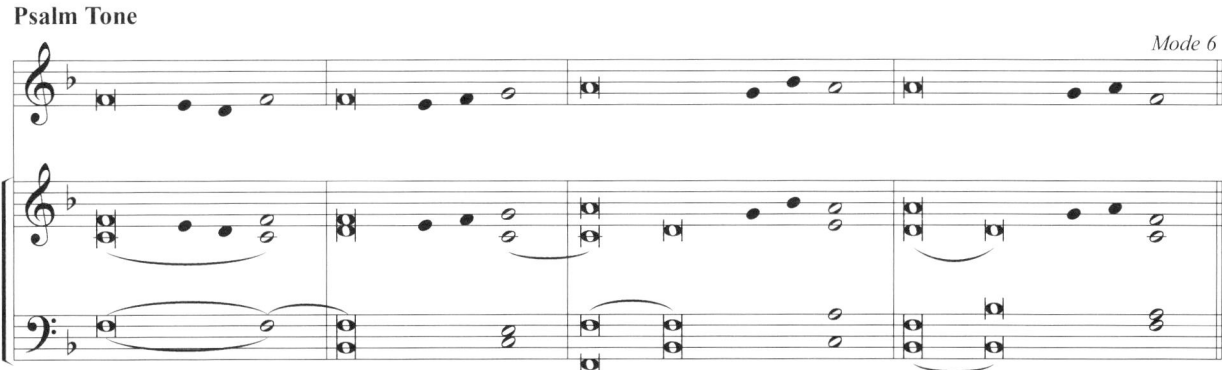

Psalm 92:2-3, 13-14, 15-16. R/ cf. v. 2a

1. It is good to give thanks to the Lord,
   to sing praise to your name, Most High,
   to proclaim your kindness at dawn
   and your faithfulness throughout the night. *R/*

2. The just one shall flourish like the palm tree,
   like a cedar of Lebanon shall he grow.
   They that are planted in the house of the Lord
   shall flourish in the courts of our God. *R/*

3. They shall bear fruit even in old age;
   vigorous and sturdy shall they be,
   declaring how just is the Lord,
   my rock, in whom there is no wrong. *R/*

Text: Refrain, *Lectionary for Mass,* © 1969, 1981, 1997, ICEL; verses, *Lectionary for Mass*/New American Bible, © 1970, 1986, 1991, 1997, 2001, 2010, CCD. All rights reserved.
Music: *The Collegeville Chant Psalter,* © 2019, Order of Saint Benedict, Collegeville, MN. Published and administered by Liturgical Press, Collegeville, MN 56321. All rights reserved.

Psalm 93

Christ the King, Year B

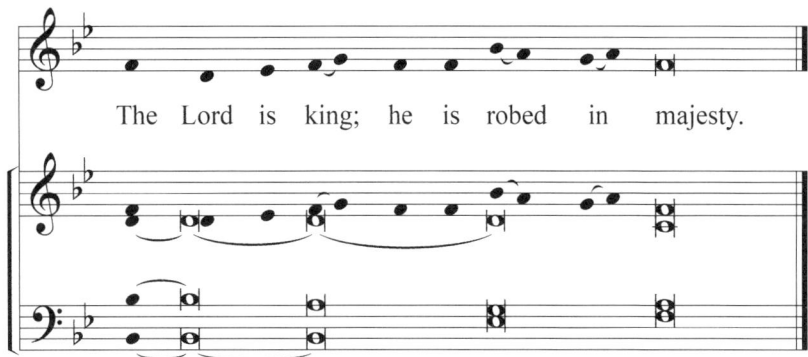

Psalm Tone

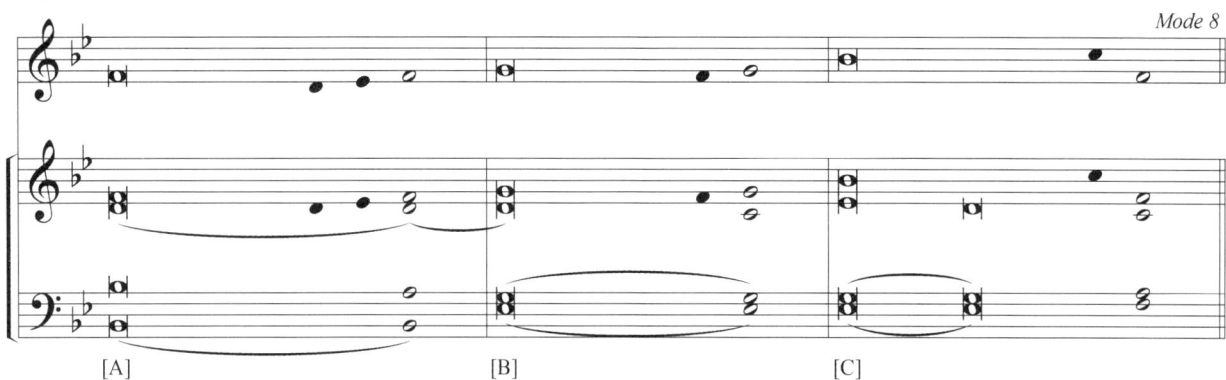

[A]   [B]   [C]

Psalm 93:1, 1-2, 5. R. v/ 1a

1. The LORD is king, in <u>splen</u>dor robed;
   [omit B]
   robed is the LORD and girt about <u>with</u> strength.   *R/*

2. And he has made the world firm,
      not <u>to</u> be moved.
   Your throne stands firm from <u>of</u> old;
   from everlasting you are, <u>O</u> LORD.   *R/*

3. Your decrees are worthy of <u>trust</u> indeed;
   holiness befits <u>your</u> house,
   O LORD, for length <u>of</u> days.   *R/*

Text: Refrain, *Lectionary for Mass,* © 1969, 1981, 1997, ICEL; verses, *Lectionary for Mass*/New American Bible, © 1970, 1986, 1991, 1997, 2001, 2010, CCD. All rights reserved.
Music: *The Collegeville Chant Psalter,* © 2019, Order of Saint Benedict, Collegeville, MN. Published and administered by Liturgical Press, Collegeville, MN 56321. All rights reserved.

Psalm 95

3rd Sunday of Lent, Year A • 23rd Sunday in Ordinary Time, Year A •
4th Sunday in Ordinary Time, Year B • 27th Sunday in Ordinary Time, Year C •
Common Ordinary Time 5

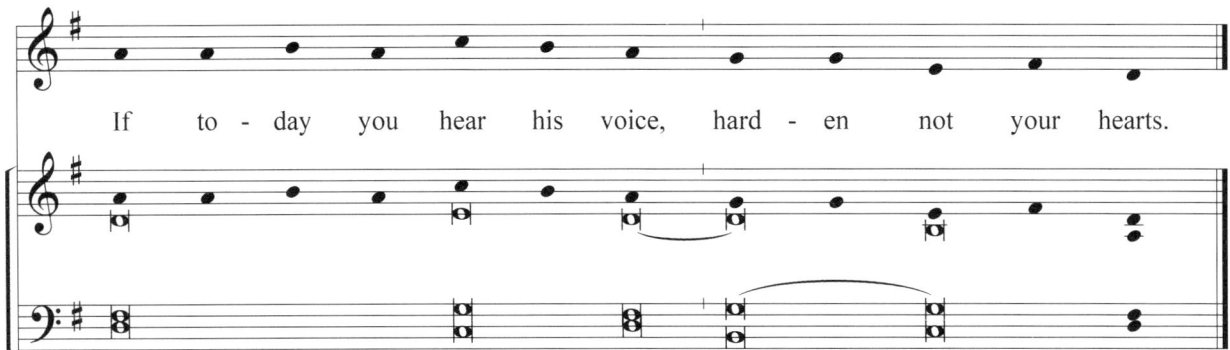

If to-day you hear his voice, hard-en not your hearts.

Psalm Tone

Mode 7

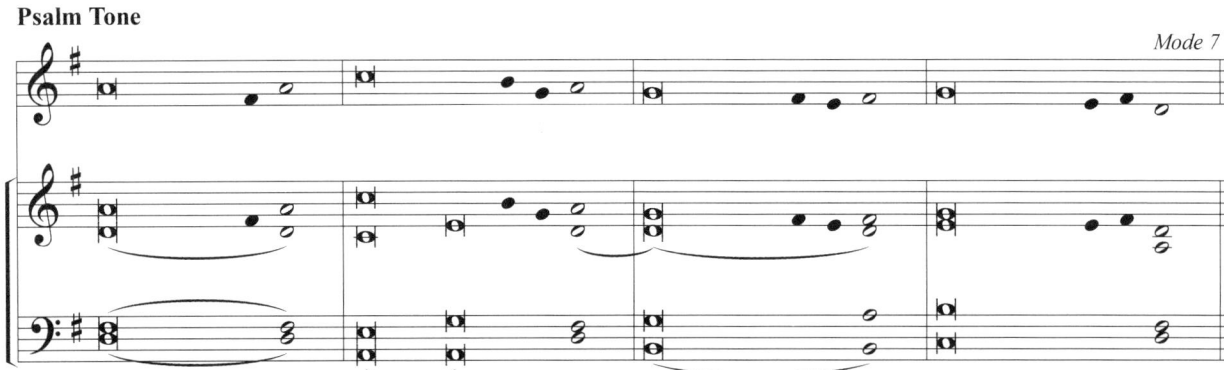

Psalm 95:1-2, 6-7, 8-9. R/ v. 8

1. Come, let us sing joyfully to the LORD;
   let us acclaim the rock of our salvation.
   Let us come into his presence with thanksgiving;
   let us joyfully sing psalms to him. *R/*

2. Come, let us bow down in worship;
   let us kneel before the LORD who made us.
   For he is our God,
   and we are the people he shepherds, the flock he guides. *R/*

3. Oh, that today you would hear his voice:
   "Harden not your hearts as at Meribah,
   as in the day of Massah in the desert,
   where your fathers tempted me;
      they tested me though they had seen my works." *R/*

Text: Refrain, *Lectionary for Mass,* © 1969, 1981, 1997, ICEL; verses, *Lectionary for Mass*/New American Bible, © 1970, 1986, 1991, 1997, 2001, 2010, CCD. All rights reserved.
Music: *The Collegeville Chant Psalter,* © 2019, Order of Saint Benedict, Collegeville, MN. Published and administered by Liturgical Press, Collegeville, MN 56321. All rights reserved.

Anniversary of Dedication of a Church, option 4

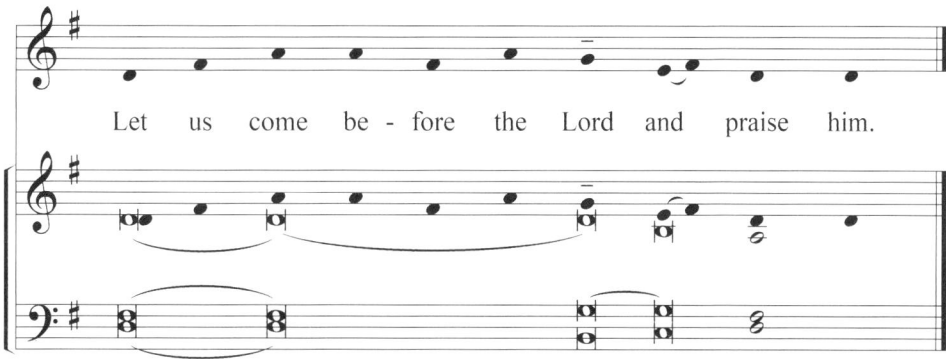

Let us come before the Lord and praise him.

Psalm Tone

Mode 7

[A] [B] [C] [D] [E] [F]

Psalm 95:1-2, 3-5, 6-7. R/ v. 2

1. Come, let us sing joyfully to <u>the</u> L<small>ORD</small>;
   let us acclaim the Rock of <u>our</u> salvation.
   [omit C, D]
   Let us come into his presence <u>with</u> thanksgiving;
   let us joyfully sing <u>psalms</u> to him.   *R/*

2. For the L<small>ORD</small> is <u>a</u> great God,
   and a great king a<u>bove</u> all gods;
   In his hands are the depths of <u>the</u> earth,
   and the tops of the mountains <u>are</u> his.
   His is the sea, for <u>he</u> has made it,
   and the dry land, which his <u>hands</u> have formed.   *R/*

3. Come, let us bow down <u>in</u> worship;
   let us kneel before the L<small>ORD</small> who made us.
   [omit C, D]
   For he <u>is</u> our God,
   and we are the people he shepherds, the <u>flock</u> he guides.   *R/*

Text: Refrain, *Lectionary for Mass,* © 1969, 1981, 1997, ICEL; verses, *Lectionary for Mass*/New American Bible, © 1970, 1986, 1991, 1997, 2001, 2010, CCD. All rights reserved.
Music: *The Collegeville Chant Psalter,* © 2019, Order of Saint Benedict, Collegeville, MN. Published and administered by Liturgical Press, Collegeville, MN 56321. All rights reserved.

Psalm 96

Christmas Midnight

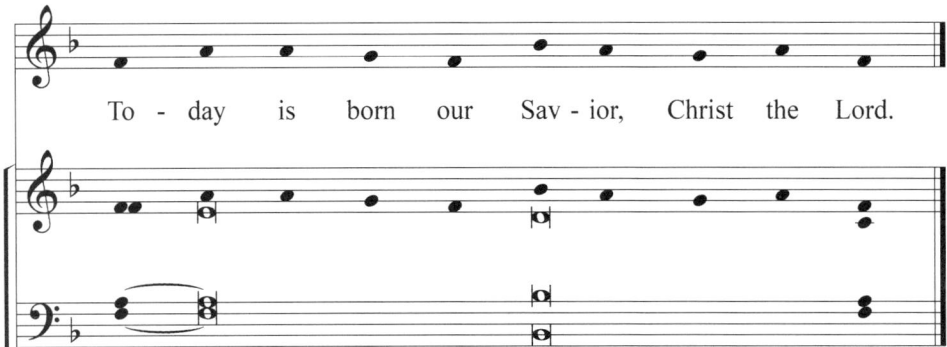

Today is born our Savior, Christ the Lord.

29th Sunday in Ordinary Time, Year A

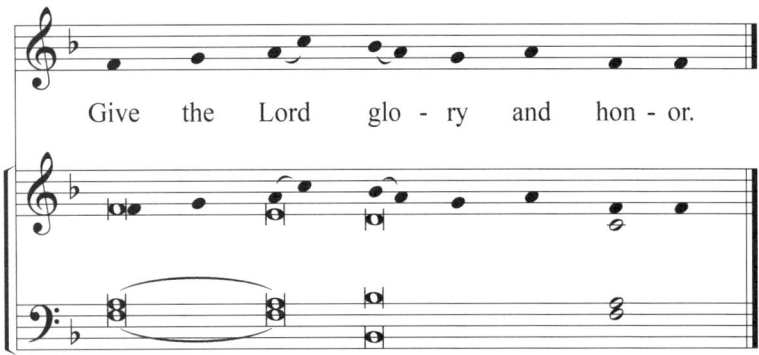

Give the Lord glory and honor.

2nd Sunday in Ordinary Time, Year C

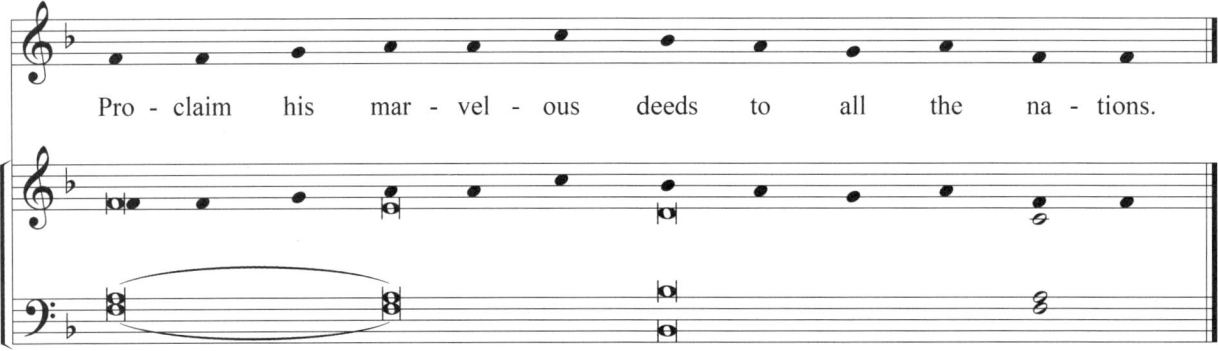

Proclaim his marvelous deeds to all the nations.

Psalm Tone

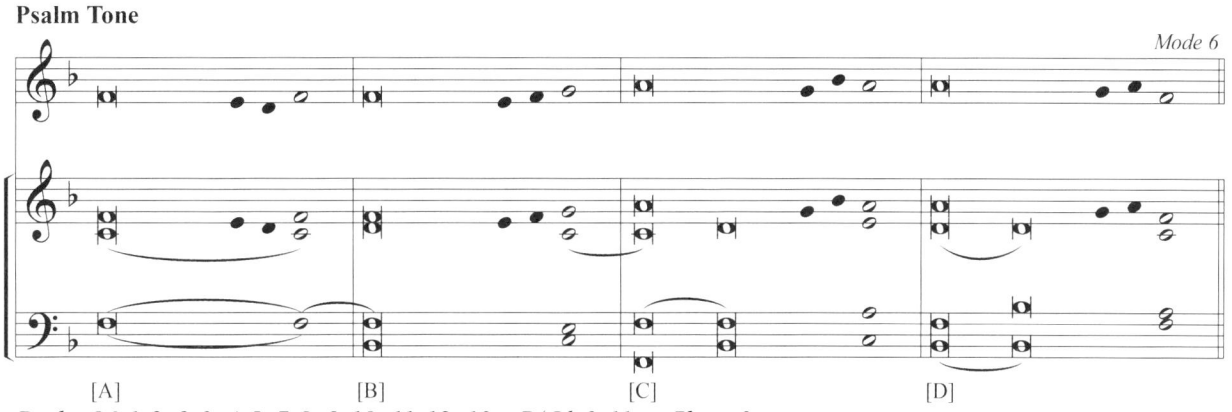

Mode 6

[A]   [B]   [C]   [D]

Psalm 96:1-2, 2-3, 4-5, 7-8, 9-10, 11-12, 13.   R/ Lk 2:11; v. 7b; v. 3

Christmas Midnight and 2 OT C only
1. Sing to the LORD <u>a</u> new song;
   sing to the LORD, <u>all</u> you lands.
   [omit C]
   Sing to the LORD; <u>bless</u> his name.   R/

Christmas Midnight and 2 OT C only
2. Announce his salvation, day <u>af</u>ter day.
   Tell his glory a<u>mong</u> the nations;
   [omit C]
   among all peoples, his <u>won</u>drous deeds.   R/

Christmas Midnight only
3. Let the heavens be glad and the <u>earth</u> rejoice;
   let the sea and what fills <u>it</u> resound;
   let the plains be joyful and all <u>that</u> is in them!
   Then shall all the trees of the for<u>est</u> exult.   R/

Christmas Midnight only
4. They shall exult before the LORD, <u>for</u> he comes;
   for he comes to <u>rule</u> the earth.
   He shall rule the <u>world</u> with justice
   and the peoples <u>with</u> his constancy.   R/

29 OT A only
1a. Sing to the LORD <u>a</u> new song;
    sing to the LORD, <u>all</u> you lands.
    Tell his glory a<u>mong</u> the nations;
    among all peoples, his <u>won</u>drous deeds.   R/

29 OT A only
2a. For great is the LORD and highly <u>to</u> be praised;
    awesome is he, be<u>yond</u> all gods.
    For all the gods of the nations are <u>things</u> of nought,
    but the LORD <u>made</u> the heavens.   R/

29 OT A and 2 OT C only
3a. Give to the LORD, you fami<u>lies</u> of nations,
    give to the LORD glo<u>ry</u> and praise;
    [omit C]
    give to the LORD the glory <u>due</u> his name!   [R/]
29 OT A only
[*] Bring gifts and en<u>ter</u> his courts.   R/

* *For 29 OT A, treat v. 3a as a four-measure verse.*

29 OT A and 2 OT C only
4a. Worship the LORD in ho<u>ly</u> attire.
    Tremble before him, <u>all</u> the earth;
    say among the nations: The LORD is king.
    He governs the peo<u>ples</u> with equity.   R/

Text: Refrain, *Lectionary for Mass,* © 1969, 1981, 1997, ICEL; verses, *Lectionary for Mass*/New American Bible, © 1970, 1986, 1991, 1997, 2001, 2010, CCD. All rights reserved.
Music: *The Collegeville Chant Psalter,* © 2019, Order of Saint Benedict, Collegeville, MN. Published and administered by Liturgical Press, Collegeville, MN 56321. All rights reserved.

| **Christmas Midnight** |
| 1. - 2. - 3. - 4. |
| **29 OT A** |
| 1a. - 2a. - *3a. - 4a. |
| **2 OT C** |
| 1. - 2. - 3a. - 4a. |

Psalm 97

Christmas Dawn

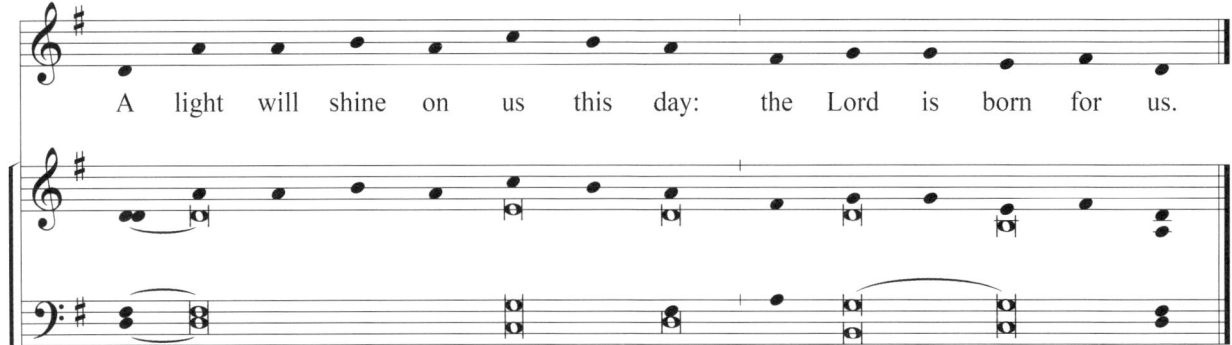

A light will shine on us this day: the Lord is born for us.

Transfiguration (August 6)

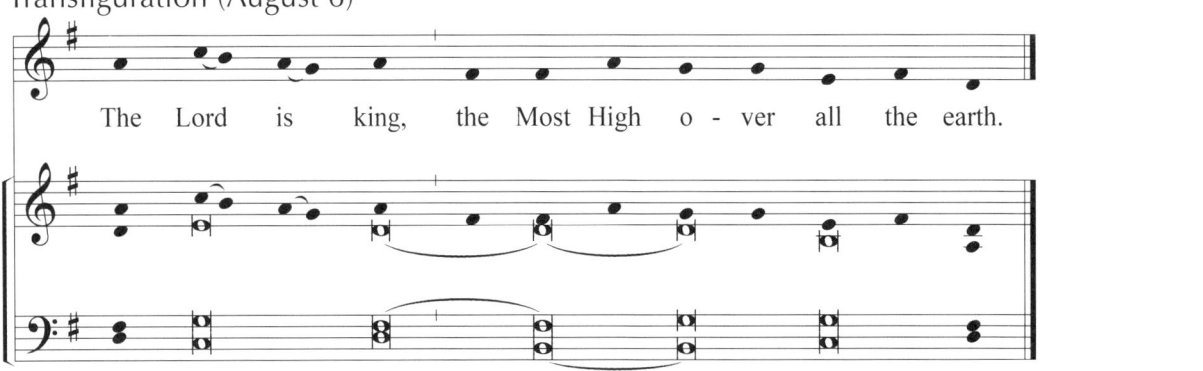

The Lord is king, the Most High o-ver all the earth.

Psalm Tone

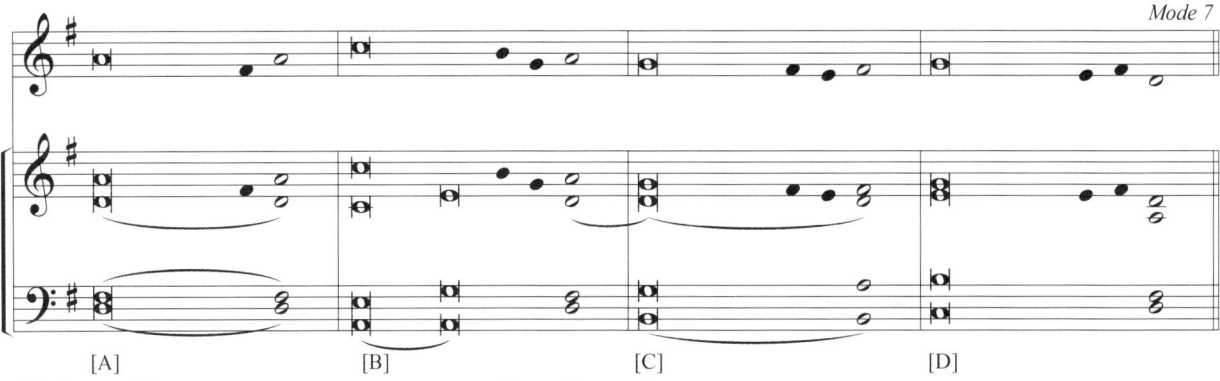

Mode 7

[A]   [B]   [C]   [D]

Christmas Dawn
Psalm 97:1, 6, 11-12.

1. The Lord is king; let the earth re<u>joice</u>;
   let the many <u>isles</u> be glad.
   The heavens pro<u>claim</u> his justice,
   and all peoples <u>see</u> his glory. *R/*

2. Light dawns for <u>the</u> just;
   and gladness, for the up<u>right</u> of heart.
   Be glad in the <u>Lord</u>, you just,
   and give thanks to his <u>holy</u> name. *R/*

Transfiguration
Psalm 97:1-2, 5-6, 9. R/ vv. 1 and 9

1. The Lord is king; let the earth re<u>joice</u>;
   let the many is<u>lands</u> be glad.
   Clouds and darkness are <u>round</u> about him,
   justice and judgment are the foundation <u>of</u> his throne. *R/*

2. The mountains melt like wax before <u>the</u> Lord,
   before the Lord of <u>all</u> the earth.
   The heavens pro<u>claim</u> his justice,
   and all peoples <u>see</u> his glory. *R/*

3. [A] Because you, O Lord, are the Most High over all <u>the</u> earth,
   [D] exalted far a<u>bove</u> all gods. *R/*

Text: Refrain, *Lectionary for Mass,* © 1969, 1981, 1997, ICEL; verses, *Lectionary for Mass*/New American Bible, © 1970, 1986, 1991, 1997, 2001, 2010, CCD. All rights reserved.
Music: *The Collegeville Chant Psalter,* © 2019, Order of Saint Benedict, Collegeville, MN. Published and administered by Liturgical Press, Collegeville, MN 56321. All rights reserved.

7th Sunday of Easter, Year C

The Lord is king, the Most High over all the earth.

7th Sunday of Easter, Year C, *alternate response*

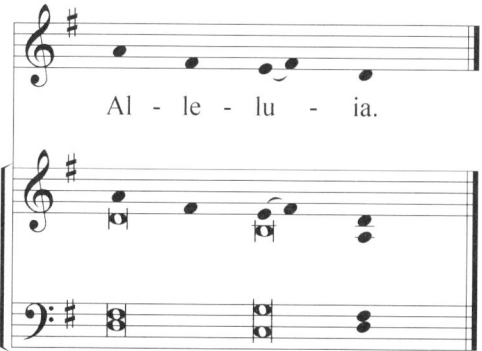

Al - le - lu - ia.

Psalm Tone

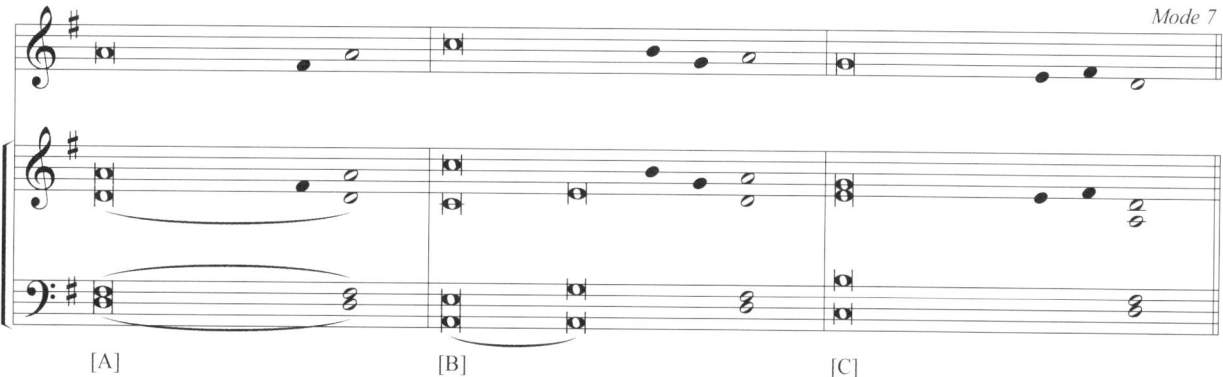

Mode 7

[A] [B] [C]

Psalm 97:1-2, 6-7, 9. R/ vv. 1 and 9

1. The Lord is king; let the earth re<u>joice</u>;
   let the many <u>islands</u> be glad.
   Justice and judgment are the foundation <u>of</u> his throne. *R/*

2. The heavens proclaim <u>his</u> justice,
   and all peoples <u>see</u> his glory.
   All gods are pros<u>trate</u> before him. *R/*

3. [A] You, O Lord, are the Most High over all <u>the</u> earth,
   [C] exalted far a<u>bove</u> all gods. *R/*

Text: Refrain, *Lectionary for Mass*, © 1969, 1981, 1997, ICEL; verses, *Lectionary for Mass*/New American Bible, © 1970, 1986, 1991, 1997, 2001, 2010, CCD. All rights reserved.
Music: *The Collegeville Chant Psalter*, © 2019, Order of Saint Benedict, Collegeville, MN. Published and administered by Liturgical Press, Collegeville, MN 56321. All rights reserved.

Psalm 98

Immaculate Conception

Christmas Day • Common Christmas

6th Sunday of Easter, Year B • 28th Sunday in Ordinary Time, Year C

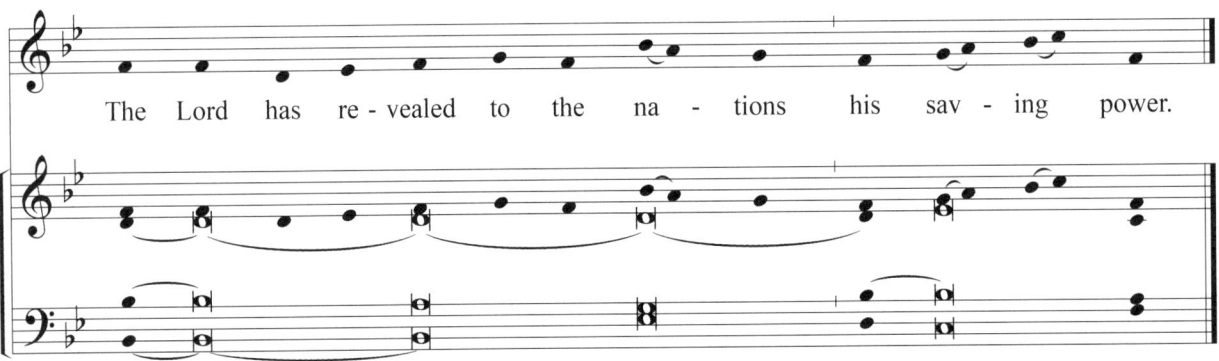

6th Sunday of Easter, Year B, *alternate response*

Psalm Tone

Psalm 98:1, 2-3ab, 3cd-4. R/ v. 1a; 3c; 2b

1. Sing to the Lord <u>a</u> new song,
   for he has done won<u>drous</u> deeds;
   his right hand has won victo<u>ry</u> for him,
   his ho<u>ly</u> arm. *R/*

2. The Lord has made his sal<u>va</u>tion known:
   in the sight of the nations he has revealed <u>his</u> justice.
   He has remembered his kindness <u>and</u> his faithfulness
   toward the house <u>of</u> Israel. *R/*

3. All the ends of the <u>earth</u> have seen
   the salvation by <u>our</u> God.
   Sing joyfully to the Lord, <u>all</u> you lands;
   break into song; <u>sing</u> praise. *R/*

Christmas Day and Common Christmas only
4. Sing praise to the Lord <u>with</u> the harp,
   with the harp and melo<u>dious</u> song.
   With trumpets and the sound <u>of</u> the horn
   sing joyfully before the King, <u>the</u> Lord. *R/*

Text: Refrain, *Lectionary for Mass,* © 1969, 1981, 1997, ICEL; verses, *Lectionary for Mass*/New American Bible, © 1970, 1986, 1991, 1997, 2001, 2010, CCD. All rights reserved.
Music: *The Collegeville Chant Psalter,* © 2019, Order of Saint Benedict, Collegeville, MN. Published and administered by Liturgical Press, Collegeville, MN 56321. All rights reserved.

33rd Sunday in Ordinary Time, Year C

Psalm Tone Mode 6

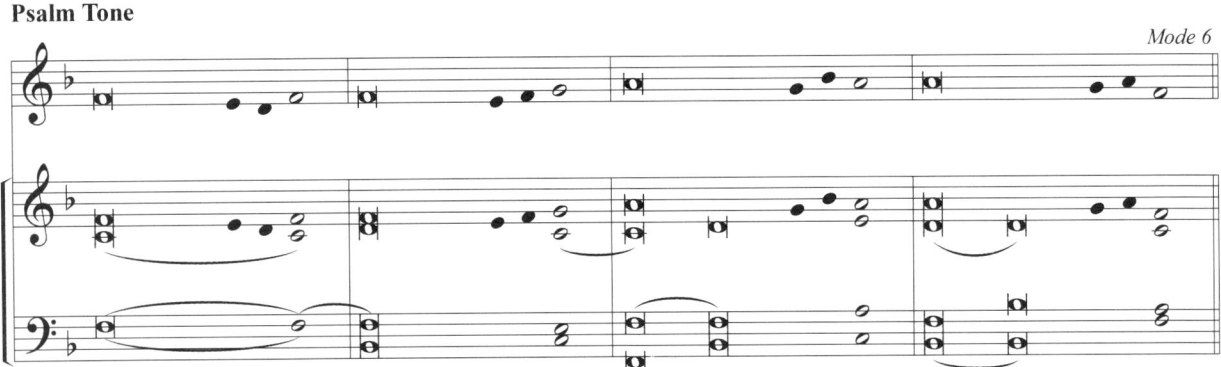

Psalm 98:5-6, 7-8, 9. R/ cf. v. 9

1. Sing praise to the Lord <u>with</u> the harp,
   with the harp and mel<u>o</u>dious song.
   With trumpets and the sound <u>of</u> the horn
   sing joyfully before the <u>King</u>, the Lord. *R/*

2. Let the sea and what fills <u>it</u> resound,
   the world and <u>those</u> who dwell in it;
   let the rivers <u>clap</u> their hands,
   the mountains shout with <u>them</u> for joy. *R/*

3. Before the Lord, <u>for</u> he comes,
   for he comes to <u>rule</u> the earth,
   he will rule the <u>world</u> with justice;
   and the peo<u>ples</u> with equity. *R/*

Text: Refrain, *Lectionary for Mass,* © 1969, 1981, 1997, ICEL; verses, *Lectionary for Mass*/New American Bible, © 1970, 1986, 1991, 1997, 2001, 2010, CCD. All rights reserved.
Music: *The Collegeville Chant Psalter,* © 2019, Order of Saint Benedict, Collegeville, MN. Published and administered by Liturgical Press, Collegeville, MN 56321. All rights reserved.

Psalm 100

11th Sunday in Ordinary Time, Year A • 4th Sunday of Easter, Year C •
Common Ordinary Time 6

We are his peo-ple, the sheep of his flock.

4th Sunday of Easter, Year C, *alternate response*

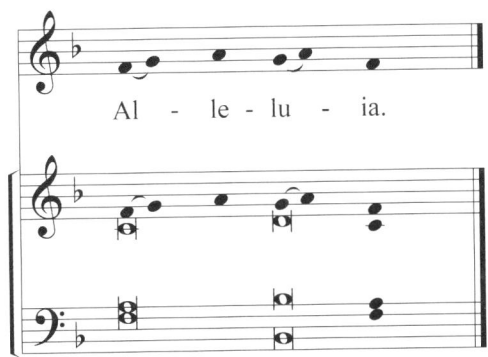

Al - le - lu - ia.

Psalm Tone   Mode 6

Psalm 100:1-2, 3, 5. R/ v. 3c

1. Sing joyfully to the L<small>ORD</small>, <u>all</u> you lands;
   serve the L<small>ORD</small> with gladness;
   come before him with <u>joy</u>ful song. R/

2. Know that the L<small>ORD</small> is God,
   he made us, <u>his</u> we are;
   his people, the <u>flock</u> he tends. R/

3. The L<small>ORD</small> is good:
   his kindness en<u>dures</u> forever,
   and his faithfulness, to all <u>gen</u>erations. R/

Text: Refrain, *Lectionary for Mass,* © 1969, 1981, 1997, ICEL; verses, *Lectionary for Mass*/New American Bible, © 1970, 1986, 1991, 1997, 2001, 2010, CCD. All rights reserved.
Music: *The Collegeville Chant Psalter,* © 2019, Order of Saint Benedict, Collegeville, MN. Published and administered by Liturgical Press, Collegeville, MN 56321. All rights reserved.

Psalm 103

7th Sunday in Ordinary Time, Year A • 8th Sunday in Ordinary Time, Year B •
3rd Sunday of Lent, Year C • 7th Sunday in Ordinary Time, Year C • Common Ordinary Time 7

The Lord is kind and merciful.

24th Sunday in Ordinary Time, Year A

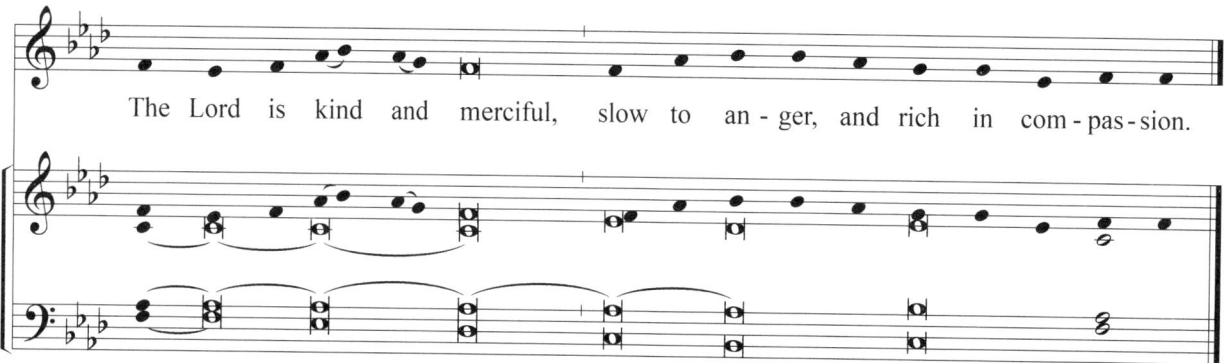

The Lord is kind and merciful, slow to an-ger, and rich in com-pas-sion.

Psalm Tone

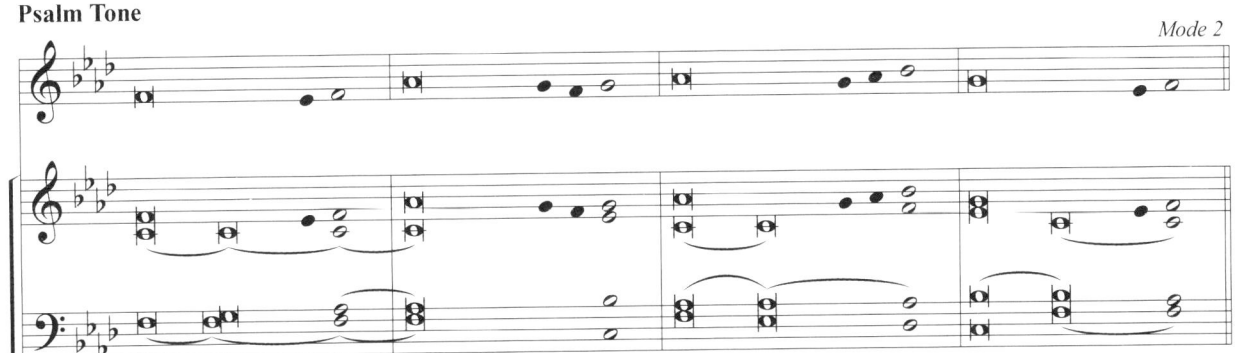

Mode 2

Psalm 103:1-2, 3-4, 6-7, 8, 9, 10, 12-13. R/ v. 8a; v. 8

1. Bless the LORD, O <u>my</u> soul;
   and all my being, bless his <u>ho</u>ly name.
   Bless the LORD, <u>O</u> my soul,
   and forget not all <u>his</u> benefits. *R/*

2. He pardons all your <u>in</u>iquities,
   heals <u>all</u> your ills.
   He redeems your life <u>from</u> destruction,
   crowns you with kindness and com<u>pas</u>sion. *R/*

3 Lent C only

3. The LORD se<u>cures</u> justice
   and the rights of all <u>the</u> oppressed.
   He has made known his <u>ways</u> to Moses,
   and his deeds to the children <u>of</u> Israel. *R/*

4. Merciful and gracious is <u>the</u> LORD,
   slow to anger, and abound<u>ing</u> in kindness.
   Not according to our sins <u>does</u> he deal with us,
   nor does he requite us according to <u>our</u> crimes. *R/*

5. As far as the east is from <u>the</u> west,
   so far has he put our trans<u>gres</u>sions from us.
   As a father has compassion <u>on</u> his children,
   so the LORD has compassion on those
   <u>who</u> fear him. *R/*

7 OT A, 8 OT B, 7 OT C, Common OT 7
   1. - 2. - 4.- 5.
24 OT A
   1. - 2. - 4b. - 5a.
3 Lent C
   1. - 2. - 3. - 4a.

3 Lent C only

4a. Merciful and gracious is <u>the</u> LORD,
    slow to anger and abound<u>ing</u> in kindness.
    For as the heavens are high a<u>bove</u> the earth,
    so surpassing is his kindness toward those
    <u>who</u> fear him. *R/*

24 OT A only

4b. He will not al<u>ways</u> chide,
    nor does he keep his <u>wrath</u> forever.
    Not according to our sins <u>does</u> he deal with us,
    nor does he requite us according to
    <u>our</u> crimes. *R/*

24 OT A only

5a. For as the heavens are high above <u>the</u> earth,
    so surpassing is his kindness toward
    <u>those</u> who fear him.
    As far as the east is <u>from</u> the west,
    so far has he put our transgres<u>sions</u>
    from us. *R/*

Text: Refrain, *Lectionary for Mass*, © 1969, 1981, 1997, ICEL; verses, *Lectionary for Mass*/New American Bible, © 1970, 1986, 1991, 1997, 2001, 2010, CCD. All rights reserved.
Music: *The Collegeville Chant Psalter*, © 2019, Order of Saint Benedict, Collegeville, MN. Published and administered by Liturgical Press, Collegeville, MN 56321. All rights reserved.

7th Sunday of Easter, Year B

The Lord has set his throne in heaven.

7th Sunday of Easter, Year B, *alternate response*

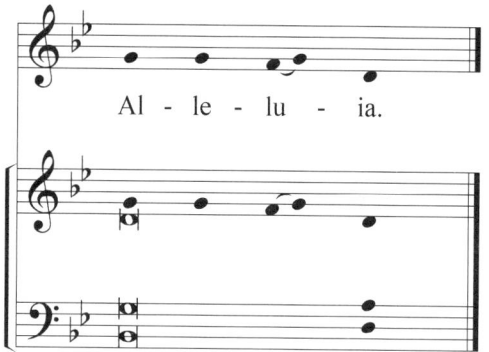

Alleluia.

Psalm Tone

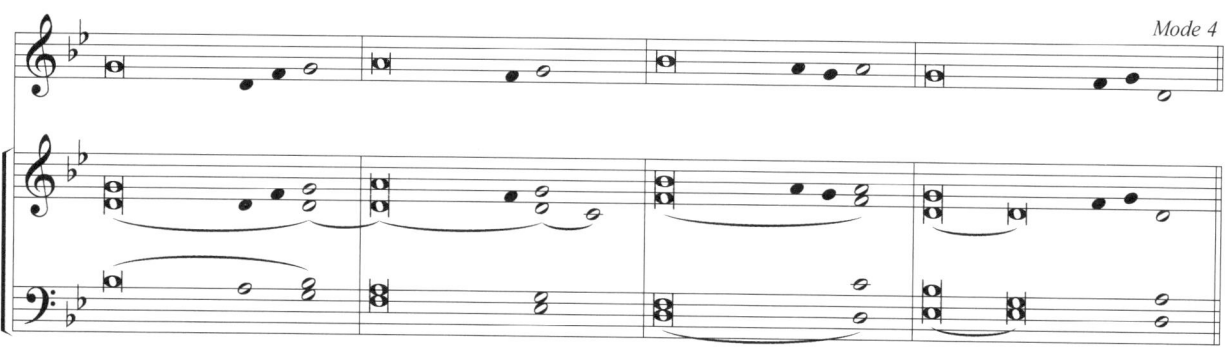

Mode 4

Psalm 103:1-2, 11-12, 19-20. R/ v. 19a

1. Bless the Lord, O my soul;
   and all my being, bless his holy name.
   Bless the Lord, O my soul,
   and forget not all his benefits. *R/*

2. For as the heavens are high above the earth,
   so surpassing is his kindness toward those who fear him.
   As far as the east is from the west,
   so far has he put our transgressions from us. *R/*

3. The Lord has established his throne in heaven,
   and his kingdom rules over all.
   Bless the Lord, all you his angels,
   you mighty in strength, who do his bidding. *R/*

Text: Refrain, *Lectionary for Mass*, © 1969, 1981, 1997, ICEL; verses, *Lectionary for Mass*/New American Bible, © 1970, 1986, 1991, 1997, 2001, 2010, CCD. All rights reserved.
Music: *The Collegeville Chant Psalter*, © 2019, Order of Saint Benedict, Collegeville, MN. Published and administered by Liturgical Press, Collegeville, MN 56321. All rights reserved.

Sacred Heart, Year A

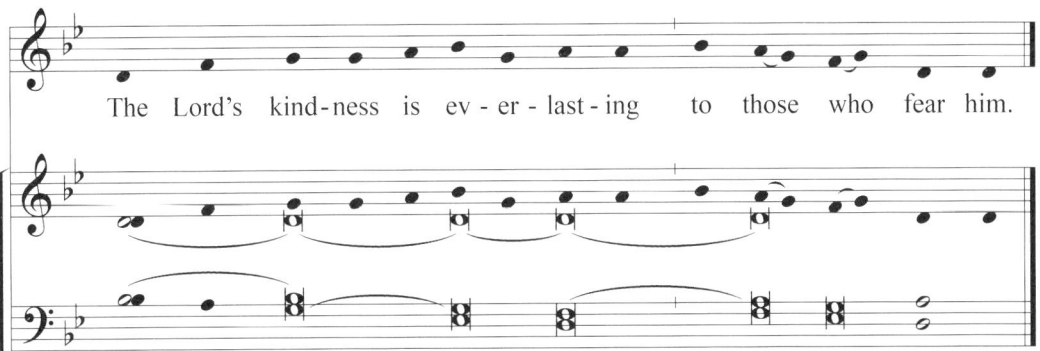

The Lord's kind-ness is ev-er-last-ing to those who fear him.

Psalm Tone
Mode 4

Psalm 103:1-2, 3-4, 6-7, 8, 10. R/ cf. v. 17

1. Bless the LORD, O my soul;
   and all my being, bless his ho<u>ly</u> name.
   Bless the LORD, <u>O</u> my soul,
   and forget not <u>all</u> his benefits.   *R/*

2. He pardons all <u>your</u> iniquities,
   heals all <u>your</u> ills.
   He redeems your life <u>from</u> destruction,
   crowns you with kindness <u>and</u> compassion.   *R/*

3. Merciful and gracious <u>is</u> the LORD,
   slow to anger, and abounding <u>in</u> kindness.
   Not according to our sins <u>does</u> he deal with us,
   nor does he requite us according <u>to</u> our crimes.   *R/*

Text: Refrain, *Lectionary for Mass,* © 1969, 1981, 1997, ICEL; verses, *Lectionary for Mass*/New American Bible, © 1970, 1986, 1991, 1997, 2001, 2010, CCD. All rights reserved.
Music: *The Collegeville Chant Psalter,* © 2019, Order of Saint Benedict, Collegeville, MN. Published and administered by Liturgical Press, Collegeville, MN 56321. All rights reserved.

Psalm 104

Easter Vigil 1 • Pentecost Vigil 4 (and Pentecost Simple Vigil) • Pentecost Day • Common Pentecost

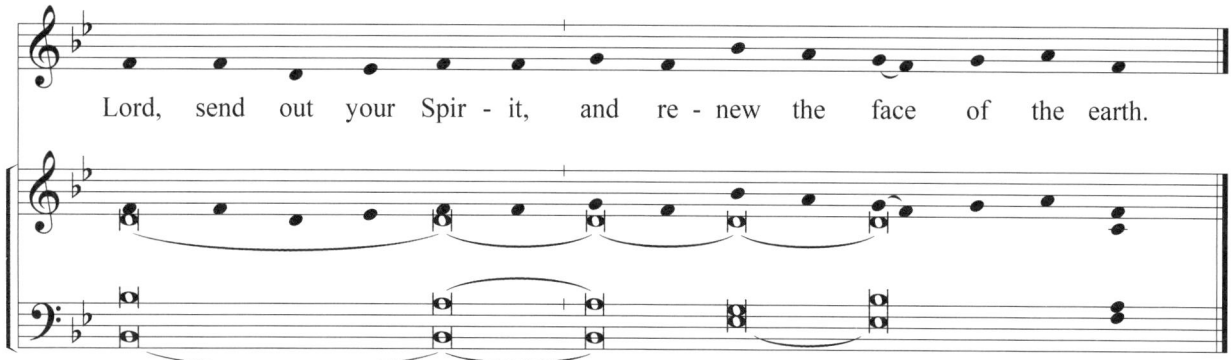

Pentecost Vigil 4 (and Pentecost Simple Vigil), *alternate response* • Pentecost Day, *alternate response*

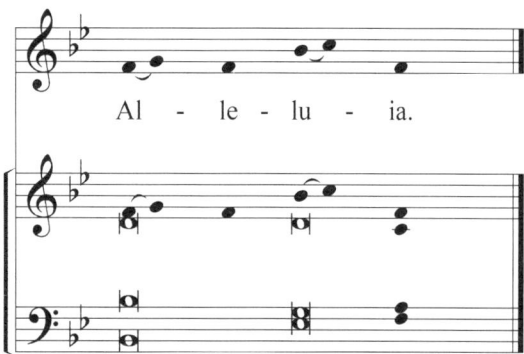

Psalm Tone

Mode 8

Easter Vigil 1
Psalm 104:1-2, 5-6, 10, 12, 13-14, 24, 35. R/ cf. v. 30

1. Bless the Lord, O my soul!
   O Lord, my God, you are great indeed!
   You are clothed with majesty and glory,
   robed in light as with a cloak.   *R/*

2. You fixed the earth upon its foundation,
   not to be moved forever;
   with the ocean, as with a garment, you covered it;
   above the mountains the waters stood.   *R/*

3. You send forth springs into the watercourses
   that wind among the mountains.
   Beside them the birds of heaven dwell;
   from among the branches they send forth
                                                            their song.   *R/*

4. You water the mountains from your palace;
   the earth is replete with the fruit of your works.
   You raise grass for the cattle,
      and vegetation for man's use,
   producing bread from the earth.   *R/*

5. How manifold are your works, O Lord!
   In wisdom you have wrought them all—
   the earth is full of your creatures.
   Bless the Lord, O my soul!   *R/*

Pentecost Vigil 4 (and Pentecost Simple Vigil)
Psalm 104:1-2, 24, 35, 27-28, 29, 30. R/ cf. v. 30

1a. = *v. 1 opposite*

2a. How manifold are your works, O Lord!
    In wisdom you have wrought them all—
    the earth is full of your creatures.
    Bless the Lord, O my soul! Alleluia.   *R/*

3a. Creatures all look to you
    to give them food in due time.
    When you give it to them, they gather it;
    when you open your hand, they are filled with
                                                 good things.   *R/*

4a. If you take away their breath, they perish
    and return to their dust.
    When you send forth your spirit, they
                                                 are created,
    and you renew the face of the earth.   *R/*

Pentecost Day, Common Pentecost
Psalm 104:1, 24, 29-30, 31, 34. R/ cf. v. 30

1b. = *v. 1 above*

2b. = *v. 4a above*

3b. May the glory of the Lord endure forever;
    may the Lord be glad in his works!
    Pleasing to him be my theme;
    I will be glad in the Lord.   *R/*

Text: Refrain, *Lectionary for Mass*, © 1969, 1981, 1997, ICEL; verses, *Lectionary for Mass*/New American Bible, © 1970, 1986, 1991, 1997, 2001, 2010, CCD. All rights reserved.
Music: *The Collegeville Chant Psalter*, © 2019, Order of Saint Benedict, Collegeville, MN. Published and administered by Liturgical Press, Collegeville, MN 56321. All rights reserved.

Baptism of the Lord, Year C

Psalm Tone

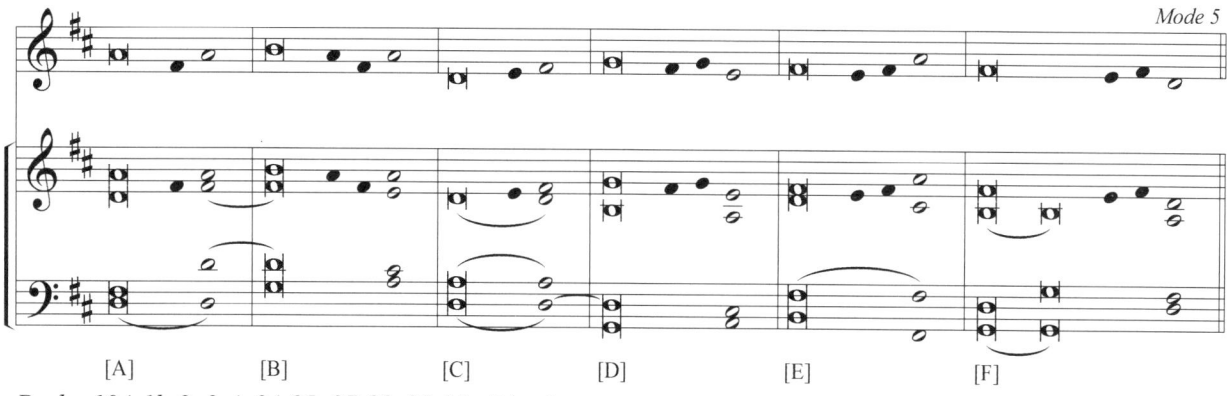

[A] [B] [C] [D] [E] [F]

Psalm 104:1b-2, 3-4, 24-25, 27-28, 29-30. R/ v. 1

1. O Lord, my God, you are great in<u>deed</u>!
   You are clothed with majes<u>ty</u> and glory,
   [omit C, D]
   robed in light as <u>with</u> a cloak.
   You have spread out the heavens
   <u>like</u> a tent-cloth.   *R/*

2. You have constructed your palace upon
   <u>the</u> waters.
   You make the clouds your chariot;
   you travel on the wings <u>of</u> the wind.
   [omit C, D]
   You make the <u>winds</u> your messengers,
   and flaming <u>fire</u> your ministers.   *R/*

3. How manifold are your works, <u>O</u> Lord!
   In wisdom you have <u>wrought</u> them all —
   the earth is full of <u>your</u> creatures;
   the sea also, <u>great</u> and wide,
   in which are schools <u>without</u> number
   of living things both <u>small</u> and great.   *R/*

4. They look to you to give them food in <u>due</u> time.
   When you give it to <u>them</u>, they gather it;
   [omit C, D]
   when you o<u>pen</u> your hand,
   they are filled <u>with</u> good things.   *R/*

5. If you take away <u>their</u> breath,
   they perish and return <u>to</u> the dust.
   [omit C, D]
   When you send forth your spirit, they <u>are</u> created,
   and you renew the face <u>of</u> the earth.   *R/*

Psalm 105

Holy Family, Year B

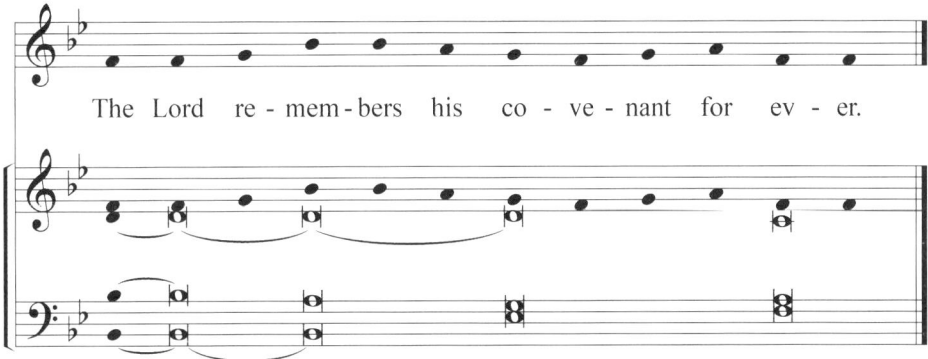

Psalm Tone

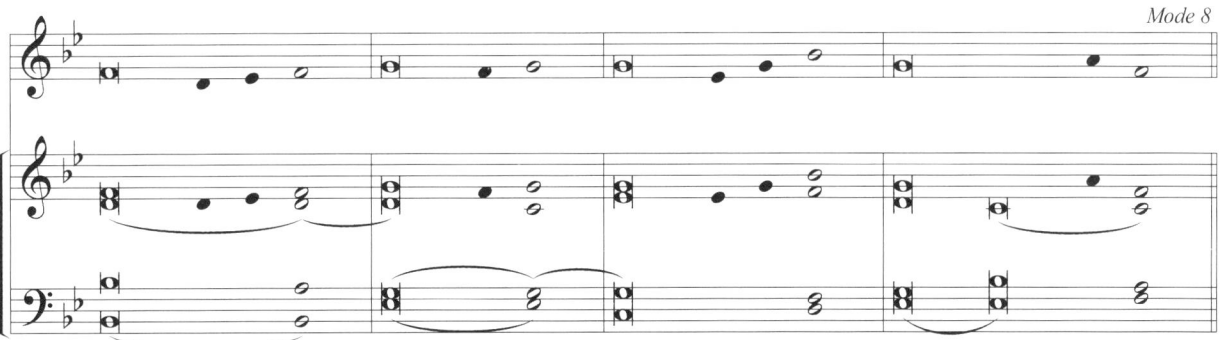

Psalm 105:1-2, 3-4, 5-6, 8-9. R/ vv. 7a, 8a

1. Give thanks to the Lord, in<u>voke</u> his name;
   make known among the nations <u>his</u> deeds.
   Sing to him, <u>sing</u> his praise,
   proclaim all his won<u>drous</u> deeds. *R/*

2. Glory in his <u>holy</u> name;
   rejoice, O hearts that seek <u>the</u> Lord!
   Look to the Lord <u>in</u> his strength;
   constantly seek <u>his</u> face. *R/*

3. You descendants of Abra<u>ham</u>, his servants,
   sons of Jacob, his cho<u>sen</u> ones!
   He, the Lord, <u>is</u> our God;
   throughout the earth his judgments pre<u>vail</u>. *R/*

4. He remembers forev<u>er</u> his covenant
   which he made binding for a thousand gen<u>er</u>ations
   which he entered in<u>to</u> with Abraham
   and by his oath <u>to</u> Isaac. *R/*

Text: Refrain, *Lectionary for Mass,* © 1969, 1981, 1997, ICEL; verses, *Lectionary for Mass*/New American Bible, © 1970, 1986, 1991, 1997, 2001, 2010, CCD. All rights reserved.
Music: *The Collegeville Chant Psalter,* © 2019, Order of Saint Benedict, Collegeville, MN. Published and administered by Liturgical Press, Collegeville, MN 56321. All rights reserved.

Psalm 107

Pentecost Vigil 3 • 12th Sunday in Ordinary Time, Year B

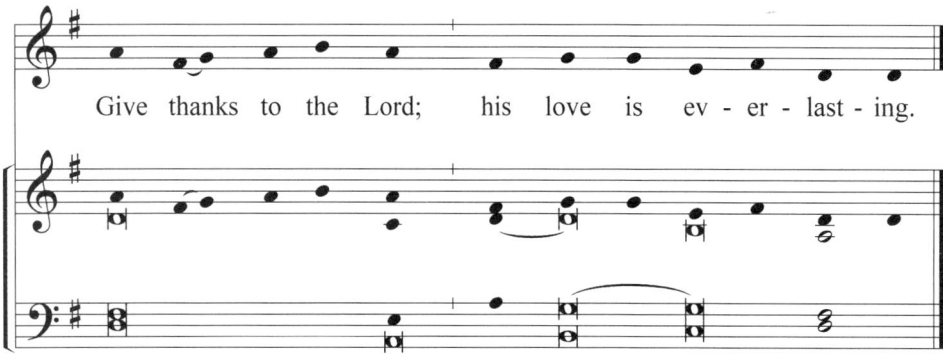

Pentecost Vigil 3, *alternate response* • 12th Sunday in Ordinary Time, *alternate response*

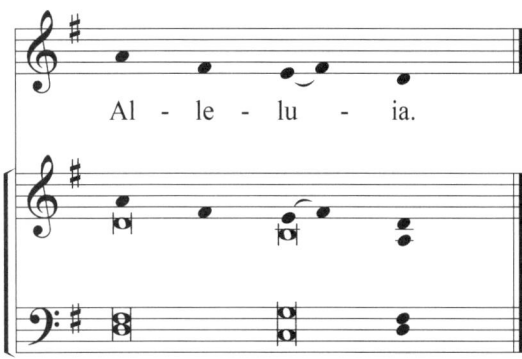

Notes:
The Lectionary Response for 12 OT B has a comma instead of a semicolon after "Lord."
The Alleluia alternate response for 12 OT B is an addition in the 1981 edition of the Lectionary, bringing it into line with the Pentecost Vigil alternate response.

Psalm Tone

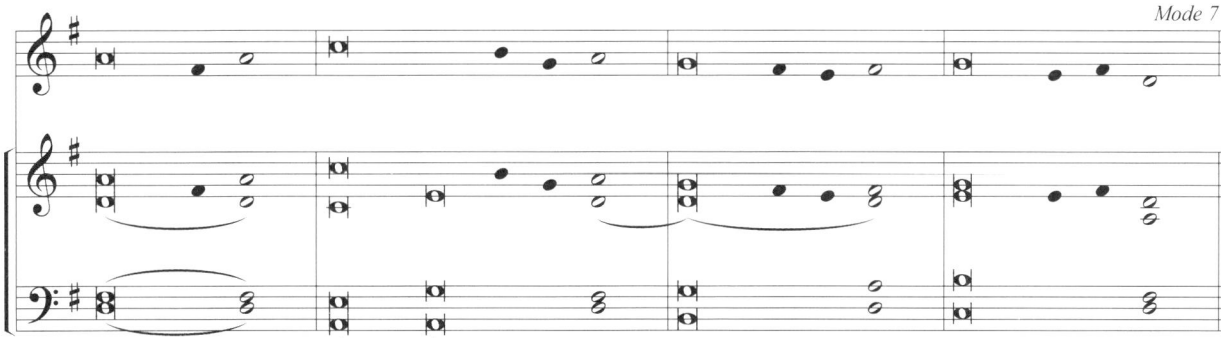

Mode 7

Pentecost Vigil 3
Psalm 107:2-3, 4-5, 6-7, 8-9. R/ v. 1b

1. Let the redeemed of <u>the</u> L<small>ORD</small> say,
   those whom he has redeemed from the hand
           <u>of</u> the foe
   And gathered <u>from</u> the lands,
   from the east and the west, from the north
           <u>and</u> the south. *R/*

2. They went astray in the de<u>sert</u> wilderness;
   the way to an inhabited city they <u>did</u> not find.
   Hun<u>gry</u> and thirsty,
   their life was wasting a<u>way</u> within them. *R/*

3. They cried to the L<small>ORD</small> in their <u>distress</u>;
   from their straits he <u>rescued</u> them.
   And he led them by a <u>direct</u> way
   to reach an inhab<u>it</u>ed city. *R/*

4. Let them give thanks to the L<small>ORD</small> for <u>his</u> mercy
   and his wondrous deeds to the child<u>ren</u> of men,
   Because he satisfied the <u>longing</u> soul
   and filled the hungry soul <u>with</u> good things. *R/*

12 OT B
Psalm 107:23-24, 25-26, 28-29, 30-31. R/ v. 1b

1. They who sailed the sea <u>in</u> ships,
   trading on <u>the</u> deep waters,
   these saw the works <u>of</u> the L<small>ORD</small>
   and his wonders in <u>the</u> abyss. *R/*

2. His command raised up <u>a</u> storm wind
   which tossed its <u>waves</u> on high.
   They mounted up to heaven; they sank
           <u>to</u> the depths;
   their hearts melted away <u>in</u> their plight. *R/*

3. They cried to the L<small>ORD</small> in their <u>distress</u>;
   from their <u>straits</u> he rescued them,
   he hushed the storm to a <u>gentle</u> breeze,
   and the billows of the <u>sea</u> were stilled. *R/*

4. They rejoiced that they <u>were</u> calmed,
   and he brought them to their <u>desired</u> haven.
   Let them give thanks to the L<small>ORD</small> <u>for</u> his kindness
   and his wondrous deeds to the child<u>ren</u> of men. *R/*

Text: Refrain, *Lectionary for Mass,* © 1969, 1981, 1997, ICEL; verses, *Lectionary for Mass*/New American Bible, © 1970, 1986, 1991, 1997, 2001, 2010, CCD. All rights reserved.
Music: *The Collegeville Chant Psalter,* © 2019, Order of Saint Benedict, Collegeville, MN. Published and administered by Liturgical Press, Collegeville, MN 56321. All rights reserved.

Note:
Verse 1 for the Pentecost Vigil erroneously has an uppercase A at the beginning of line 3, even though the sentence continues.

Psalm 110

Body and Blood of Christ, Year C

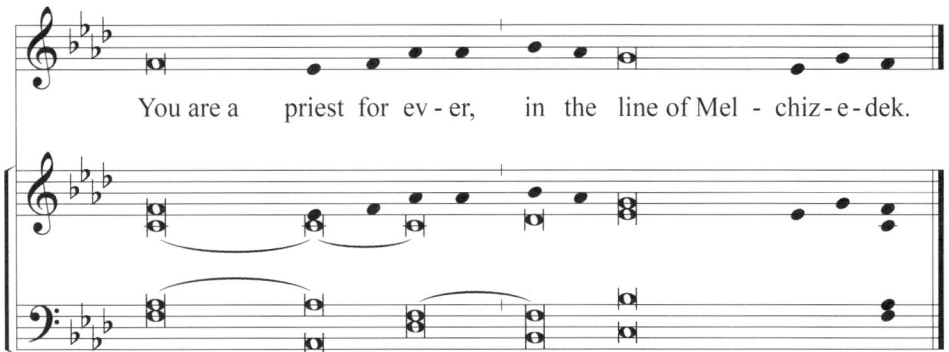

Psalm Tone

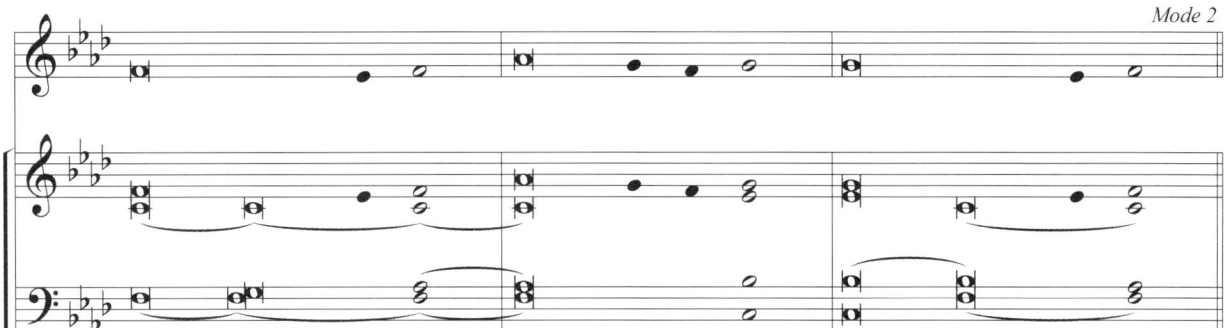

Psalm 110:1, 2, 3, 4. R/ v. 4b

1. The Lord said <u>to</u> my Lord:
   "Sit <u>at</u> my right hand
   till I make your enemies <u>your</u> footstool." *R/*

2. The scepter of <u>your</u> power
   the Lord will stretch <u>forth</u> from Zion:
   "Rule in the midst of <u>your</u> enemies." *R/*

3. "Yours is princely power in the day of <u>your</u> birth,
   in <u>holy</u> splendor;
   before the daystar, like the dew, I have <u>begotten</u> you." *R/*

4. The Lord has sworn, and he will not <u>repent</u>:
   "You are a <u>priest</u> forever,
   according to the order of <u>Melchizedek</u>." *R/*

Text: Refrain, *Lectionary for Mass,* © 1969, 1981, 1997, ICEL; verses, *Lectionary for Mass*/New American Bible, © 1970, 1986, 1991, 1997, 2001, 2010, CCD. All rights reserved.
Music: *The Collegeville Chant Psalter,* © 2019, Order of Saint Benedict, Collegeville, MN. Published and administered by Liturgical Press, Collegeville, MN 56321. All rights reserved.

Psalm 112

5th Sunday in Ordinary Time, Year A

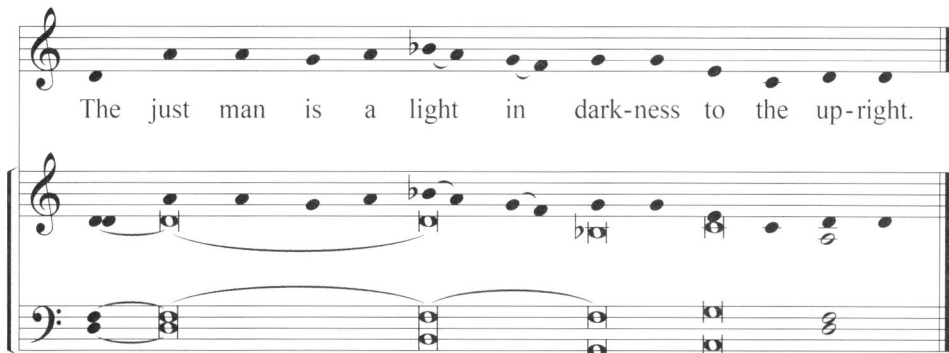

5th Sunday in Ordinary Time, Year A, *alternate response*

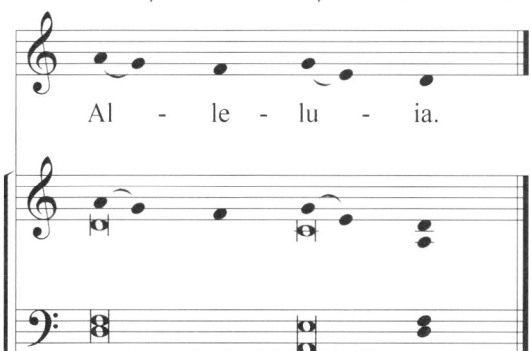

Note:
The alternate response is an addition in the 1981 Lectionary.

Psalm Tone

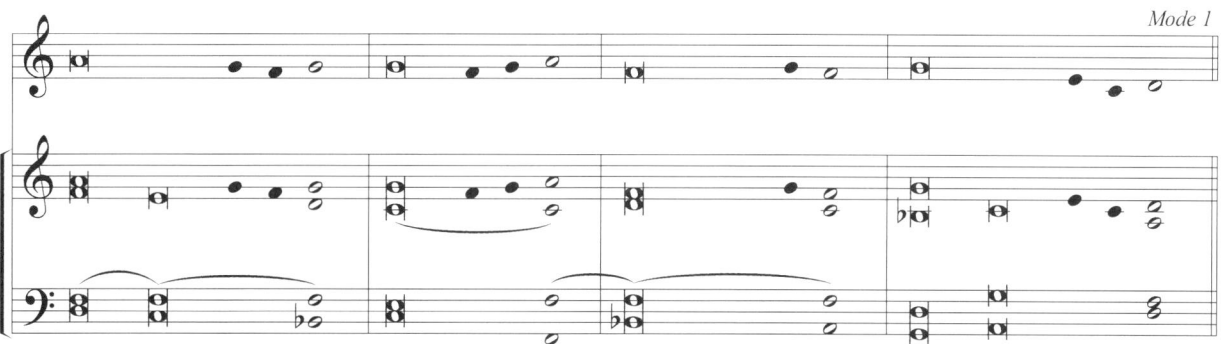

Psalm 112:4-5, 6-7, 8-9. R/ v. 4a

1. Light shines through the darkness <u>for</u> the upright;
   he is gracious and merci<u>ful</u> and just.
   Well for the man who is gracious <u>and</u> lends,
   who conducts his af<u>fairs</u> with justice. *R/*

2. He shall nev<u>er</u> be moved;
   the just one shall be in everlast<u>ing</u> remembrance.
   An evil report he shall <u>not</u> fear;
   his heart is firm, trusting <u>in</u> the Lord. *R/*

3. His heart is steadfast; he <u>shall</u> not fear.
   Lavishly he gives <u>to</u> the poor;
   his justice shall endure for<u>ever</u>;
   his horn shall be exal<u>ted</u> in glory. *R/*

Text: Refrain, *Lectionary for Mass*, © 1969, 1981, 1997, ICEL; verses, *Lectionary for Mass*/New American Bible, © 1970, 1986, 1991, 1997, 2001, 2010, CCD. All rights reserved.
Music: *The Collegeville Chant Psalter*, © 2019, Order of Saint Benedict, Collegeville, MN. Published and administered by Liturgical Press, Collegeville, MN 56321. All rights reserved.

Psalm 113

25th Sunday in Ordinary Time, Year C

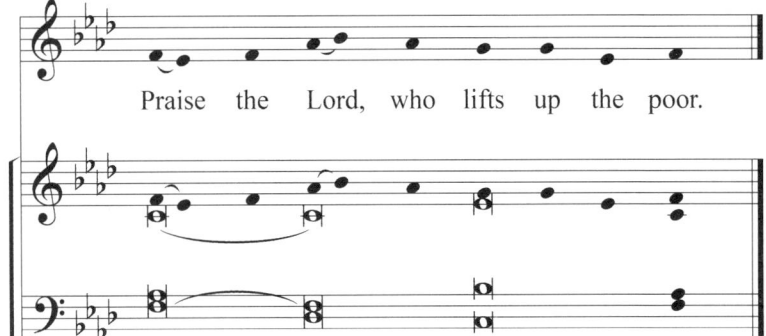

Note:
Some Lectionaries have no comma after 'Lord' in the response.

25th Sunday in Ordinary Time, Year C, *alternate response*

Psalm Tone

Psalm 113:1-2, 4-6, 7-8. R/ vv. 1a, 7b

1. Praise, you servants of the Lord,
   praise the name of the Lord.
   Blessed be the name of the Lord
   both now and forever. *R/*

2. High above all nations is the Lord;
   above the heavens is his glory.
   Who is like the Lord, our God, who is enthroned on high
   and looks upon the heavens and the earth below? *R/*

3. He raises up the lowly from the dust;
   from the dunghill he lifts up the poor
   to seat them with princes,
   with the princes of his own people. *R/*

Text: Refrain, *Lectionary for Mass*, © 1969, 1981, 1997, ICEL; verses, *Lectionary for Mass*/New American Bible, © 1970, 1986, 1991, 1997, 2001, 2010, CCD. All rights reserved.
Music: *The Collegeville Chant Psalter*, © 2019, Order of Saint Benedict, Collegeville, MN. Published and administered by Liturgical Press, Collegeville, MN 56321. All rights reserved.

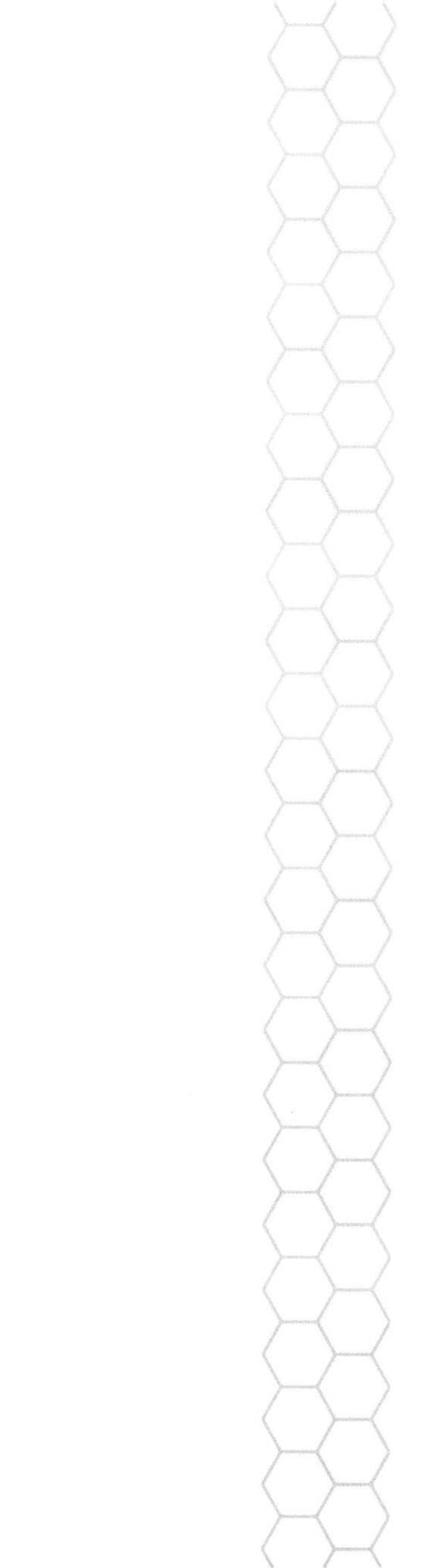

Psalm 116

2nd Sunday of Lent, Year B • 24th Sunday in Ordinary Time, Year B

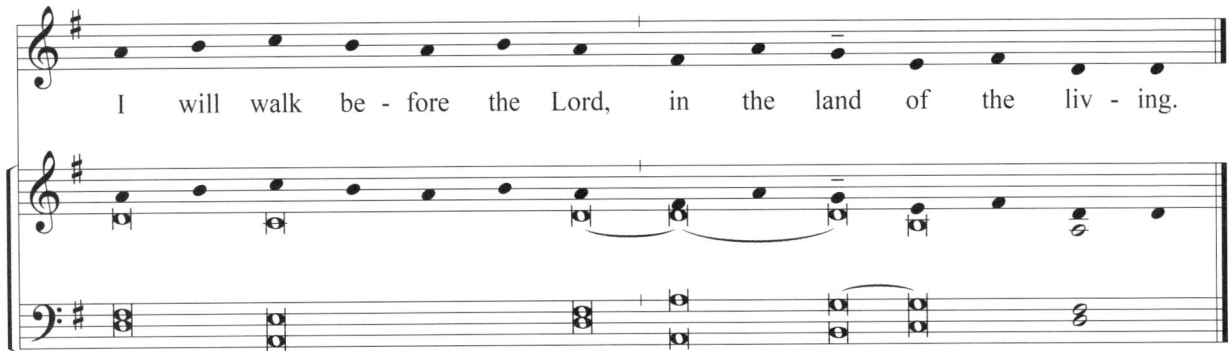

24th Sunday in Ordinary Time, Year B, *alternate response*

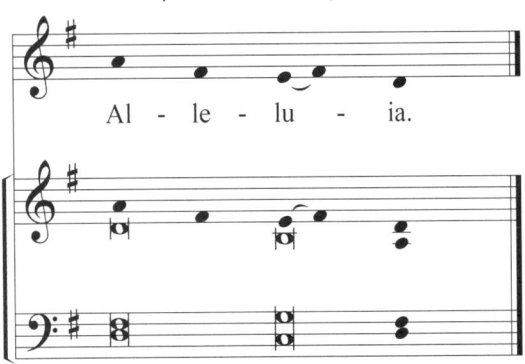

Psalm Tone

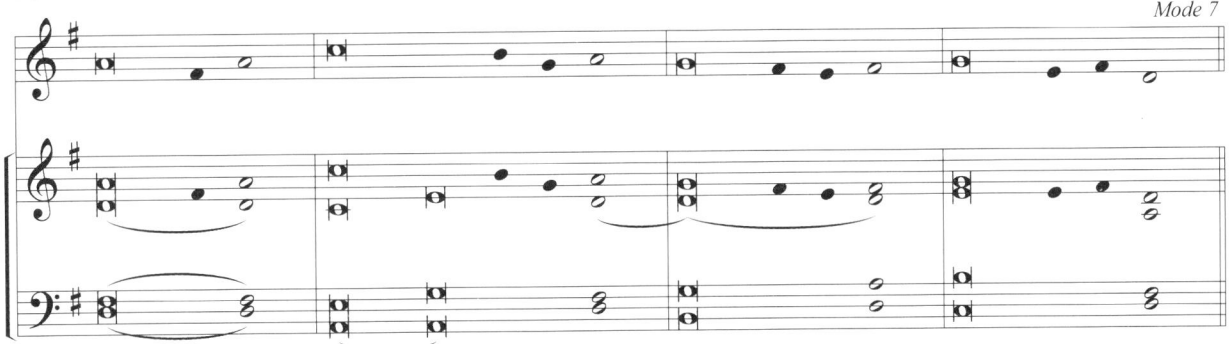

Mode 7

24 OT B
Psalm 116:1-2, 3-4, 5-6, 8-9. R/ v. 9

1. I love the Lord because he <u>has</u> heard
    my voice in <u>sup</u>plication,
     because he has inclined his <u>ear</u> to me
    the <u>day</u> I called.   *R/*

2. The cords of death <u>en</u>compassed me;
    the snares of the netherworld <u>seized</u> upon me;
     I fell into <u>dis</u>tress and sorrow,
    and I called upon the name of the Lord,
       "O Lord, <u>save</u> my life!"   *R/*

3. Gracious is the Lord <u>and</u> just;
    yes, our <u>God</u> is merciful.
     The Lord <u>keeps</u> the little ones;
    I was brought low, <u>and</u> he saved me.   *R/*

4. For he has freed my soul <u>from</u> death,
    my eyes from tears, my <u>feet</u> from stumbling.
     I shall walk be<u>fore</u> the Lord
    in the land <u>of</u> the living.   *R/*

2 Lent B
Psalm 116:10, 15, 16-17, 18-19. R/ v. 9

1. I believed, even when <u>I</u> said,
    "I am greatly <u>af</u>flicted."
     Precious in the eyes <u>of</u> the Lord
    is the death <u>of</u> his faithful ones.   *R/*

2. O Lord, I am <u>your</u> servant;
    I am your servant, the son <u>of</u> your handmaid;
     you have <u>loosed</u> my bonds.
    To you will I offer sacrifice of thanksgiving,
       and I will call upon the name <u>of</u> the Lord.   *R/*

3. My vows to the Lord I <u>will</u> pay
    in the presence of <u>all</u> his people,
     In the courts of the house <u>of</u> the Lord,
    in your midst, <u>O</u> Jerusalem.   *R/*

Text: Refrain, *Lectionary for Mass,* © 1969, 1981, 1997, ICEL; verses, *Lectionary for Mass*/New American Bible, © 1970, 1986, 1991, 1997, 2001, 2010, CCD. All rights reserved.
Music: *The Collegeville Chant Psalter,* © 2019, Order of Saint Benedict, Collegeville, MN. Published and administered by Liturgical Press, Collegeville, MN 56321. All rights reserved.

Holy Thursday, Evening Mass of the Lord's Supper

Body and Blood of Christ, Year B

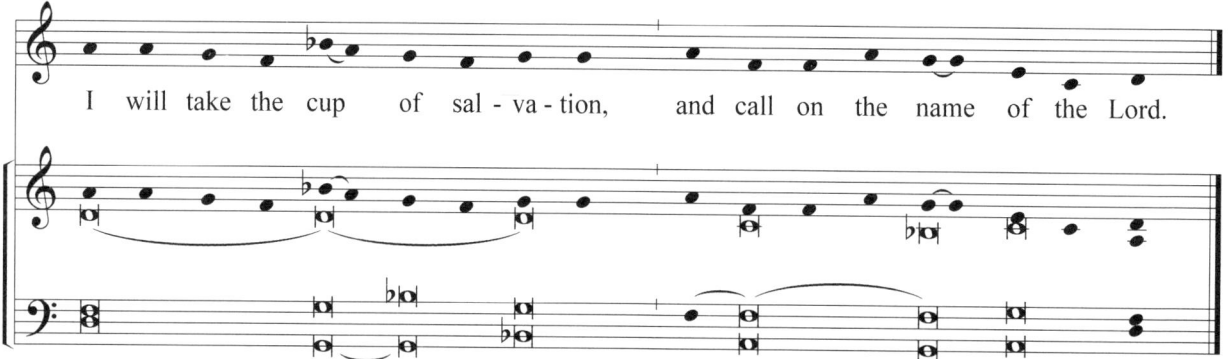

Body and Blood of Christ, Year B, *alternate response*

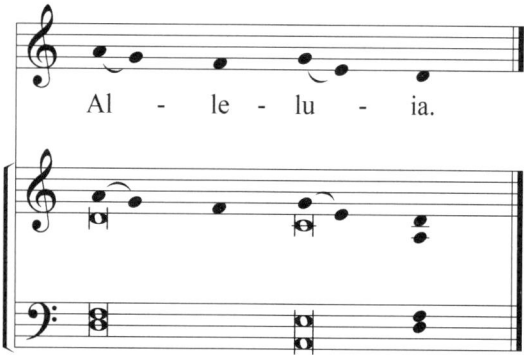

Psalm Tone

Mode 1

Psalm 116:12-13, 15-16bc, 17-18. R/ cf. 1 Cor 10:16; v. 13

1. How shall I make a return <u>to</u> the Lord
   for all the good he has <u>done</u> for me?
   The cup of salvation I will <u>take</u> up,
   and I will call upon the name <u>of</u> the Lord. R/

2. Precious in the eyes <u>of</u> the Lord
   is the death <u>of</u> his faithful ones.
   I am your servant, the son of <u>your</u> handmaid;
   you have <u>loosed</u> my bonds. R/

3. To you will I offer sacrifice <u>of</u> thanksgiving,
   and I will call upon the name <u>of</u> the Lord.
   My vows to the Lord I <u>will</u> pay
   in the presence of <u>all</u> his people. R/

Text: Refrain, *Lectionary for Mass,* © 1969, 1981, 1997, ICEL; verses, *Lectionary for Mass*/New American Bible, © 1970, 1986, 1991, 1997, 2001, 2010, CCD. All rights reserved.
Music: *The Collegeville Chant Psalter*, © 2019, Order of Saint Benedict, Collegeville, MN. Published and administered by Liturgical Press, Collegeville, MN 56321. All rights reserved.

Psalm 117

9th Sunday in Ordinary Time, Year C • 21st Sunday in Ordinary Time, Year C

Go out to all the world and tell the Good News.

Alternate response (both Sundays)

Alleluia.

Psalm Tone

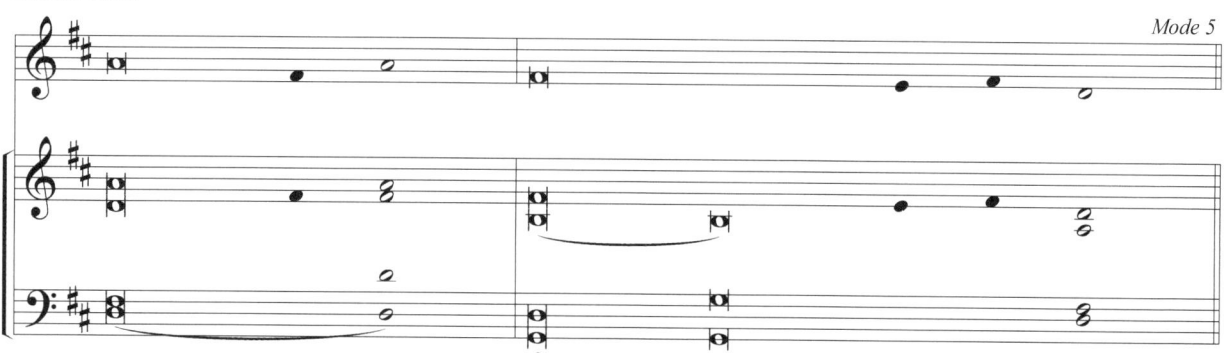

Mode 5

Psalm 117:1, 2. R/ Mk 16:15

1. Praise the Lord, all <u>you</u> nations;
   glorify him, <u>all</u> you peoples! *R/*

2. For steadfast is his kindness <u>toward</u> us,
   and the fidelity of the Lord en<u>dures</u> forever. *R/*

<sub>Text: Refrain, *Lectionary for Mass*, © 1969, 1981, 1997, ICEL; verses, *Lectionary for Mass*/New American Bible, © 1970, 1986, 1991, 1997, 2001, 2010, CCD. All rights reserved.
Music: *The Collegeville Chant Psalter*, © 2019, Order of Saint Benedict, Collegeville, MN. Published and administered by Liturgical Press, Collegeville, MN 56321. All rights reserved.</sub>

Note:
Some Lectionaries have lowercase 'good news' in 9 OT C response.

Psalm 118

Easter Vigil Alleluia Psalm • Easter Day, *alternate response*

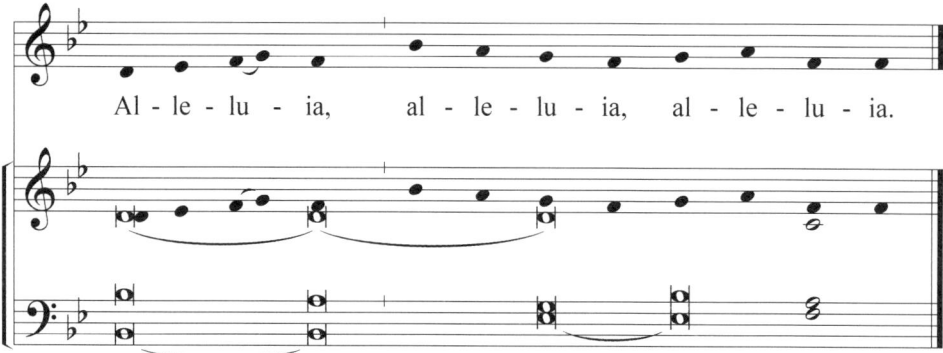

Easter Day • Easter Common 1

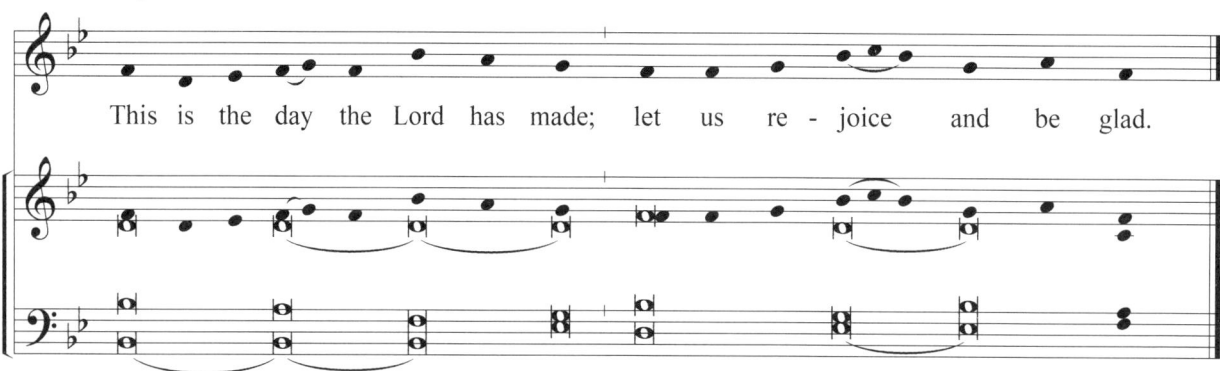

Psalm Tone

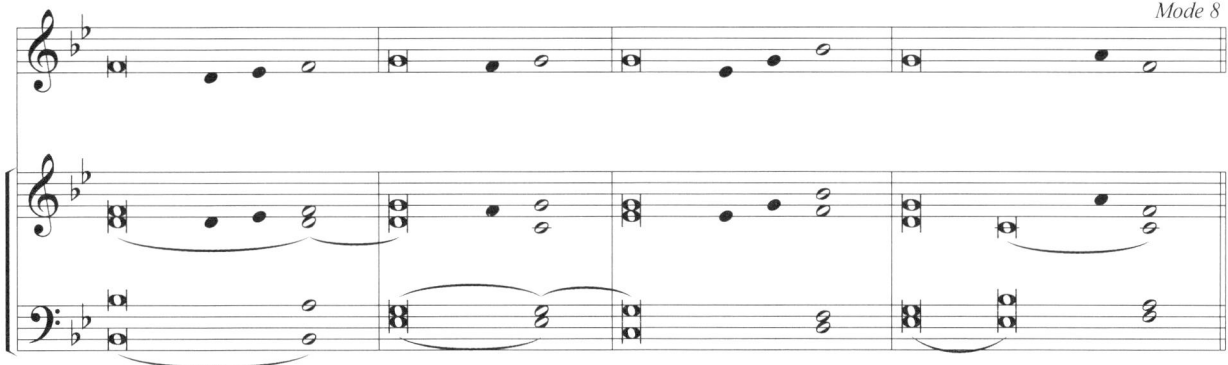

Mode 8

Psalm 118:1-2, 16-17, 22-23. R/ v. 24

1. Give thanks to the LORD, for <u>he</u> is good,
   for his mercy endures <u>for</u>ever.
   Let the house of <u>Is</u>rael say,
   "His mercy endures <u>for</u>ever." *R/*

2. The right hand of the LORD has <u>struck</u> with power;
   the right hand of the LORD is <u>ex</u>alted.
   I shall not <u>die</u>, but live,
   and declare the works of <u>the</u> LORD. *R/*

3. The stone the buil<u>ders</u> rejected
   has become <u>the</u> cornerstone.
   By the LORD has <u>this</u> been done;
   it is wonderful in <u>our</u> eyes. *R/*

Note:
Lectionary for **Easter Sunday** has the whole of v. 2 in quotation marks.
Lectionary for **Easter Common Psalm 1** reverses the first two lines of v. 2.

Text: Refrain, *Lectionary for Mass,* © 1969, 1981, 1997, ICEL; verses, *Lectionary for Mass*/New American Bible, © 1970, 1986, 1991, 1997, 2001, 2010, CCD. All rights reserved.
Music: *The Collegeville Chant Psalter,* © 2019, Order of Saint Benedict, Collegeville, MN. Published and administered by Liturgical Press, Collegeville, MN 56321. All rights reserved.

2nd Sunday of Easter, Years A-B-C

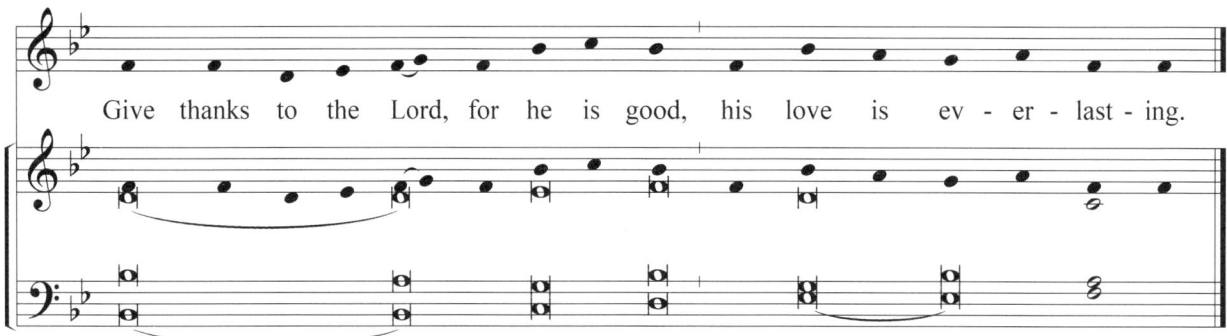

Give thanks to the Lord, for he is good, his love is ev - er - last - ing.

4th Sunday of Easter, Year B

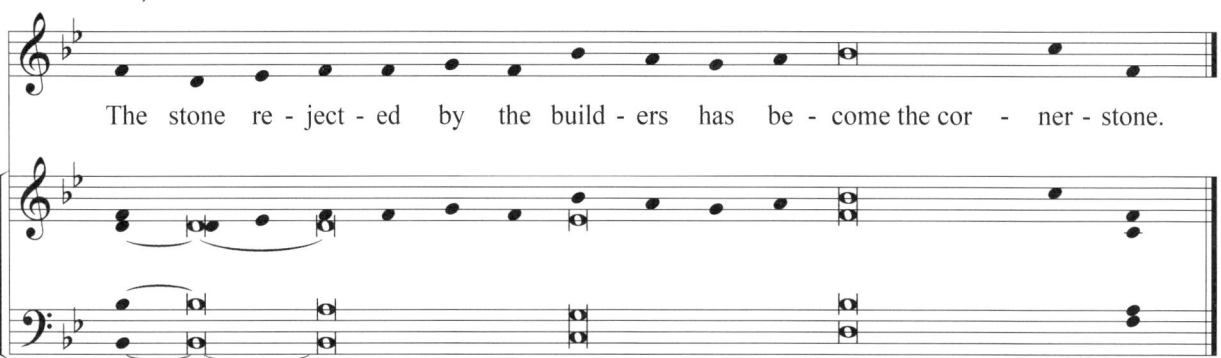

The stone re - ject - ed by the build - ers has be - come the cor - ner - stone.

2nd Sunday of Easter, Years A-B-C, *alternate response* •
4th Sunday of Easter, Year B, *alternate response*

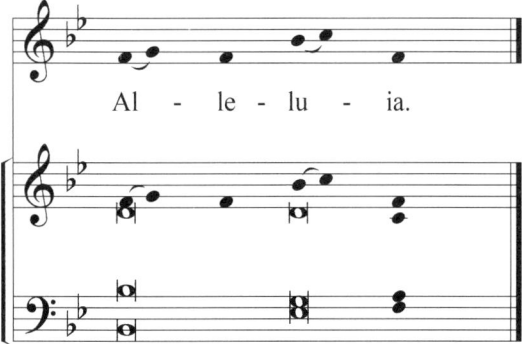

Al - le - lu - ia.

Psalm Tone

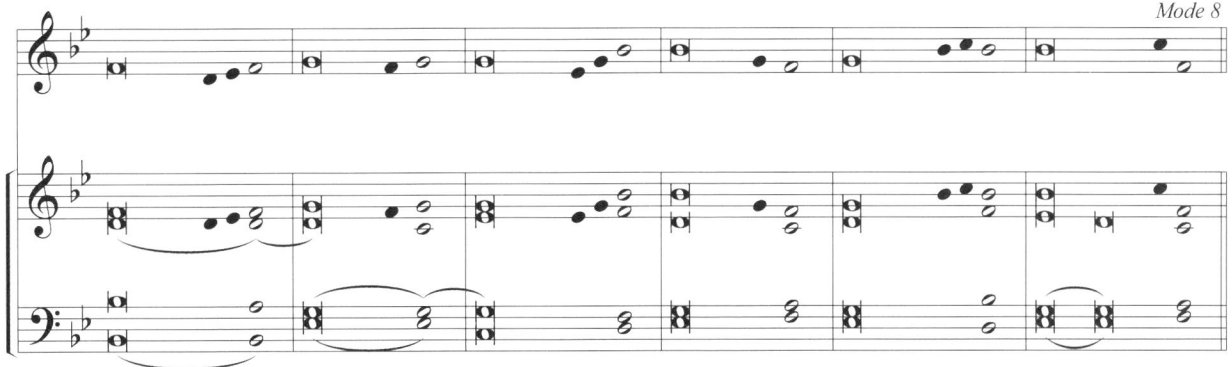

Mode 8

2 Easter A-B-C
Psalm 118:2-4, 13-15, 22-24. R/ v. 1

1. Let the house of <u>Is</u>rael say,
   "His mercy endures for<u>ev</u>er."
   Let the house of <u>Aa</u>ron say,
   "His mercy endures for<u>ev</u>er."
   Let those who <u>fear</u> the Lord say,
   "His mercy endures for<u>ev</u>er." R/

2. I was hard pressed <u>and</u> was falling,
   but the Lord helped me.
   My strength and my courage <u>is</u> the Lord,
   and he has been <u>my</u> savior.
   The joyful <u>shout</u> of victory
   in the tents of <u>the</u> just: R/

3. The stone which the buil<u>ders</u> rejected
   has become <u>the</u> cornerstone.
   By the Lord has <u>this</u> been done;
   it is wonderful in <u>our</u> eyes.
   This is the day the <u>Lord</u> has made;
   let us be glad and re<u>joice</u> in it. R/

4 Easter B
Psalm 118:1, 8-9, 21-23, 26, 28, 29. R/ v. 22

1. Give thanks to the Lord, for <u>he</u> is good,
   for his mercy endures for<u>ev</u>er.
   It is better to take refuge <u>in</u> the Lord
   than to trust <u>in</u> man.
   It is better to take refuge <u>in</u> the Lord
   than to trust <u>in</u> princes. R/

2. I will give thanks to you, for <u>you</u> have answered me
   and have been <u>my</u> savior.
   The stone which the buil<u>ders</u> rejected
   has become <u>the</u> cornerstone.
   By the Lord has <u>this</u> been done;
   it is wonderful in <u>our</u> eyes. R/

3. Blessed is he who comes in the name <u>of</u> the Lord;
   we bless you from the house of <u>the</u> Lord.
   I will give thanks to you, for <u>you</u> have answered me
   and have been <u>my</u> savior.
   Give thanks to the Lord, for <u>he</u> is good;
   for his kindness endures for<u>ev</u>er. R/

Text: Refrain, *Lectionary for Mass*, © 1969, 1981, 1997, ICEL; verses, *Lectionary for Mass*/New American Bible, © 1970, 1986, 1991, 1997, 2001, 2010, CCD. All rights reserved.
Music: *The Collegeville Chant Psalter*, © 2019, Order of Saint Benedict, Collegeville, MN. Published and administered by Liturgical Press, Collegeville, MN 56321. All rights reserved.

Psalm 119

6th Sunday in Ordinary Time, Year A

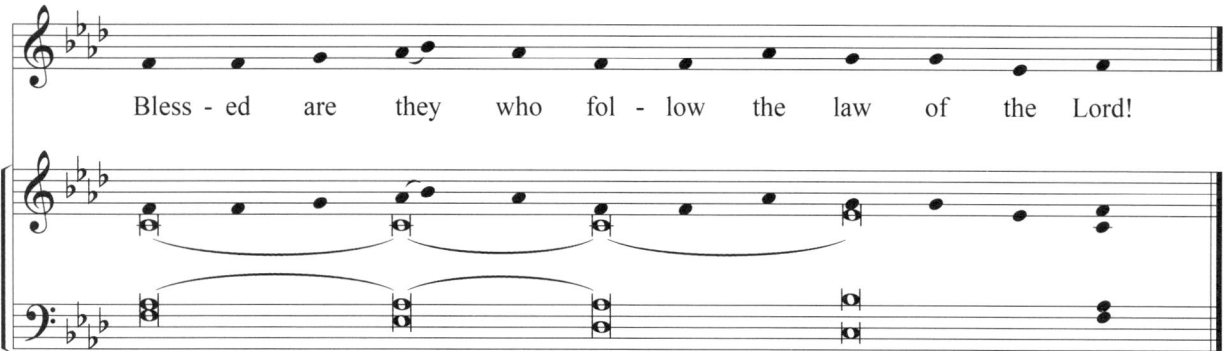

17th Sunday in Ordinary Time, Year A

Psalm Tone

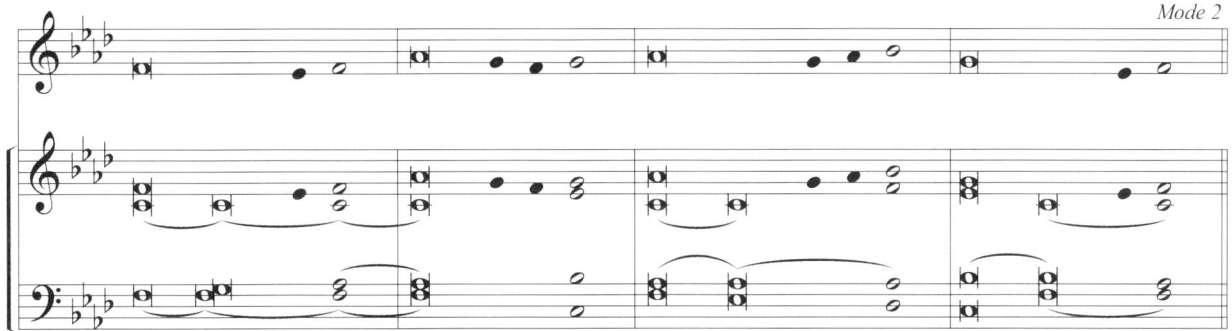

Mode 2

6 OT A
Psalm 119:1-2, 4-5, 17-18, 33-34. R/ v. 1b

1. Blessed are they whose way <u>is</u> blameless,
   who walk in the law <u>of</u> the L<small>ORD</small>.
   Blessed are they who observe <u>his</u> decrees,
   who seek him with all <u>their</u> heart.   *R/*

2. You have commanded that <u>your</u> precepts
   be dili<u>gent</u>ly kept.
   Oh, that I might be firm <u>in</u> the ways
   of keeping <u>your</u> statutes!   *R/*

3. Be good to your servant, that I <u>may</u> live
   and <u>keep</u> your words.
   Open my eyes, that I <u>may</u> consider
   the wonders of <u>your</u> law.   *R/*

4. Instruct me, O L<small>ORD</small>, in the way of <u>your</u> statutes,
   that I may exact<u>ly</u> observe them.
   Give me discernment, that I may ob<u>serve</u> your law
   and keep it with all <u>my</u> heart.   *R/*

17 OT A
Psalm 119:57, 72, 76-77, 127-128, 129-130. R/ v. 97a

1. I have said, O L<small>ORD</small>, that <u>my</u> part
   is to <u>keep</u> your words.
   The law of your mouth is to <u>me</u> more precious
   than thousands of gold and sil<u>ver</u> pieces.   *R/*

2. Let your kind<u>ness</u> comfort me
   according to your promise <u>to</u> your servants.
   Let your compassion come to me that <u>I</u> may live,
   for your law is my de<u>light</u>.   *R/*

3. For I love your <u>command</u>
   more than gold, howev<u>er</u> fine.
   For in all your precepts <u>I</u> go forward;
   every false way <u>I</u> hate.   *R/*

4. Wonderful are your <u>de</u>crees;
   therefore <u>I</u> observe them.
   The revelation of your <u>words</u> sheds light,
   giving understanding to <u>the</u> simple.   *R/*

Text: Refrain, *Lectionary for Mass,* © 1969, 1981, 1997, ICEL; verses, *Lectionary for Mass*/New American Bible, © 1970, 1986, 1991, 1997, 2001, 2010, CCD. All rights reserved.
Music: *The Collegeville Chant Psalter,* © 2019, Order of Saint Benedict, Collegeville, MN. Published and administered by Liturgical Press, Collegeville, MN 56321. All rights reserved.

Psalm 121

29th Sunday in Ordinary Time, Year C

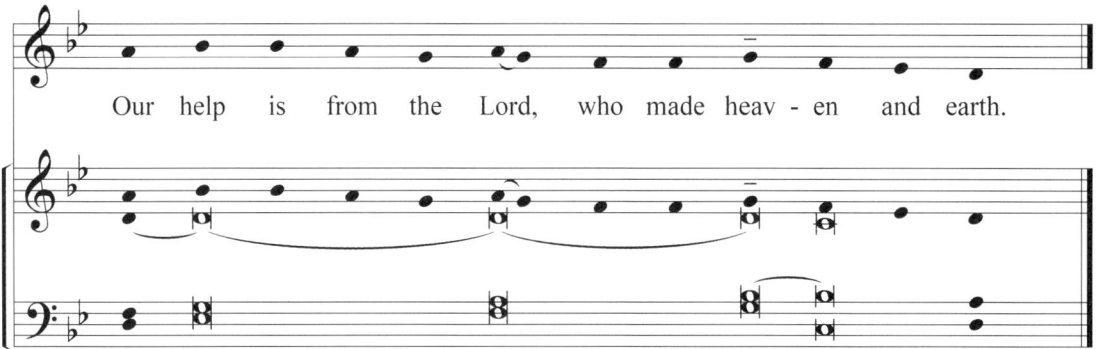

Psalm Tone

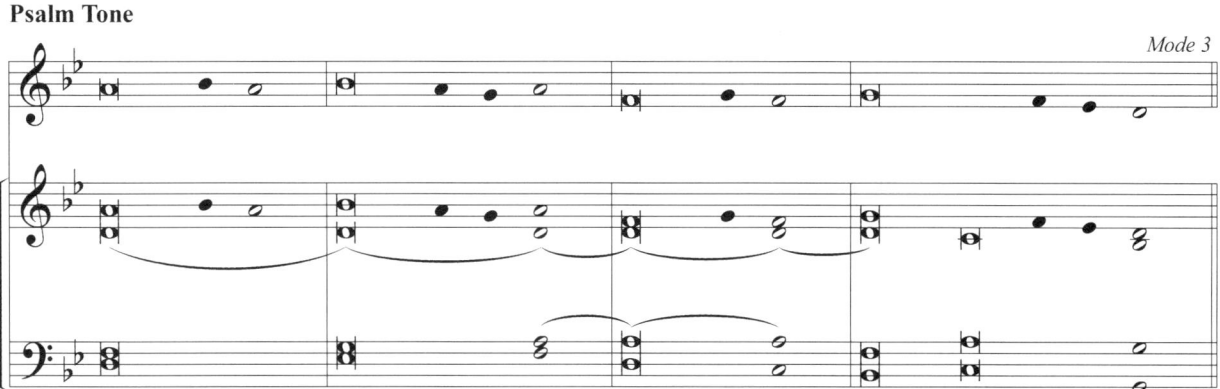

Psalm 121:1-2, 3-4, 5-6, 7-8. R/ cf. v. 2

1. I lift up my eyes toward <u>the</u> mountains;
   whence shall help <u>come</u> to me?
   My help is from <u>the</u> L<small>ORD</small>,
   who made heav<u>en</u> and earth. *R/*

2. May he not suffer your foot <u>to</u> slip;
   may he slumber <u>not</u> who guards you:
   indeed he neither slumbers <u>nor</u> sleeps,
   the guard<u>ian</u> of Israel. *R/*

3. The L<small>ORD</small> is your guardian; the L<small>ORD</small> is <u>your</u> shade;
   he is beside you <u>at</u> your right hand.
   The sun shall not harm you <u>by</u> day,
   nor the <u>moon</u> by night. *R/*

4. The L<small>ORD</small> will guard you from <u>all</u> evil;
   he will <u>guard</u> your life.
   The L<small>ORD</small> will guard your coming and <u>your</u> going,
   both now <u>and</u> forever. *R/*

Text: Refrain, *Lectionary for Mass,* © 1969, 1981, 1997, ICEL; verses, *Lectionary for Mass*/New American Bible, © 1970, 1986, 1991, 1997, 2001, 2010, CCD. All rights reserved.
Music: *The Collegeville Chant Psalter,* © 2019, Order of Saint Benedict, Collegeville, MN. Published and administered by Liturgical Press, Collegeville, MN 56321. All rights reserved.

Psalm 122

1st Sunday of Advent, Year A • Christ the King, Year C •
Common Ordinary Time 9 (last weeks) • Anniversary of Dedication of a Church, option 5

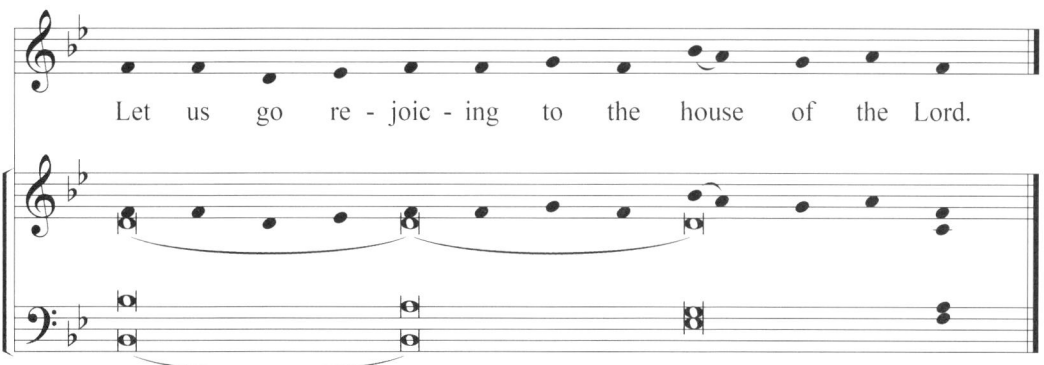

Psalm 122:1-2, 3-4, 4-5, 6-7, 8-9. R/ cf. v. 1

1. I rejoiced because they said to me,
   "We will go up to the house of the LORD."
   And now we have set foot
   within your gates, O Jerusalem. *R/*

2. Jerusalem, built as a city
   with compact unity.
   To it the tribes go up,
   the tribes of the LORD. *R/*

1 Advent A, Common OT 9
   1. - 2. - 3. - 4. - 5.
Christ the King C
   1. - 2. - 3.
Anniversary of Dedication 5
   1. - 2. - 5.

Omit on Anniversary of Dedication
3. According to the decree for Israel,
   to give thanks to the name of the LORD.
   In it are set up judgment seats,
   seats for the house of David. *R/*

***Omit on Christ the King C and
Anniversary of Dedication***
4. Pray for the peace of Jerusalem!
   May those who love you prosper!
   May peace be within your walls,
   prosperity in your buildings. *R/*

5. Because of my brothers and friends
   I will say, "Peace be within you!"
   Because of the house of the LORD, our God,
   I will pray for your good. *R/*

Note:
Anniversary of Dedication 5, v. 5, line 1, has
"Because of my relatives and friends"

Text: Refrain, *Lectionary for Mass,* © 1969, 1981, 1997, ICEL; verses, *Lectionary for Mass*/New American Bible, © 1970, 1986, 1991, 1997, 2001, 2010, CCD. All rights reserved.
Music: *The Collegeville Chant Psalter,* © 2019, Order of Saint Benedict, Collegeville, MN. Published and administered by Liturgical Press, Collegeville, MN 56321. All rights reserved.

Psalm 123

14th Sunday in Ordinary Time, Year B

Psalm Tone

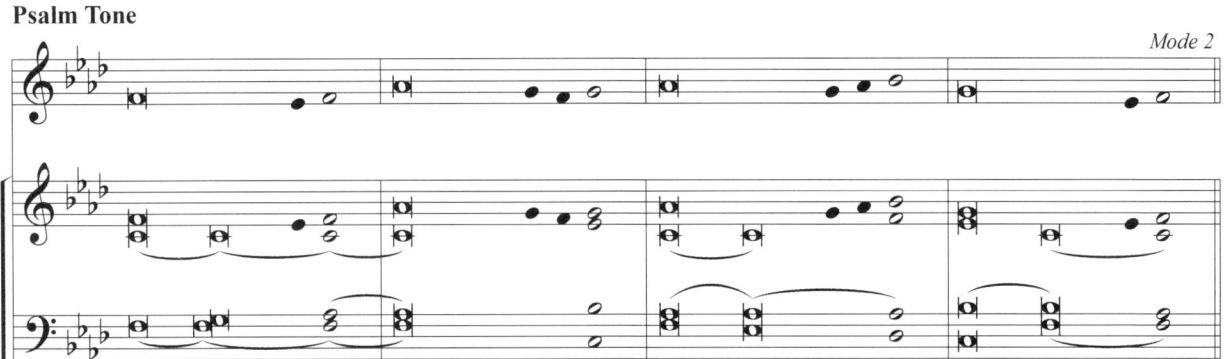

Mode 2

Psalm 123:1-2, 2, 3-4. R/ v. 2cd

1. To you I lift up my eyes
   who are enthroned in heaven—
   as the eyes of servants
   are on the hands of their masters. *R/*

2. As the eyes of a maid
   are on the hands of her mistress,
   so are our eyes on the Lord, our God,
   till he have pity on us. *R/*

3. Have pity on us, O Lord, have pity on us,
   for we are more than sated with contempt;
   our souls are more than sated
      with the mockery of the arrogant,
   with the contempt of the proud. *R/*

Text: Refrain, *Lectionary for Mass,* © 1969, 1981, 1997, ICEL; verses, *Lectionary for Mass*/New American Bible, © 1970, 1986, 1991, 1997, 2001, 2010, CCD. All rights reserved.
Music: *The Collegeville Chant Psalter,* © 2019, Order of Saint Benedict, Collegeville, MN. Published and administered by Liturgical Press, Collegeville, MN 56321. All rights reserved.

Psalm 126

30th Sunday in Ordinary Time, Year B • 2nd Sunday of Advent, Year C •
5th Sunday of Lent, Year C

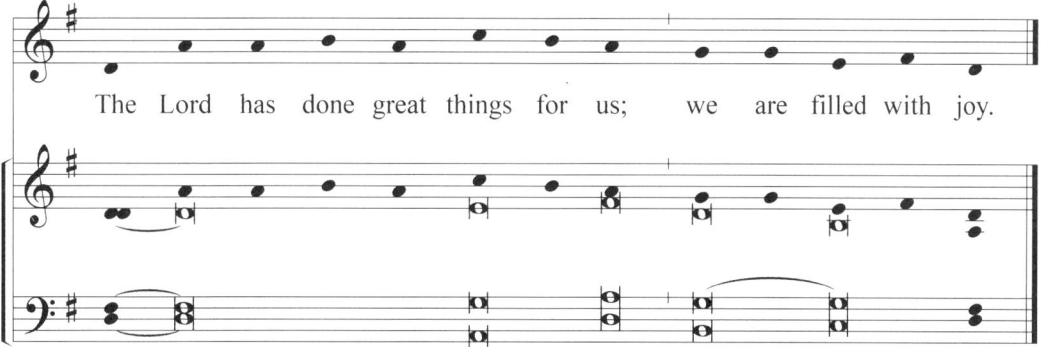

Psalm Tone

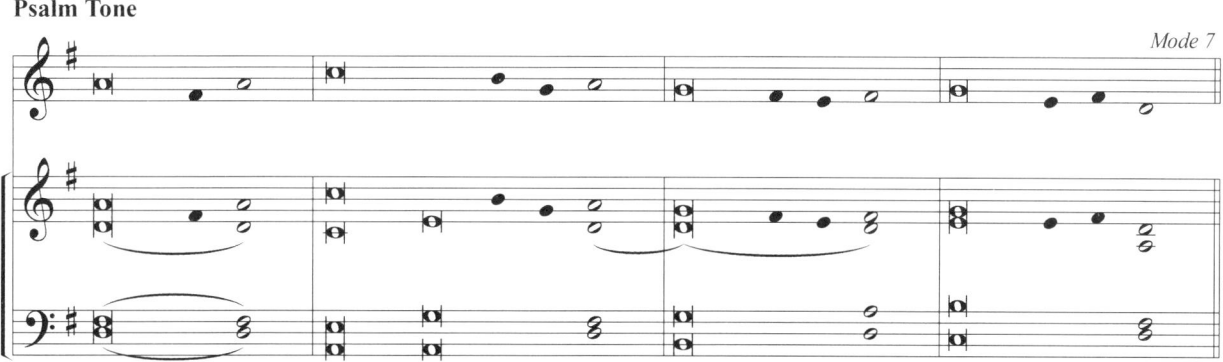

Psalm 126:1-2, 2-3, 4-5, 6. R/ v. 3

1. When the Lord brought back the captives <u>of</u> Zion,
   we were <u>like</u> men dreaming.
   Then our mouth was <u>filled</u> with laughter,
   and our tongue <u>with</u> rejoicing. *R/*

2. Then they said among <u>the</u> nations,
   "The Lord has done great <u>things</u> for them."
   The Lord has done great <u>things</u> for us;
   we are <u>glad</u> indeed. *R/*

3. Restore our fortunes, <u>O</u> Lord,
   like the torrents in the <u>southern</u> desert.
   Those who <u>sow</u> in tears
   shall <u>reap</u> rejoicing. *R/*

4. Although they go <u>forth</u> weeping,
   carrying the seed <u>to</u> be sown,
   they shall come <u>back</u> rejoicing,
   carry<u>ing</u> their sheaves. *R/*

Text: Refrain, *Lectionary for Mass*, © 1969, 1981, 1997, ICEL; verses, *Lectionary for Mass*/New American Bible, © 1970, 1986, 1991, 1997, 2001, 2010, CCD. All rights reserved.
Music: *The Collegeville Chant Psalter*, © 2019, Order of Saint Benedict, Collegeville, MN. Published and administered by Liturgical Press, Collegeville, MN 56321. All rights reserved.

Psalm 128

Holy Family

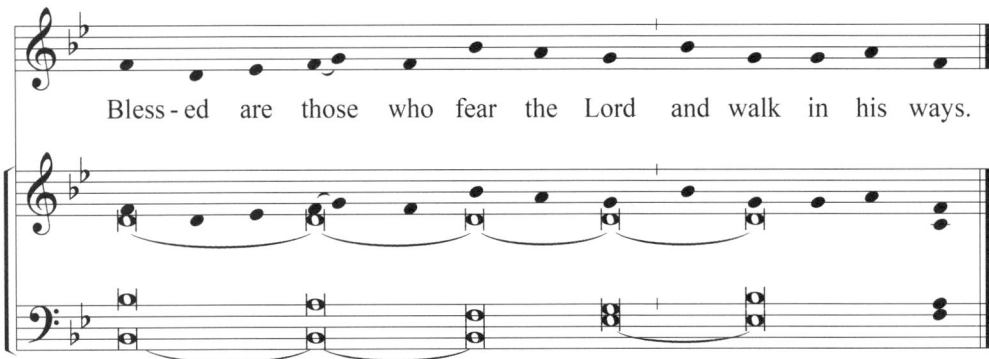

Bless-ed are those who fear the Lord and walk in his ways.

27th Sunday in Ordinary Time, Year B

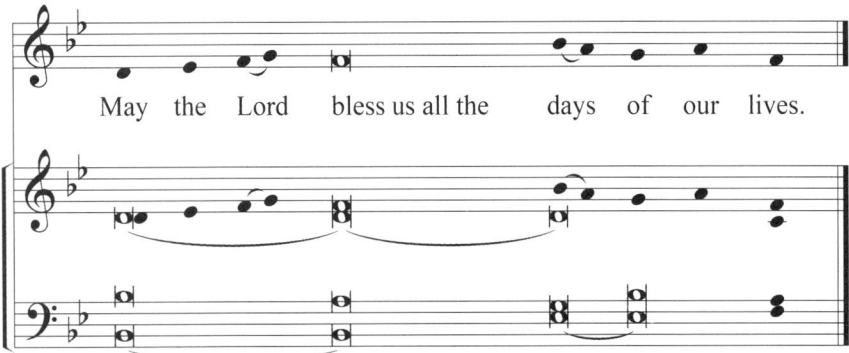

May the Lord bless us all the days of our lives.

33rd Sunday in Ordinary Time, Year A

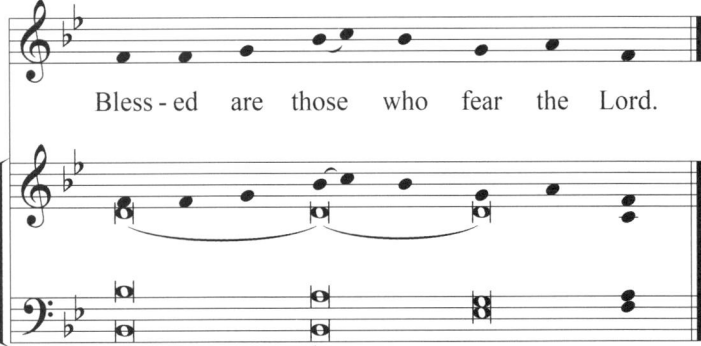

Bless-ed are those who fear the Lord.

Psalm Tone

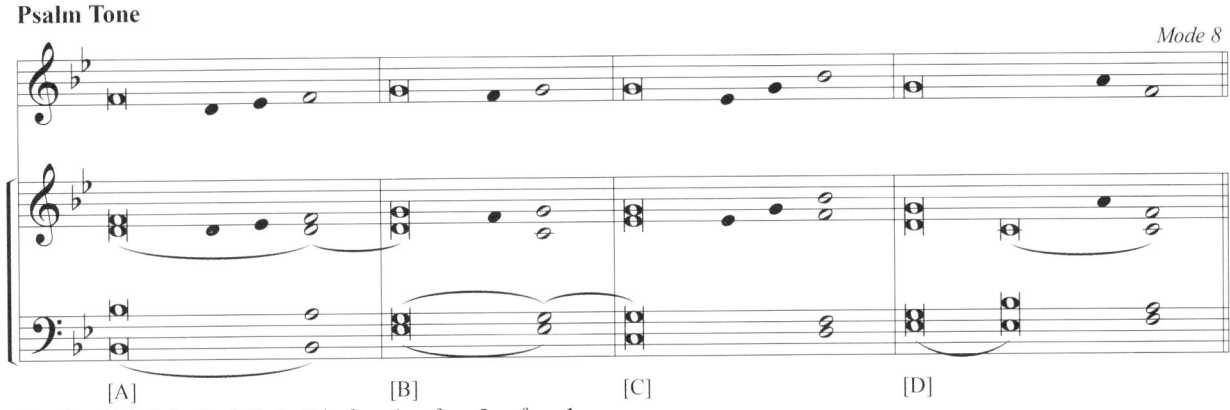

[A] [B] [C] [D]

Psalm 128:1-2, 3, 4-5, 6 R/ cf. v. 1; cf. v. 5; cf. v. 1a

Holy Family only
1. Blessed is everyone who <u>fears</u> the Lord,
    who walks in <u>his</u> ways!
    For you shall eat the fruit <u>of</u> your handiwork;
    blessed shall you be, <u>and</u> favored. *R/*

27 OT B and 33 OT A only
1a. Blessed are you who <u>fear</u> the Lord,
    who walk in <u>his</u> ways!
    For you shall eat the fruit <u>of</u> your handiwork;
    blessed shall you be, <u>and</u> favored. *R/*

2. Your wife shall be like a <u>fruitful</u> vine
    in the recesses of <u>your</u> home;
    your children like <u>olive</u> plants
    around <u>your</u> table. *R/*

3. Behold, thus is the man blessed
        who <u>fears</u> the Lord.
    The Lord bless you <u>from</u> Zion:
    may you see the prosperity <u>of</u> Jerusalem
    all the days of <u>your</u> life. *R/*

27 OT B only
4. May you see your <u>children</u>'s children.
    [omit B, C]
    Peace be up<u>on</u> Israel! *R/*

Text: Refrain, *Lectionary for Mass,* © 1969, 1981, 1997, ICEL; verses, *Lectionary for Mass*/New American Bible, © 1970, 1986, 1991, 1997, 2001, 2010, CCD. All rights reserved.
Music: *The Collegeville Chant Psalter,* © 2019, Order of Saint Benedict, Collegeville, MN. Published and administered by Liturgical Press, Collegeville, MN 56321. All rights reserved.

> **Holy Family**
>   1. - 2. - 3.
> **27 OT B**
>   1a. - 2. - 3. - 4.
> **33 OT A**
>   1a. - 2. - 3.

Psalm 130

5th Sunday of Lent, Year A • 10th Sunday in Ordinary Time, Year B • Common Lent 3

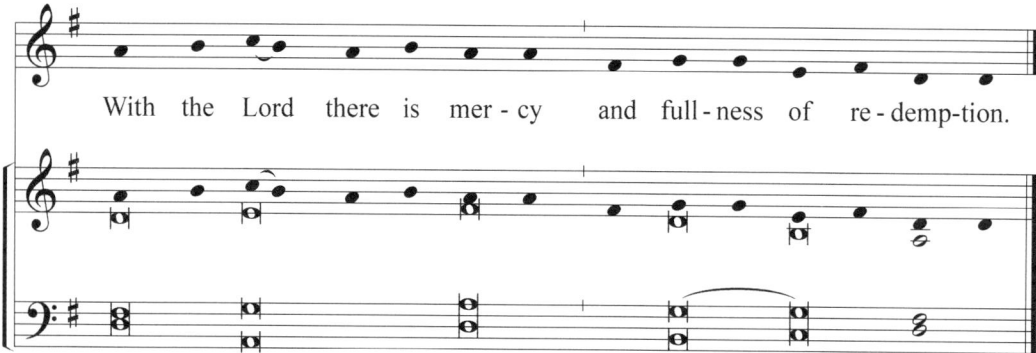

With the Lord there is mer-cy and full-ness of re-demp-tion.

Psalm Tone

Mode 7

5 Lent A, 10 OT B
Psalm 130:1-2, 3-4, 5-6, 7-8. R/ v. 7bc

1. Out of the depths I cry to you, O Lord;
   Lord, <u>hear</u> my voice!
   Let your ears <u>be</u> attentive
   to my voice in <u>sup</u>plication. *R/*

2. If you, O Lord, mark <u>i</u>niquities,
   Lord, <u>who</u> can stand?
   But with you <u>is</u> forgiveness,
   that you may <u>be</u> revered. *R/*

3. I trust in <u>the</u> Lord;
   my soul trusts <u>in</u> his word.
   More than sentinels wait <u>for</u> the dawn,
   let Israel wait <u>for</u> the Lord. *R/*

4. For with the Lord <u>is</u> kindness
   and with him is plente<u>ous</u> redemption;
   and he will <u>re</u>deem Israel
   from all <u>their</u> iniquities. *R/*

Common Lent 3
Psalm 130:1-2, 3-4, 4-6, 7-8. R/ v. 7bc

1. Out of the depths I cry to you, O Lord;
   Lord, <u>hear</u> my voice!
   Let your ears <u>be</u> attentive
   to my voice in <u>sup</u>plication. *R/*

2. If you, O Lord, mark <u>i</u>niquities,
   Lord, <u>who</u> can stand?
   But with you <u>is</u> forgiveness,
   and so you may <u>be</u> revered. *R/*

3. I trust in <u>the</u> Lord;
   my soul trusts <u>in</u> his word.
   My soul waits <u>for</u> the Lord
   more than sentinels wait <u>for</u> the dawn. *R/*

4. For with the Lord <u>is</u> kindness
   and with him is plente<u>ous</u> redemption;
   and he will <u>re</u>deem Israel
   from all <u>their</u> iniquities. *R/*

Text: Refrain, *Lectionary for Mass*, © 1969, 1981, 1997, ICEL; verses, *Lectionary for Mass*/New American Bible, © 1970, 1986, 1991, 1997, 2001, 2010, CCD. All rights reserved.
Music: *The Collegeville Chant Psalter*, © 2019, Order of Saint Benedict, Collegeville, MN. Published and administered by Liturgical Press, Collegeville, MN 56321. All rights reserved.

Psalm 131

31st Sunday in Ordinary Time, Year A

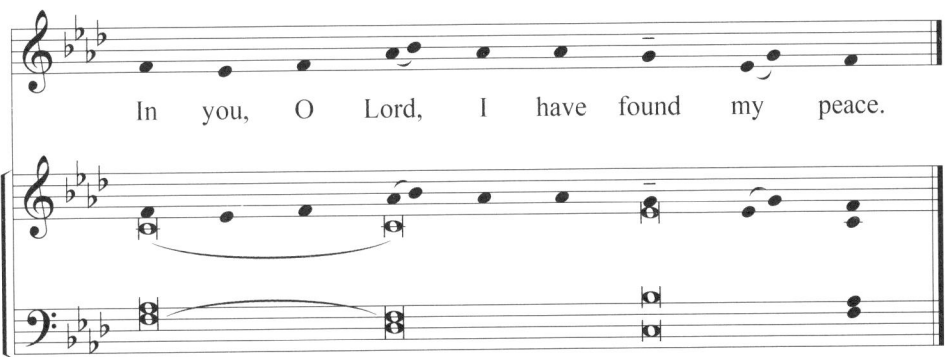

Psalm Tone

Mode 2

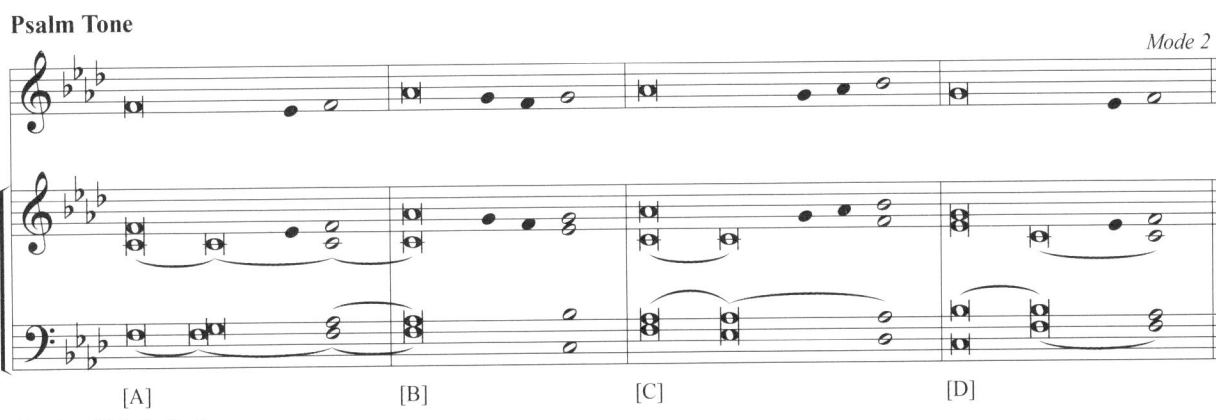

[A]   [B]   [C]   [D]

Psalm 131:1, 2, 3

1. O Lord, my heart is <u>not</u> proud,
   nor are <u>my</u> eyes haughty;
   I busy not myself <u>with</u> great things,
   nor with things too <u>sub</u>lime for me. *R/*

2. Nay rather, I have stilled <u>and</u> quieted
   my soul like <u>a</u> weaned child.
   Like a weaned child on its <u>moth</u>er's lap,
   so is my soul <u>with</u>in me. *R/*

3. O Israel, hope in <u>the</u> Lord,
   [omit B, C]
   both now and <u>for</u>ever. *R/*

Text: Refrain, *Lectionary for Mass,* © 1969, 1981, 1997, ICEL; verses, *Lectionary for Mass/*New American Bible, © 1970, 1986, 1991, 1997, 2001, 2010, CCD. All rights reserved.
Music: *The Collegeville Chant Psalter,* © 2019, Order of Saint Benedict, Collegeville, MN. Published and administered by Liturgical Press, Collegeville, MN 56321. All rights reserved.

Psalm 132

Assumption Vigil

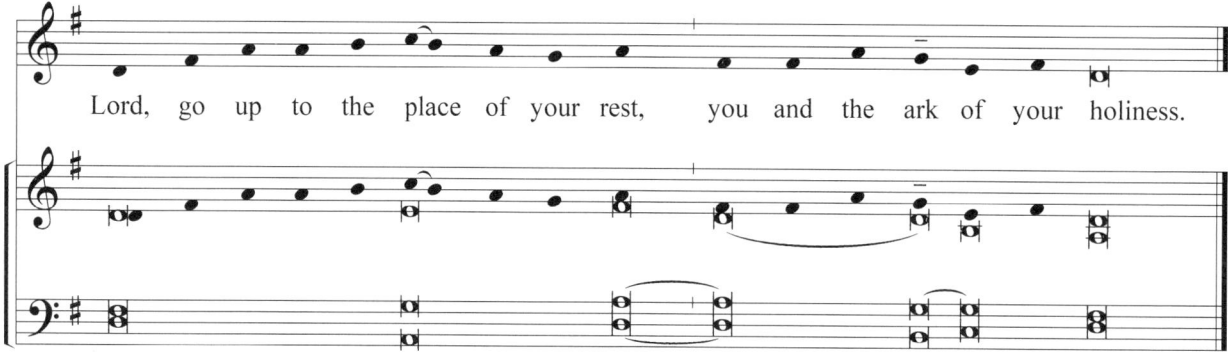

Psalm Tone

Psalm 132:6-7, 9-10, 13-14. R/ v. 8

1. Behold, we heard of it <u>in</u> Ephrathah;
   we found it in the <u>fields</u> of Jaar.
   Let us en<u>ter</u> his dwelling,
   let us worship <u>at</u> his footstool. *R/*

2. May your priests be clothed <u>with</u> justice;
   let your faithful ones shout merri<u>ly</u> for joy.
   For the sake of Da<u>vid</u> your servant,
   reject not the plea of <u>your</u> anointed. *R/*

3. For the LORD has cho<u>sen</u> Zion;
   he prefers her <u>for</u> his dwelling.
   "Zion is my resting <u>place</u> forever;
   in her will I dwell, for <u>I</u> prefer her." *R/*

Text: Refrain, *Lectionary for Mass*, © 1969, 1981, 1997, ICEL; verses, *Lectionary for Mass*/New American Bible, © 1970, 1986, 1991, 1997, 2001, 2010, CCD. All rights reserved.
Music: *The Collegeville Chant Psalter*, © 2019, Order of Saint Benedict, Collegeville, MN. Published and administered by Liturgical Press, Collegeville, MN 56321. All rights reserved.

Psalm 136

Common Easter Vigil 1 and 2

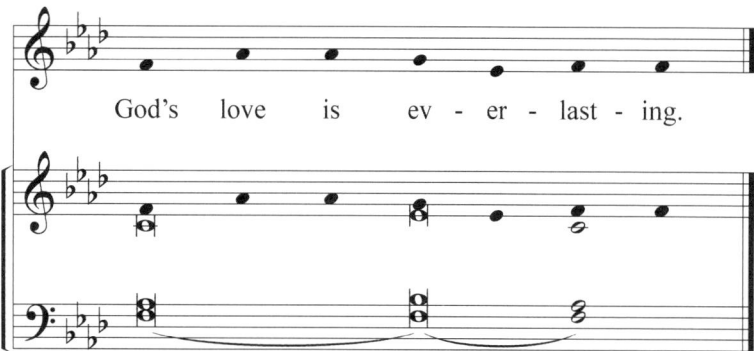

God's love is ev-er-last-ing.

Psalm Tone

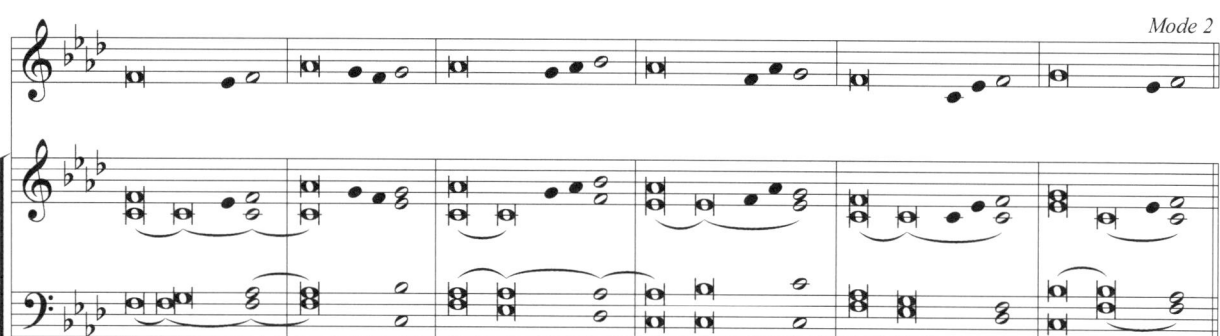

Mode 2

Common Easter Vigil 1
Psalm 136:1-3, 4-6, 7-9, 24-26.

1. Give thanks to the L<small>ORD</small>, for he <u>is</u> good,
    for his mercy en<u>dures</u> forever;
   give thanks to the <u>God</u> of gods,
    for his mercy en<u>dures</u> forever;
   give thanks to the L<small>ORD</small> of lords,
    for his mercy endures <u>for</u>ever. *R/*

2. Who alone does <u>great</u> wonders,
    for his mercy en<u>dures</u> forever;
   who made the heav<u>ens</u> in wisdom,
    for his mercy en<u>dures</u> forever;
   who spread out the earth up<u>on</u> the waters,
    for his mercy endures <u>for</u>ever. *R/*

3. Who made the <u>great</u> lights,
    for his mercy en<u>dures</u> forever;
   the sun to rule o<u>ver</u> the day,
    for his mercy en<u>dures</u> forever;
   the moon and the stars to rule o<u>ver</u> the night,
    for his mercy endures <u>for</u>ever. *R/*

4. Who freed us from <u>our</u> foes,
    for his mercy en<u>dures</u> forever;
   who gives food <u>to</u> all flesh,
    for his mercy en<u>dures</u> forever;
   give thanks to the <u>God</u> of heaven,
    for his mercy endures <u>for</u>ever. *R/*

Common Easter Vigil 2
Psalm 136:1, 3, 16, 21-23, 24-26.

1. Give thanks to the L<small>ORD</small>, for he <u>is</u> good,
    for his mercy en<u>dures</u> forever;
   give thanks to the L<small>ORD</small> of lords,
    for his mercy en<u>dures</u> forever;
   who led his people <u>through</u> the wilderness,
    for his mercy endures <u>for</u>ever. *R/*

2. Who made their land <u>a</u> heritage,
    for his mercy en<u>dures</u> forever;
   the heritage of Isra<u>el</u>, his servant,
    for his mercy en<u>dures</u> forever;
   who remembered us in <u>our</u> abjection,
    for his mercy endures <u>for</u>ever. *R/*

3. Who freed us from <u>our</u> foes,
    for his mercy en<u>dures</u> forever;
   who gives food <u>to</u> all flesh,
    for his mercy en<u>dures</u> forever;
   give thanks to the <u>God</u> of heaven,
    for his mercy endures <u>for</u>ever. *R/*

Text: Refrain, *Lectionary for Mass,* © 1969, 1981, 1997, ICEL; verses, *Lectionary for Mass*/New American Bible, © 1970, 1986, 1991, 1997, 2001, 2010, CCD. All rights reserved.
Music: *The Collegeville Chant Psalter,* © 2019, Order of Saint Benedict, Collegeville, MN. Published and administered by Liturgical Press, Collegeville, MN 56321. All rights reserved.

Psalm 137

4th Sunday of Lent, Year B

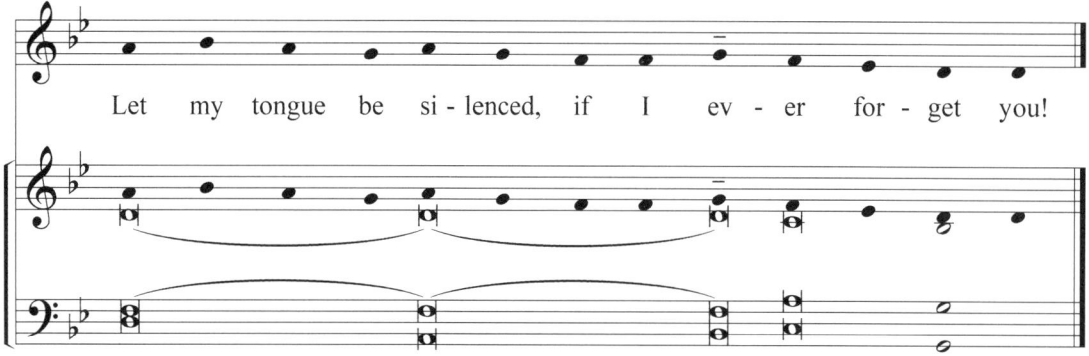

Psalm Tone

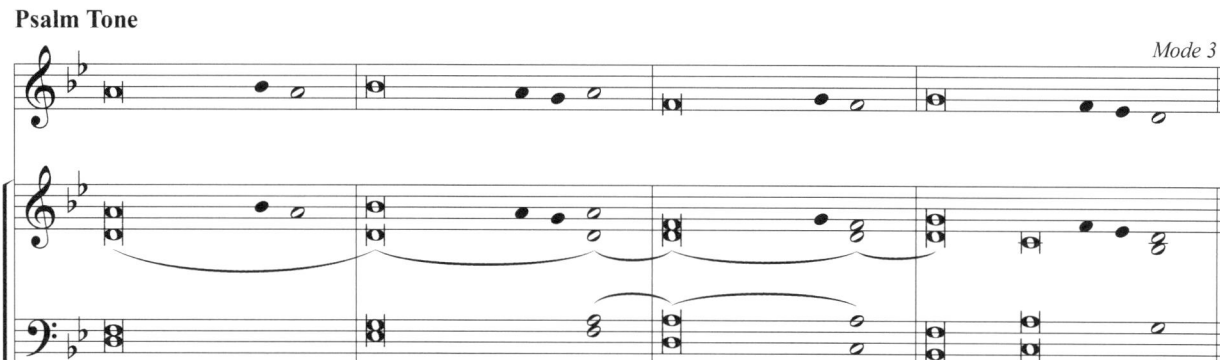

Psalm 137:1-2, 3, 4-5, 6. R/ v. 6ab

1. By the streams of Ba<u>by</u>lon
   we sat and wept
      when we re<u>mem</u>bered Zion.
   On the aspens of <u>that</u> land
   we hung <u>up</u> our harps. *R/*

2. For there our captors asked <u>of</u> us
   the lyrics <u>of</u> our songs,
      and our despoilers urged us to <u>be</u> joyous:
   "Sing for us the <u>songs</u> of Zion!" *R/*

3. How could we sing a song of <u>the</u> Lord
   in a <u>foreign</u> land?
   If I forget you, <u>Jerusalem</u>,
   may my right hand <u>be</u> forgotten! *R/*

4. May my tongue cleave to <u>my</u> palate
   if I remem<u>ber</u> you not,
   if I place not <u>Jerusalem</u>
   ahead <u>of</u> my joy. *R/*

Text: Refrain, *Lectionary for Mass*, © 1969, 1981, 1997, ICEL; verses, *Lectionary for Mass*/New American Bible, © 1970, 1986, 1991, 1997, 2001, 2010, CCD. All rights reserved.
Music: *The Collegeville Chant Psalter*, © 2019, Order of Saint Benedict, Collegeville, MN. Published and administered by Liturgical Press, Collegeville, MN 56321. All rights reserved.

Psalm 138

21st Sunday in Ordinary Time, Year A

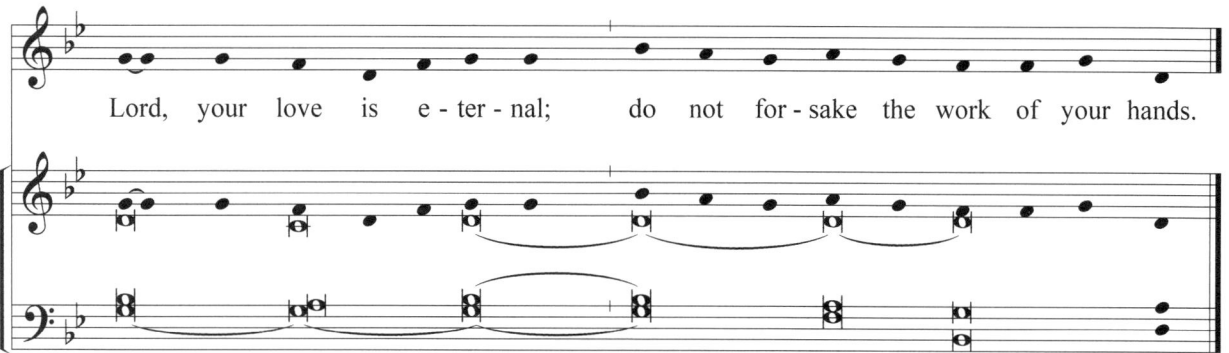

Lord, your love is e-ter-nal; do not for-sake the work of your hands.

5th Sunday in Ordinary Time, Year C

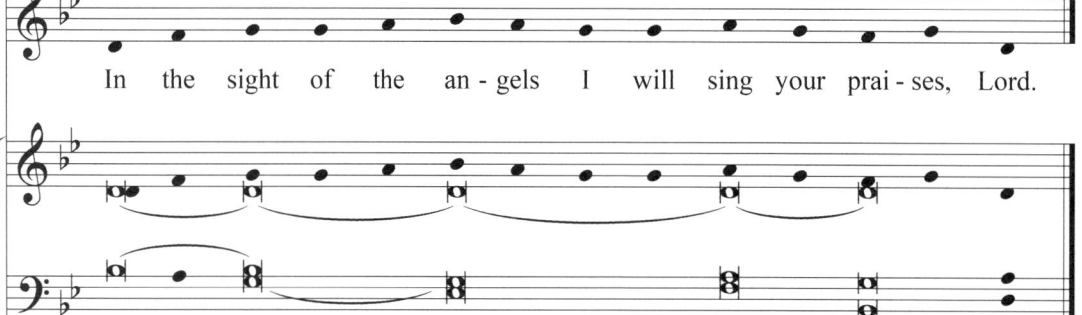

In the sight of the an-gels I will sing your prai-ses, Lord.

17th Sunday in Ordinary Time, Year C

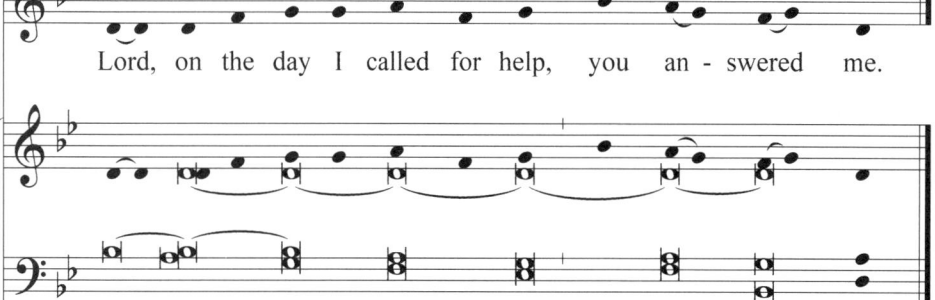

Lord, on the day I called for help, you an-swered me.

Thanksgiving, option 3

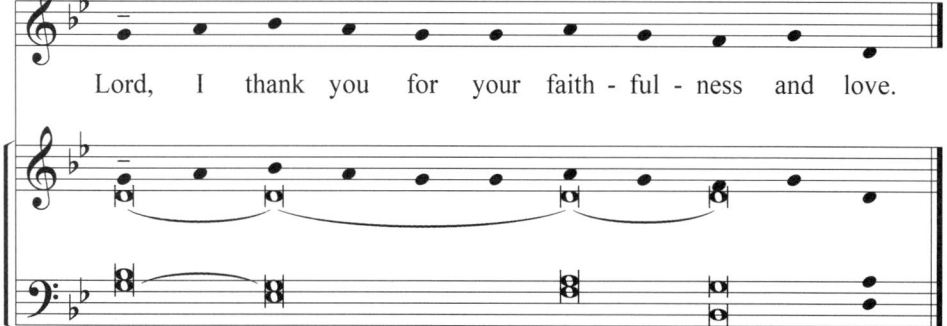

Lord, I thank you for your faith-ful-ness and love.

Psalm 138, pg. 2

Psalm Tone

Mode 4

Thanksgiving 3
Psalm 138:1-2ab, 2cde-3, 4-5. R/ v. 2bc

1. I will give thanks to you, O Lord,
   with <u>all</u> my heart,
   for you have heard the words of <u>my</u> mouth;
   in the presence of the angels I will
   <u>sing</u> your praise;
   I will worship at your <u>ho</u>ly temple. R/

2. I will give thanks <u>to</u> your name,
   because of your kindness and <u>your</u> truth.
   When I called, you <u>answered</u> me;
   you built up <u>strength</u> within me. R/

3. All the kings of the earth shall give thanks to
   <u>you</u>, O Lord,
   when they hear the words of <u>your</u> mouth;
   And they shall sing of the ways <u>of</u> the Lord:
   "Great is the glory <u>of</u> the Lord." R/

21 OT A
Psalm 138:1-2, 2-3, 6, 8. R/ v. 8bc

1., 2. *as above*

3b. The Lord is exalted, yet the low<u>ly</u> he sees,
   and the proud he knows from <u>a</u>far.
   Your kindness, O Lord, en<u>dures</u> forever;
   forsake not the work <u>of</u> your hands. R/

5 OT C
Psalm 138:1-2, 2-3, 4-5, 7-8. R/ v. 1c

1a. I will give thanks to you, O Lord, with <u>all</u> my heart,
   for you have heard the words of <u>my</u> mouth;
   in the presence of the angels I will <u>sing</u> your praise;
   I will worship at your holy temple and give thanks
   <u>to</u> your name. R/

2a. Because of your kindness <u>and</u> your truth;
   for you have made great above all things
   your name and <u>your</u> promise.
   When I called, you <u>answered</u> me;
   you built up <u>strength</u> within me. R/

3. *as opposite*

4. Your <u>right</u> hand saves me.
   The Lord will complete what he has done
   <u>for</u> me;
   your kindness, O Lord, en<u>dures</u> forever;
   forsake not the work <u>of</u> your hands. R/

17 OT C
Psalm 138:1-2, 2-3, 6-7, 7-8. R/ v. 3a

1a., 2a. *as above*

3a. The Lord is exalted, yet the low<u>ly</u> he sees,
   and the proud he knows from <u>a</u>far.
   Though I walk amid distress, <u>you</u> preserve me;
   against the anger of my enemies you
   <u>raise</u> your hand. R/

4. = *4 above*

Text: Refrain, *Lectionary for Mass*, © 1969, 1981, 1997, ICEL; verses, *Lectionary for Mass*/New American Bible, © 1970, 1986, 1991, 1997, 2001, 2010, CCD. All rights reserved.
Music: *The Collegeville Chant Psalter*, © 2019, Order of Saint Benedict, Collegeville, MN. Published and administered by Liturgical Press, Collegeville, MN 56321. All rights reserved.

Thanksgiving	5 OT C
1. - 2. - 3.	1a. - 2a. - 3. - 4.
21 OT A	**17 OT C**
1. - 2. - 3b.	1a. - 2a. - 3a. - 4.

Psalm 139

St. John the Baptist Day

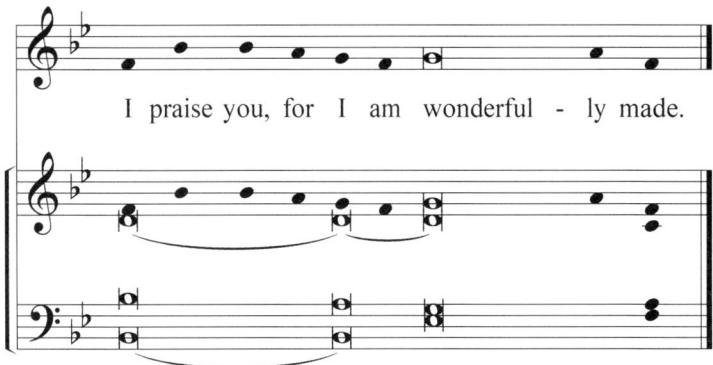

Psalm Tone

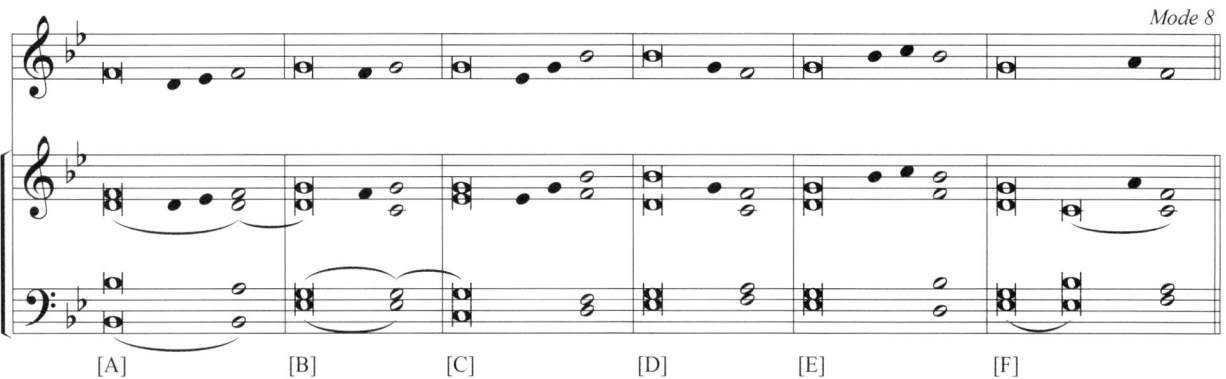

Mode 8

[A]   [B]   [C]   [D]   [E]   [F]

Psalm 139:1b-3, 13-14ab, 14c-15. R/ v. 14

1. O Lord, you have probed <u>me</u>, you know me:
   you know when I sit and when <u>I</u> stand;
   [omit C]
   you understand my thoughts from <u>a</u>far.
   My journeys and my <u>rest</u> you scrutinize,
   with all my ways you are <u>fa</u>miliar. *R/*

2. Truly you have formed my <u>in</u>most being;
   you knit me in my moth<u>er's</u> womb.
   I give you thanks that I am fearfully, wonder<u>ful</u>ly made;
   [omit D, E]
   wonderful are <u>your</u> works. *R/*

3. My soul also you <u>knew</u> full well;
   nor was my frame unknown <u>to</u> you
   When I was <u>made</u> in secret,
   [omit D, E]
   when I was fashioned in the depths of <u>the</u> earth. *R/*

Text: Refrain, *Lectionary for Mass*, © 1969, 1981, 1997, ICEL; verses, *Lectionary for Mass/New American Bible*, © 1970, 1986, 1991, 1997, 2001, 2010, CCD. All rights reserved.
Music: *The Collegeville Chant Psalter*, © 2019, Order of Saint Benedict, Collegeville, MN. Published and administered by Liturgical Press, Collegeville, MN 56321. All rights reserved.

Psalm 145

**14th Sunday in Ordinary Time, Year A • 5th Sunday of Easter, Year C •
31st Sunday in Ordinary Time, Year C • Common Ordinary Time 8**

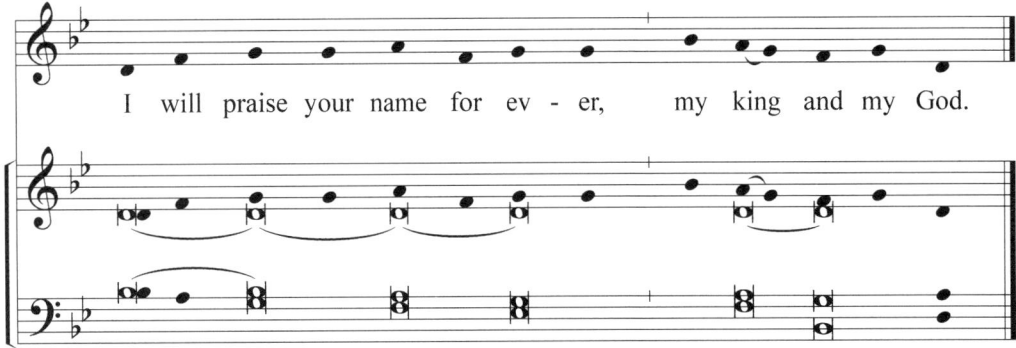

I will praise your name for ev - er, my king and my God.

Thanksgiving, option 4

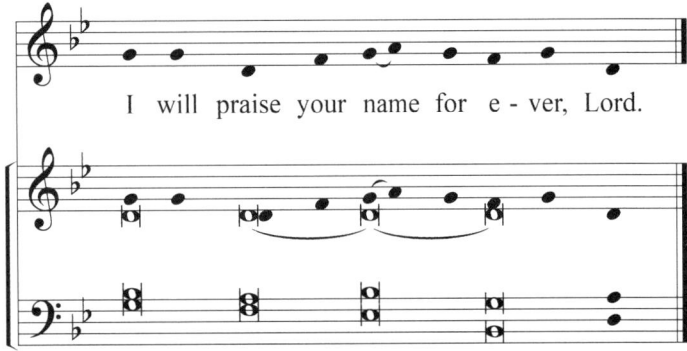

I will praise your name for e - ver, Lord.

14th Sunday in Ordinary Time, *alternate response* **•
5th Sunday of Easter, Year C,** *alternate response*

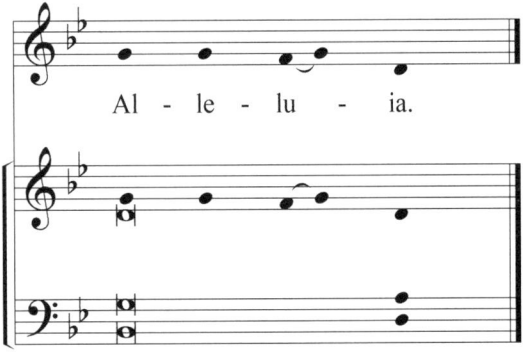

Al - le - lu - ia.

Psalm Tone

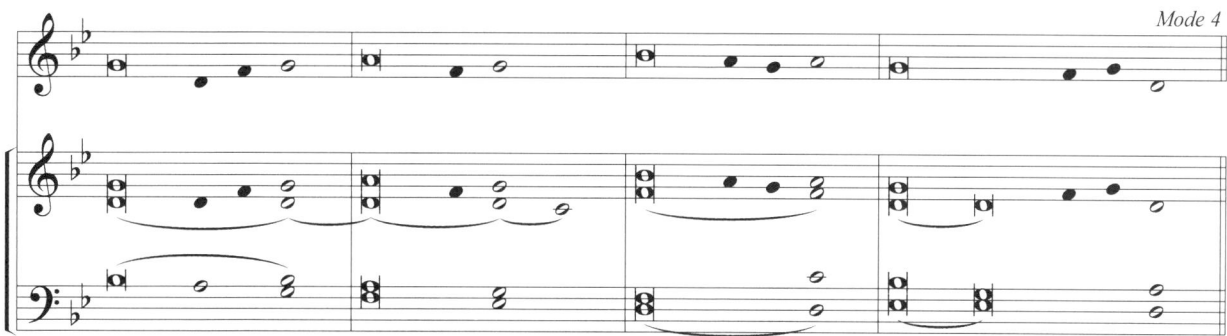

Mode 4

14 OT A, 31 OT C, Common OT 8
Psalm 145:1-2, 8-9, 10-11, 13-14. R/ cf. v. 1

1. I will extol you, O my God and King,
   and I will bless your name forever and ever.
   Every day will I bless you,
   and I will praise your name forever and ever. R/

2. The Lord is gracious and merciful,
   slow to anger and of great kindness.
   The Lord is good to all
   and compassionate toward all his works. R/

3. Let all your works give you thanks, O Lord,
   and let your faithful ones bless you.
   Let them discourse of the glory of your kingdom
   and speak of your might. R/

4. The Lord is faithful in all his words
   and holy in all his works.
   The Lord lifts up all who are falling
   and raises up all who are bowed down. R/

Thanksgiving 4
Psalm 145:2-3, 4-5, 6-7, 8-9, 10-11. R/ cf. v. 1

1a. Every day will I bless you,
    and I will praise your name forever and ever.
    Great is the Lord and highly to be praised;
    his greatness is unsearchable. R/

2a. Generation after generation praises your works
    and proclaims your might.
    They speak of the splendor of your
                                    glorious majesty
    and tell of your wondrous works. R/

3a. They discourse of the power of your
                                    terrible deeds
    and declare your greatness.
    They publish the fame of your abundant
                                    goodness
    and joyfully sing of your justice. R/

4a. = 2. opposite

5a. = 3. opposite

5 Easter C
Psalm 145:8-9, 10-11, 12-13. R/ cf. v. 1

1b. = 2. above

2b. = 3. above

3b. Let them make known your might to the children of Adam,
    and the glorious splendor of your kingdom.
    Your kingdom is a kingdom for all ages,
    and your dominion endures through all generations. R/

---

14 OT A, 31 OT C, Common OT 8
  1. - 2. - 3. - 4.
5 Easter C
  2. - 3. - 3b.
Thanksgiving 4
  1a. - 2a. - 3a. - 2. - 3.

Text: Refrain, *Lectionary for Mass*, © 1969, 1981, 1997, ICEL; verses, *Lectionary for Mass/New American Bible*, © 1970, 1986, 1991, 1997, 2001, 2010, CCD. All rights reserved.
Music: *The Collegeville Chant Psalter*, © 2019, Order of Saint Benedict, Collegeville, MN. Published and administered by Liturgical Press, Collegeville, MN 56321. All rights reserved.

18th Sunday in Ordinary Time, Year A • 17th Sunday in Ordinary Time, Year B

The hand of the Lord feeds us; he answers all our needs.

Psalm Tone   Mode 7

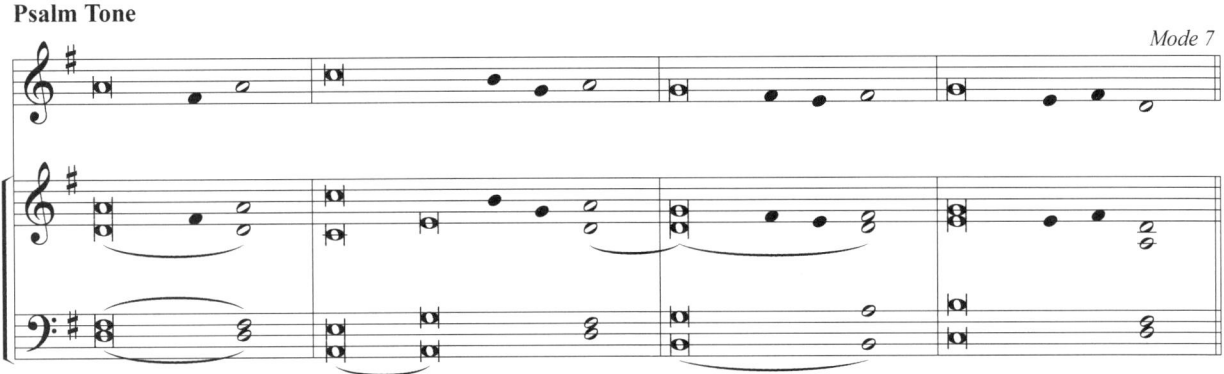

Psalm 145:8-9, 10-11, 15-16, 17-18. R/ cf. v. 16

18 OT A only
1. The LORD is gracious <u>and</u> merciful,
   slow to anger and <u>of</u> great kindness.
   The LORD is <u>good</u> to all
   and compassionate toward <u>all</u> his works. *R/*

2. The eyes of all look hopefully <u>to</u> you,
   and you give them their food <u>in</u> due season;
   you o<u>pen</u> your hand
   and satisfy the desire of every <u>living</u> thing. *R/*

3. The LORD is just in all <u>his</u> ways
   and holy in <u>all</u> his works.
   The LORD is near to all who <u>call</u> upon him,
   to all who call upon <u>him</u> in truth. *R/*

17 OT B only
1a. Let all your works give you thanks, <u>O</u> LORD,
    and let your faith<u>ful</u> ones bless you.
    Let them discourse of the glory <u>of</u> your kingdom
    and speak <u>of</u> your might. *R/*

18 OT A
  1. - 2. - 3.
17 OT B
  1a. - 2. - 3.

Text: Refrain, *Lectionary for Mass*, © 1969, 1981, 1997, ICEL; verses, *Lectionary for Mass*/New American Bible, © 1970, 1986, 1991, 1997, 2001, 2010, CCD. All rights reserved.
Music: *The Collegeville Chant Psalter*, © 2019, Order of Saint Benedict, Collegeville, MN. Published and administered by Liturgical Press, Collegeville, MN 56321. All rights reserved.

25th Sunday in Ordinary Time, Year A

The Lord is near to all who call up-on him.

Psalm Tone Mode 5

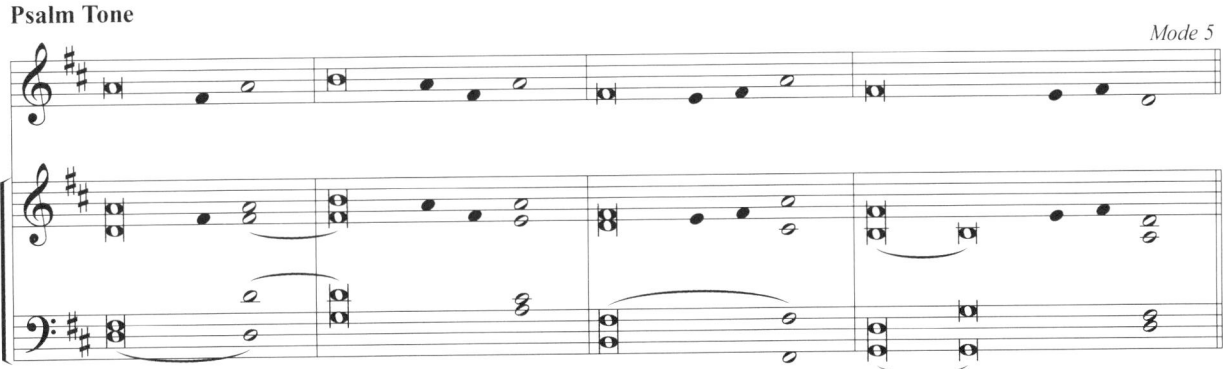

Psalm 145:2-3, 8-9, 17-18. R/ v. 18a

1. Every day will I bless you,
   and I will praise your name forev<u>er</u> and ever.
   Great is the Lord and highly <u>to</u> be praised;
   his greatness <u>is</u> unsearchable. *R/*

2. The Lord is gracious <u>and</u> merciful,
   slow to anger and <u>of</u> great kindness.
   The Lord is <u>good</u> to all
   and compassionate toward <u>all</u> his works. *R/*

3. The Lord is just in all <u>his</u> ways
   and holy in <u>all</u> his works.
   The Lord is near to all who <u>call</u> upon him,
   to all who call upon <u>him</u> in truth. *R/*

Text: Refrain, *Lectionary for Mass,* © 1969, 1981, 1997, ICEL; verses, *Lectionary for Mass*/New American Bible, © 1970, 1986, 1991, 1997, 2001, 2010, CCD. All rights reserved.
Music: *The Collegeville Chant Psalter,* © 2019, Order of Saint Benedict, Collegeville, MN. Published and administered by Liturgical Press, Collegeville, MN 56321. All rights reserved.

Psalm 146

23rd Sunday in Ordinary Time, Year B • 32nd Sunday in Ordinary Time, Year B • 26th Sunday in Ordinary Time, Year C

Praise the Lord, my soul!

3rd Sunday of Advent, Year A, *alternate response* • 23rd Sunday in Ordinary Time, Year B, *alternate response* • 32nd Sunday in Ordinary Time, Year B, *alternate response* • 26th Sunday in Ordinary Time, Year C, *alternate response*

Al - le - lu - ia.

4th Sunday in Ordinary Time, Year A

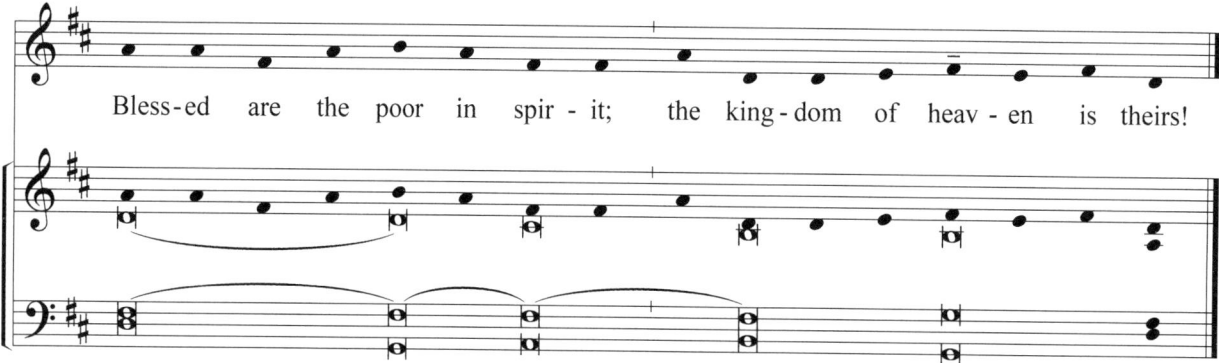

Bless-ed are the poor in spir - it; the king-dom of heav - en is theirs!

3rd Sunday of Advent, Year A

Psalm Tone

Mode 5

Psalm 146:6-7, 8-9, 9-10. R/ v. 1b; Mt 5:3; cf. Is 35:4

1. The LORD keeps faith <u>for</u>ever,
   secures justice for <u>the</u> oppressed,
   gives food <u>to</u> the hungry.
   The LORD sets <u>cap</u>tives free. *R/*

2. The LORD gives sight to <u>the</u> blind;
   the LORD raises up those who <u>were</u> bowed down.
   The LORD <u>loves</u> the just;
   the LORD <u>pro</u>tects strangers. *R/*

3. The fatherless and the widow the LORD <u>sus</u>tains,
   but the way of the wi<u>cked</u> he thwarts.
   The LORD shall <u>reign</u> forever;
   your God, O Zion, through all generations. <u>Alle</u>luia. *R/*

3 Adv A, v. 1, line 1
1. The LORD God keeps faith <u>for</u>ever,

23 OT B, v. 1, line 1
1. The God of Jacob keeps faith <u>for</u>ever,

26 OT C, v. 1, line 1
1. Blessed is he who keeps faith <u>for</u>ever.

3 Adv A, v. 3, line 4
your God, O Zion, through all <u>gen</u>erations. *R/*

Text: Refrain, *Lectionary for Mass*, © 1969, 1981, 1997, ICEL; verses, *Lectionary for Mass*/New American Bible, © 1970, 1986, 1991, 1997, 2001, 2010, CCD. All rights reserved.
Music: *The Collegeville Chant Psalter*, © 2019, Order of Saint Benedict, Collegeville, MN. Published and administered by Liturgical Press, Collegeville, MN 56321. All rights reserved.

Note:
32 OT B and **26 OT C** have minor differences of punctuation in v. 2.

Psalm 147a

5th Sunday in Ordinary Time, Year B

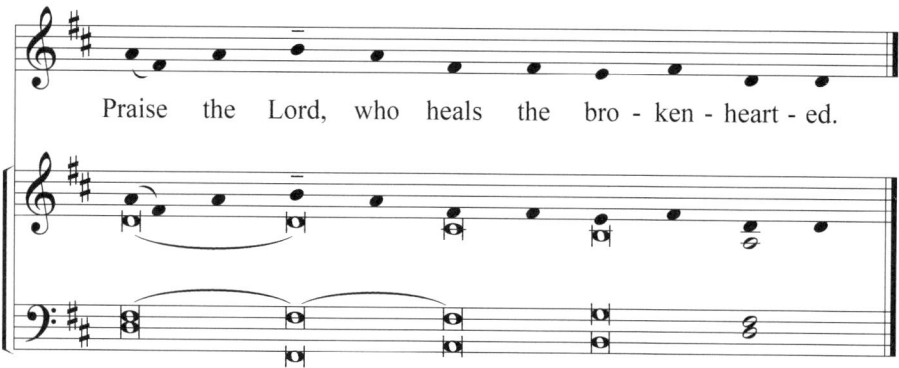

Praise the Lord, who heals the bro-ken-heart-ed.

5th Sunday in Ordinary Time, Year B, *alternate response*

Al - le - lu - ia.

Psalm Tone

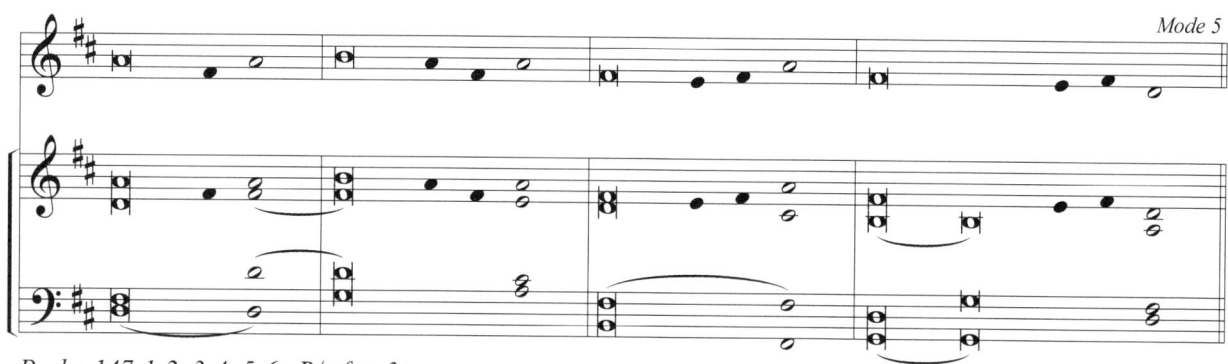

Mode 5

Psalm 147:1-2, 3-4, 5-6. R/ cf. v. 3a

1. Praise the LORD, for he <u>is</u> good;
   sing praise to our God, for he is gracious;
   it is fit<u>ting</u> to praise him.
   The LORD re<u>builds</u> Jerusalem;
   the dispersed of Is<u>rael</u> he gathers. *R/*

2. He heals the bro<u>ken</u>hearted
   and binds <u>up</u> their wounds.
   He tells the number <u>of</u> the stars;
   he calls <u>each</u> by name. *R/*

3. Great is our Lord and mighty <u>in</u> power;
   to his wisdom there <u>is</u> no limit.
   The LORD sus<u>tains</u> the lowly;
   the wicked he casts <u>to</u> the ground. *R/*

Text: Refrain, *Lectionary for Mass*, © 1969, 1981, 1997, ICEL; verses, *Lectionary for Mass*/New American Bible, © 1970, 1986, 1991, 1997, 2001, 2010, CCD. All rights reserved.
Music: *The Collegeville Chant Psalter*, © 2019, Order of Saint Benedict, Collegeville, MN. Published and administered by Liturgical Press, Collegeville, MN 56321. All rights reserved.

Psalm 147b

Body and Blood of Christ, Year A

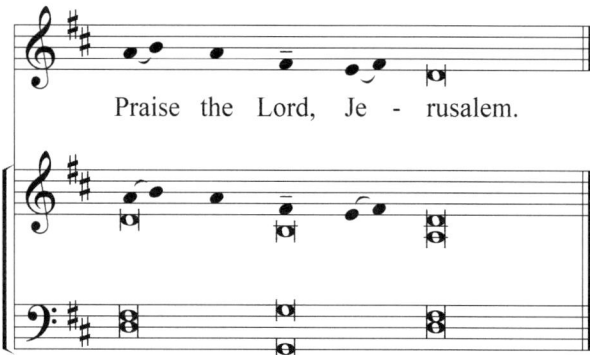

Praise the Lord, Jerusalem.

2nd Sunday after Christmas

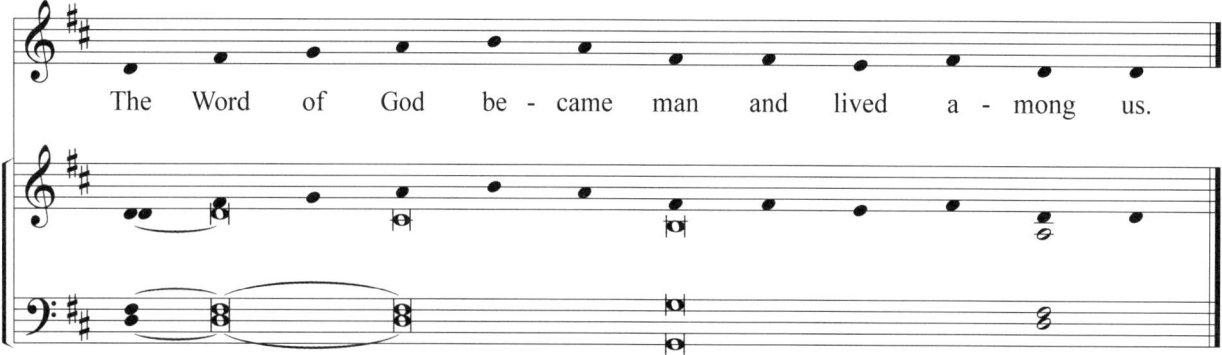

The Word of God became man and lived among us.

Body and Blood of Christ, Year A, *alternate response* •
2nd Sunday after Christmas, *alternate response*

Alleluia.

Psalm Tone

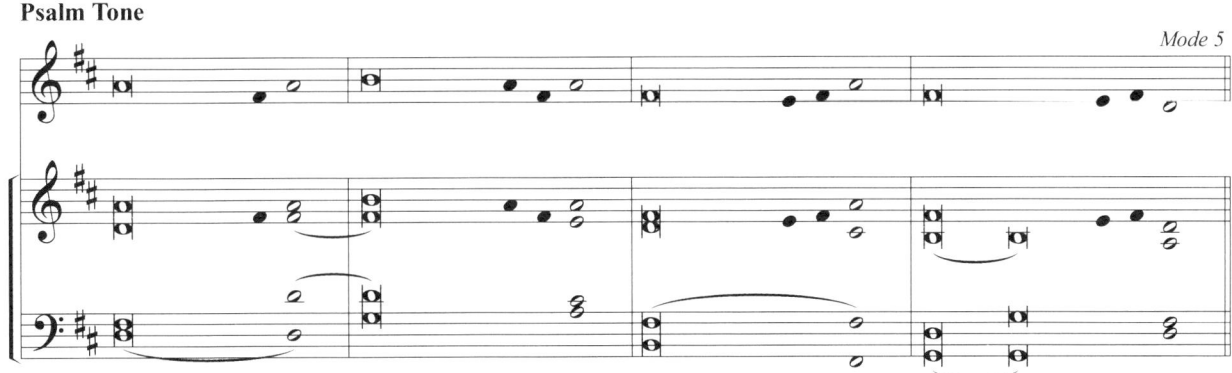

Psalm 147:12-13, 14-15, 19-20. R/ v. 12; Jn 1:14

1. Glorify the Lord, O Jerusalem;
   praise your God, O Zion.
   For he has strengthened the bars of your gates;
   he has blessed your children within you. *R/*

2. He has granted peace in your borders;
   with the best of wheat he fills you.
   He sends forth his command to the earth;
   swiftly runs his word! *R/*

3. He has proclaimed his word to Jacob,
   his statutes and his ordinances to Israel.
   He has not done thus for any other nation;
   his ordinances he has not made known to them. Alleluia. *R/*

Text: Refrain, *Lectionary for Mass,* © 1969, 1981, 1997, ICEL; verses, *Lectionary for Mass*/New American Bible, © 1970, 1986, 1991, 1997, 2001, 2010, CCD. All rights reserved.
Music: *The Collegeville Chant Psalter,* © 2019, Order of Saint Benedict, Collegeville, MN. Published and administered by Liturgical Press, Collegeville, MN 56321. All rights reserved.

Exodus 15

Easter Vigil 3

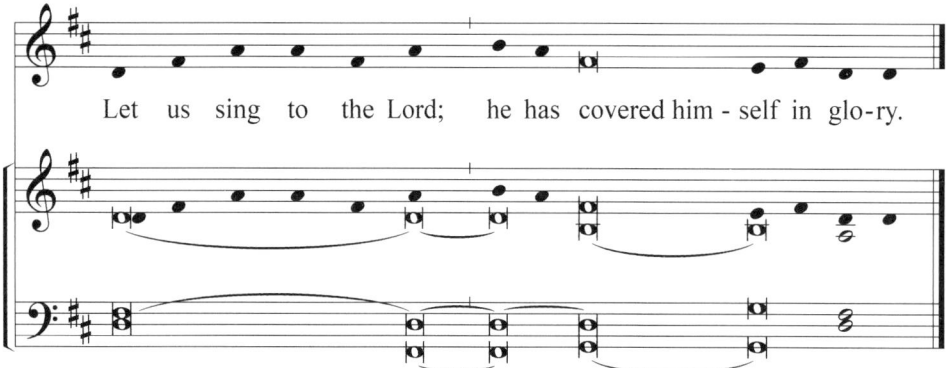

Let us sing to the Lord; he has covered him-self in glo-ry.

Canticle Tone

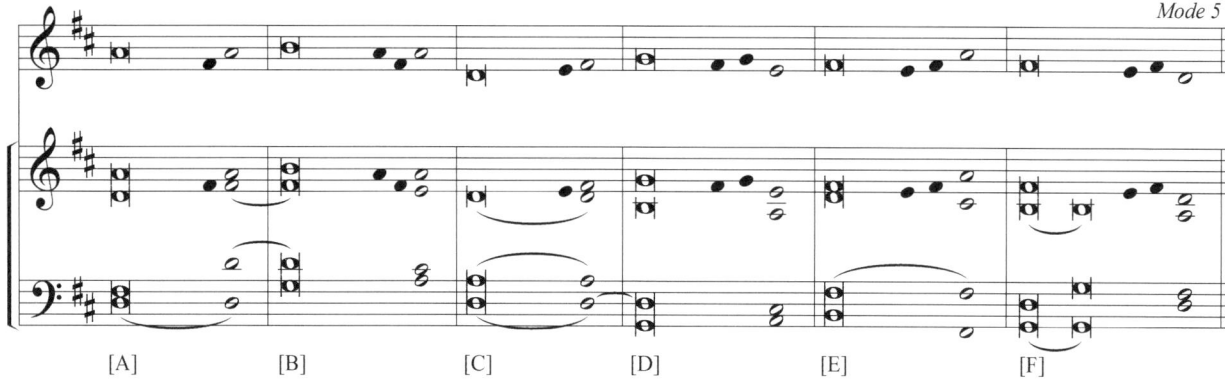

Mode 5

[A]   [B]   [C]   [D]   [E]   [F]

Exodus 15:1-2, 3-4, 5-6, 17-18. R/ v. 1b

1. I will sing to the Lord, for he is gloriously <u>tri</u>umphant;
   horse and chariot he has cast in<u>to</u> the sea.
   My strength and my courage is <u>the</u> Lord,
   and he has <u>been</u> my savior.
   He is my <u>God</u>, I praise him;
   the God of my father, <u>I</u> extol him.   *R/*

2. The Lord is <u>a</u> warrior,
   Lord <u>is</u> his name!
   [omit C, D]
   Pharaoh's chariots and army he hurled in<u>to</u> the sea;
   the elite of his officers were submerged <u>in</u> the Red Sea.   *R/*

> *Note:*
> Since 1970, the U.S. Lectionary has contained an important error at the end of the Exodus reading preceding this canticle.
>
> According to the Latin original, the reading should end with "Then Moses and the Israelites sang this song to the Lord:" (last line but two), and the Canticle then follows **immediately**, with **no other** lines of scripture and **no** concluding formula ("The word of the Lord") intervening.

3. The flood wa<u>ters</u> covered them,
   they sank into the depths <u>like</u> a stone.
   [omit C, D]
   Your right hand, O Lord, magni<u>fi</u>cent in power,
   your right hand, O Lord, has shat<u>tered</u> the enemy.   *R/*

4. You brought in the people you <u>re</u>deemed
   and planted them on the mountain of <u>your</u> inheritance
   the place where you made your seat, <u>O</u> Lord,
   the sanctuary, Lord, which your <u>hands</u> established.
   [omit E]
   The Lord shall reign fore<u>ver</u> and ever.   *R/*

Text: Refrain, *Lectionary for Mass,* © 1969, 1981, 1997, ICEL; verses, *Lectionary for Mass*/New American Bible, © 1970, 1986, 1991, 1997, 2001, 2010, CCD. All rights reserved.
Music: *The Collegeville Chant Psalter,* © 2019, Order of Saint Benedict, Collegeville, MN. Published and administered by Liturgical Press, Collegeville, MN 56321. All rights reserved.

1 Chronicles

Thanksgiving, option 1 • Anniversary of Dedication of a Church, option 1

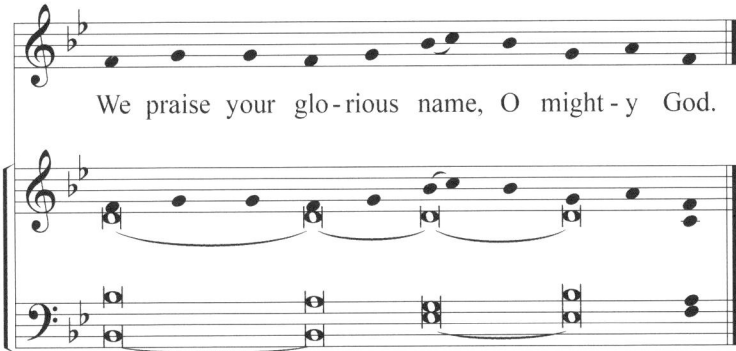

Canticle Tone

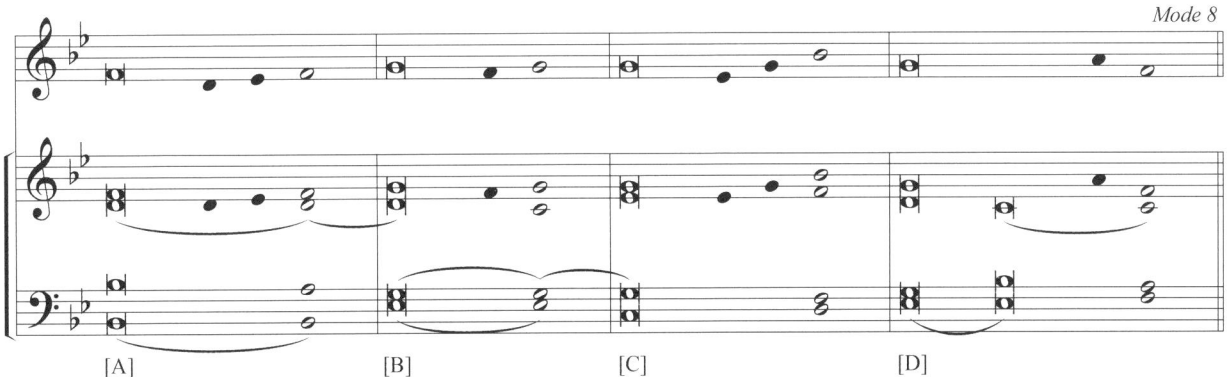

1 Chronicles 29:10bcd, 11abc, 11d-12a, 12bcd. R/ v. 13b

Thanksgiving, opt. 1

1. "Blessed may you <u>be</u>, O L<small>ORD</small>,
    God of Israel <u>our</u> father,
    [omit C]
    from eternity to <u>e</u>ternity." R/

2. "Yours, O L<small>ORD</small>, are grandeur and power,
          majesty, splen<u>dor</u>, and glory.
    For all in heaven and on earth <u>is</u> yours;
    yours, O L<small>ORD</small>, <u>is</u> the sovereignty;
    you are exalted as head <u>o</u>ver all." R/

3. "Riches and hon<u>or</u> are from you,
    and you have dominion <u>o</u>ver all.
    In your hand are pow<u>er</u> and might;
    it is yours to give grandeur and strength <u>to</u> all." R/

Anniversary of Dedication of a Church, opt. 1

1. "Blessed may you <u>be</u>, O L<small>ORD</small>,
    God of Israel <u>our</u> father,
    [omit C]
    from eternity to <u>e</u>ternity." R/

2. "Yours, O L<small>ORD</small>, are <u>grandeur</u> and power,
    majesty, splendor, <u>and</u> glory.
    [omit C]
    For all in heaven and on earth <u>is</u> yours." R/

3. "Yours, O L<small>ORD</small>, <u>is</u> the sovereignty;
    you are exalted as head <u>o</u>ver all.
    [omit C]
    Riches and honor are <u>from</u> you." R/

4. "You have dominion <u>o</u>ver all.
    In your hand are power <u>and</u> might;
    it is yours to give grandeur and strength <u>to</u> all." R/

Text: Refrain, *Lectionary for Mass,* © 1969, 1981, 1997, ICEL; verses, *Lectionary for Mass*/New American Bible, © 1970, 1986, 1991, 1997, 2001, 2010, CCD. All rights reserved.
Music: *The Collegeville Chant Psalter,* © 2019, Order of Saint Benedict, Collegeville, MN. Published and administered by Liturgical Press, Collegeville, MN 56321. All rights reserved.

Isaiah 12

Easter Vigil 5 • Easter Vigil 7, *alternate psalm* • Baptism of the Lord, Year B • Sacred Heart, Year B

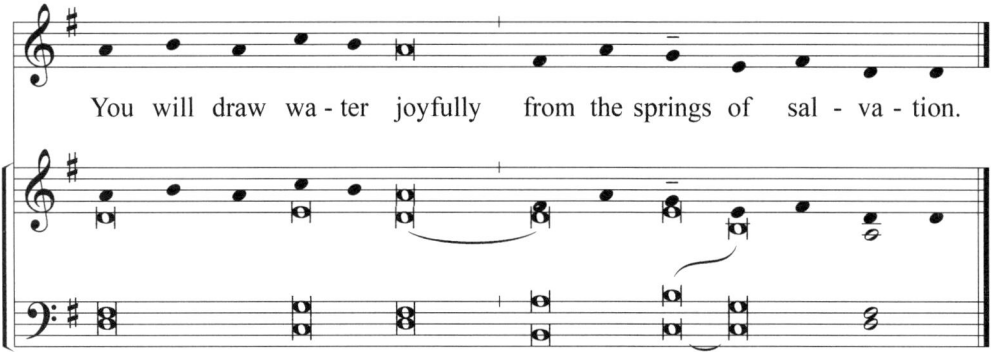

3rd Sunday of Advent, Year C

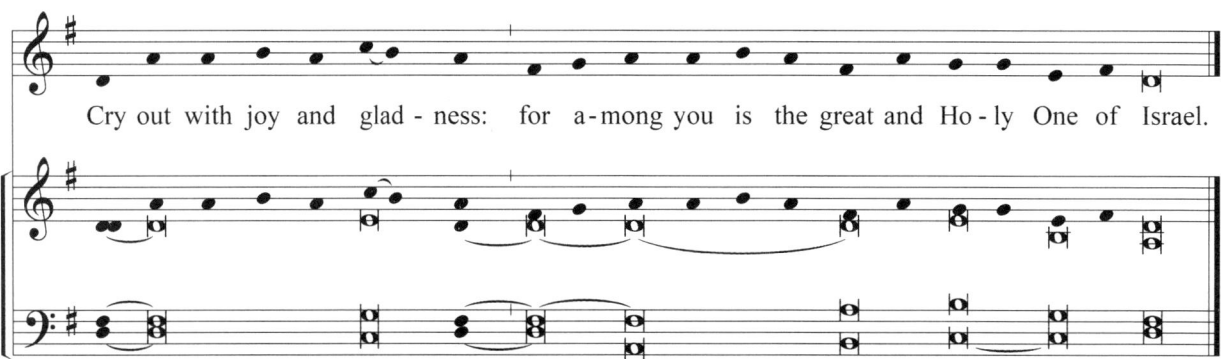

Canticle Tone

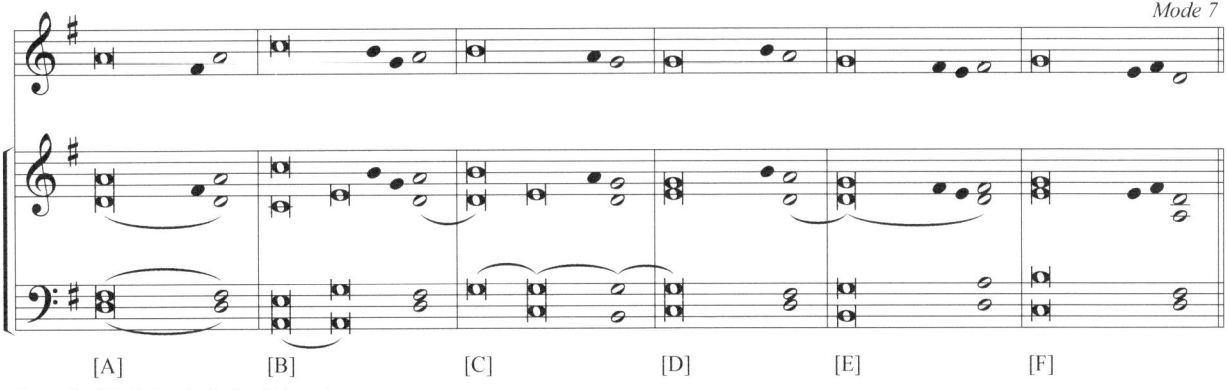

Mode 7

[A] [B] [C] [D] [E] [F]

Isaiah 12:2-3, 4, 5-6. R/ v. 6

1. God indeed is <u>my</u> savior;
   I am confident and <u>un</u>afraid.
   My strength and my courage is <u>the</u> Lord,
   and he has been <u>my</u> savior.
   With joy you <u>will</u> draw water
   at the fountain <u>of</u> salvation.   *R/*

2. Give thanks to <u>the</u> Lord,
                        ac<u>claim</u> his name;
   [omit C, D]
   among the nations make <u>known</u> his deeds,
   proclaim how exalted <u>is</u> his name.   *R/*

3. Sing praise to <u>the</u> Lord
               for his glo<u>rious</u> achievement;
   let this be known throughout all <u>the</u> earth.
   Shout with exultation, O city <u>of</u> Zion,
   for great <u>in</u> your midst
   is the Holy <u>One</u> of Israel!   *R/*

Text: Refrain, *Lectionary for Mass,* © 1969, 1981, 1997, ICEL; verses, *Lectionary for Mass*/New American Bible, © 1970, 1986, 1991, 1997, 2001, 2010, CCD. All rights reserved.
Music: *The Collegeville Chant Psalter,* © 2019, Order of Saint Benedict, Collegeville, MN. Published and administered by Liturgical Press, Collegeville, MN 56321. All rights reserved.

Daniel 3

Pentecost Vigil 2 • Trinity, Year A

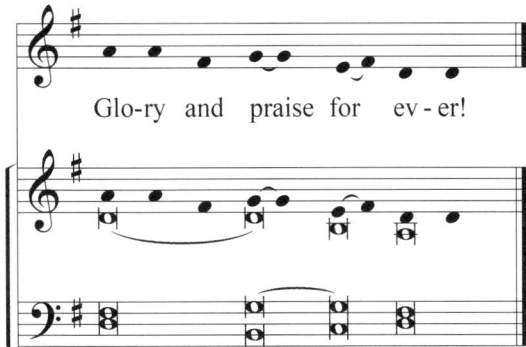

Canticle Tone

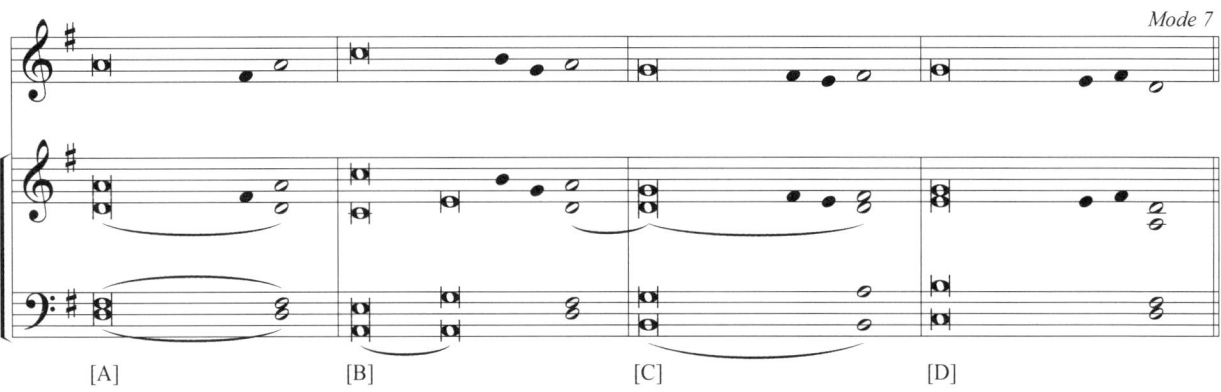

Daniel 3:52, 53, 54, 55, 56. R/ v. 52b

1. Blessed are you, O Lord, the God of <u>our</u> fathers,
   praiseworthy and exalted above <u>all</u> forever;
   and blessed is your holy and <u>glo</u>rious name,
   praiseworthy and exalted above all <u>for</u> all ages. *R/*

2. Blessed are you in the temple of your ho<u>ly</u> glory,
   [omit B, C]
   praiseworthy and glorious above <u>all</u> forever. *R/*

3. Blessed are you on the throne of <u>your</u> kingdom,
   [omit B, C]
   praiseworthy and exalted above <u>all</u> forever. *R/*

4. Blessed are you who look into <u>the</u> depths
   from your throne up<u>on</u> the cherubim,
   [omit C]
   praiseworthy and exalted above <u>all</u> forever. *R/*

Text: Refrain, *Lectionary for Mass,* © 1969, 1981, 1997, ICEL; verses, *Lectionary for Mass*/New American Bible, © 1970, 1986, 1991, 1997, 2001, 2010, CCD. All rights reserved.
Music: *The Collegeville Chant Psalter,* © 2019, Order of Saint Benedict, Collegeville, MN. Published and administered by Liturgical Press, Collegeville, MN 56321. All rights reserved.

Luke 1

3rd Sunday of Advent, Year B

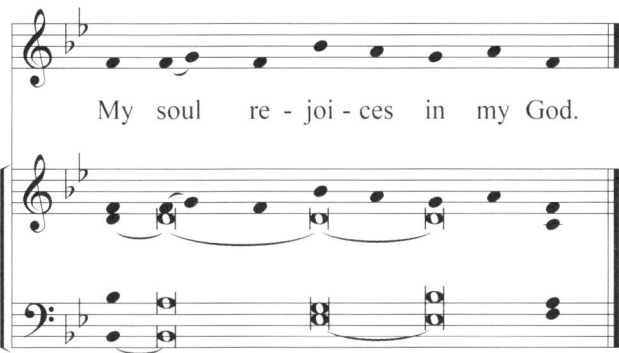

Canticle Tone

Mode 8

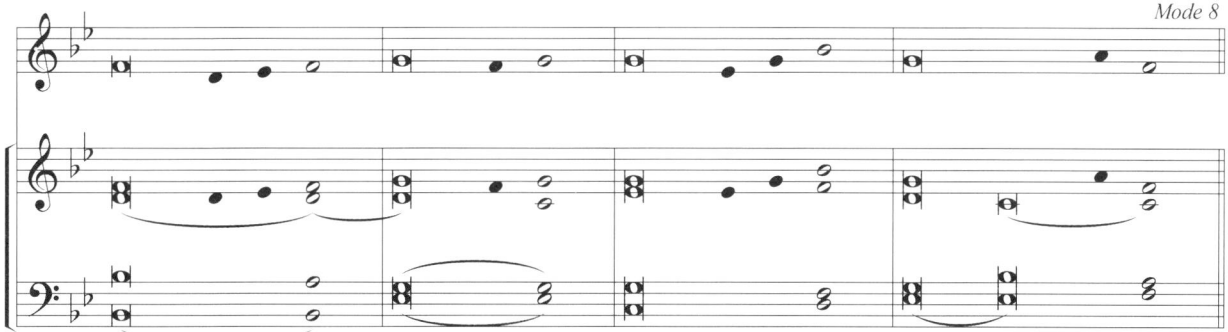

Luke 1:46-48, 49-50, 53-54. R/ cf. Is 61:10b

1. My soul proclaims the greatness <u>of</u> the Lord;
   my spirit rejoices in God <u>my</u> Savior,
   for he has looked upon his <u>low</u>ly servant.
   From this day all generations will call <u>me</u> blessed: *R/*

2. the Almighty has done great <u>things</u> for me,
   and holy is <u>his</u> Name.
   He has mercy on <u>those</u> who fear him
   in every gen<u>er</u>ation. *R/*

3. He has filled the hun<u>gry</u> with good things,
   and the rich he has sent a<u>way</u> empty.
   He has come to the help of his <u>ser</u>vant Israel
   for he has remembered his promise <u>of</u> mercy. *R/*

Text: Refrain, *Lectionary for Mass*, © 1969, 1981, 1997, ICEL; verses, *Lectionary for Mass*/New American Bible, © 1970, 1986, 1991, 1997, 2001, 2010, CCD. All rights reserved.
Music: *The Collegeville Chant Psalter*, © 2019, Order of Saint Benedict, Collegeville, MN. Published and administered by Liturgical Press, Collegeville, MN 56321. All rights reserved.

Liturgical Index by Use

NB: references are to Psalm number, not page number
Canticles are Ex (Exodus), 1 Chron (1 Chronicles), Is (Isaiah), Dan (Daniel), Lk (Luke)
See note at end re: Psalm 147a and Psalm 147b

Liturgical Day	Year A	Year B	Year C
PROPER OF TIME			
1st Sunday of Advent	122	80	25
2nd Sunday of Advent	72	85	126
3rd Sunday of Advent	146	Lk 1	Is 12
4th Sunday of Advent	24	89	80
Christmas Vigil	89	89	89
Christmas Midnight	96	96	96
Christmas Dawn	97	97	97
Christmas Day	98	98	98
Holy Family	128	105	84
Mary, Mother of God	67	67	67
2nd Sunday after Christmas	147b+	147b+	147b+
Epiphany Vigil	72	72	72
Epiphany Day	72	72	72
Baptism of the Lord	29	Is 12	104
Ash Wednesday	51	51	51
1st Sunday of Lent	51	25	91
2nd Sunday of Lent	33	116	27
3rd Sunday of Lent	95	19	103
4th Sunday of Lent	23	137	34
5th Sunday of Lent	130	51	126
Palm Sunday	22	22	22
Holy Thursday Evening	116	116	116
Good Friday	31	31	31
Easter Vigil			
Psalm 1	104	104	104
Psalm 1 *alternate*	33	33	33
Psalm 2	16	16	16
Psalm 3	Ex 15	Ex 15	Ex 15
Psalm 4	30	30	30
Psalm 5	Is 12	Is 12	Is 12
Psalm 6	19	19	19
Psalm 7	42-3	42-3	42-3
Psalm 7 *alternate 1*	Is 12	Is 12	Is 12
Psalm 7 *alternate 2*	51	51	51
Alleluia Psalm	118	118	118
Easter Day	118	118	118
2nd Sunday of Easter	118	118	118

Liturgical Day	Year A	Year B	Year C
3rd Sunday of Easter	16	4	30
4th Sunday of Easter	23	118	100
5th Sunday of Easter	33	22	145
6th Sunday of Easter	66	98	67
Ascension Vigil and Day	47	47	47
7th Sunday of Easter	27	103	97
Pentecost Extended Vigil			
Psalm 1	33	33	33
Psalm 2	Dan 3	Dan 3	Dan 3
Psalm 2 *alternate*	19	19	19
Psalm 3	107	107	107
Psalm 4 (& Simple Vigil)	104	104	104
Pentecost Day	104	104	104
Trinity Sunday	Dan 3	33	8
Body and Blood of Christ	147b+	116	110
Sacred Heart	103	Is 12	23
2nd Sunday in Ordinary Time	40	40	96
3rd Sunday in Ordinary Time	27	25	19
4th Sunday in Ordinary Time	146	95	71
5th Sunday in Ordinary Time	112	147a+	138
6th Sunday in Ordinary Time	119	32	1
7th Sunday in Ordinary Time	103	41	103
8th Sunday in Ordinary Time	62	103	92
9th Sunday in Ordinary Time	31	81	117
10th Sunday in Ordinary Time	50	130	30
11th Sunday in Ordinary Time	100	92	32
12th Sunday in Ordinary Time	69	107	63
13th Sunday in Ordinary Time	89	30	16
14th Sunday in Ordinary Time	145	123	66
15th Sunday in Ordinary Time	65	85	69
15th Sunday in Ordinary Time *alternate*			19
16th Sunday in Ordinary Time	86	23	15
17th Sunday in Ordinary Time	119	145	138
18th Sunday in Ordinary Time	145	78	90
18th Sunday in Ordinary Time *alternate*			[95]*
19th Sunday in Ordinary Time	85	34	33
20th Sunday in Ordinary Time	67	34	40
21st Sunday in Ordinary Time	138	34	117
22nd Sunday in Ordinary Time	63	15	68
23rd Sunday in Ordinary Time	95	146	90
24th Sunday in Ordinary Time	103	116	51
25th Sunday in Ordinary Time	145	54	113
26th Sunday in Ordinary Time	25	19	146
27th Sunday in Ordinary Time	80	128	95
28th Sunday in Ordinary Time	23	90	98
29th Sunday in Ordinary Time	96	33	121

Liturgical Day	Year A	Year B	Year C
30th Sunday in Ordinary Time	18	126	34
31st Sunday in Ordinary Time	131	18	145
32nd Sunday in Ordinary Time	63	146	17
33rd Sunday in Ordinary Time	128	16	98
Christ the King	23	93	122

COMMON PSALMS
(may replace the psalm proper to a particular day)

Common Psalm Advent 1	25
Common Psalm Advent 2	85
Common Psalm Christmas	98
Common Psalm Epiphany	72
Common Psalm Lent 1	51
Common Psalm Lent 2	91
Common Psalm Lent 3	130
Common Psalm Holy Week	22
Common Psalm Easter Vigil 1	136
Common Psalm Easter Vigil 2	136
Common Psalm Easter Season 1	118
Common Psalm Easter Season 2	66
Common Psalm Ascension	47
Common Psalm Pentecost	104
Common Psalm Ordinary Time 1	19
Common Psalm Ordinary Time 2	27
Common Psalm Ordinary Time 3	34
Common Psalm Ordinary Time 4	63
Common Psalm Ordinary Time 5	95
Common Psalm Ordinary Time 6	100
Common Psalm Ordinary Time 7	103
Common Psalm Ordinary Time 8	145
Common Psalm Ordinary Time 9 (last weeks)	122

PROPER OF SAINTS and OTHER DAYS WHICH MAY REPLACE A SUNDAY

Liturgical Day	Years A, B, and C		
February 2: Presentation of the Lord	24		
March 25: Annunciation of the B.V.M.	40		
June 23: St John the Baptist (Vigil)	71		
June 24: St John the Baptist (Day)	139		
June 28: Ss Peter and Paul (Vigil)	19		
June 29: Ss Peter and Paul (Day)	34		
August 6: Transfiguration of the Lord	97		
August 14: Assumption of the B.V.M. (Vigil)	132		
August 15: Assumption of the B.V.M. (Day)	45		
September 14: Exaltation of the Holy Cross	78		
November 1: All Saints	24		
November 2: All Souls (three Masses)	23	25	27

Liturgical Day	Years A, B, and C			
November 9: Dedication of the Lateran Basilica	46			
December 8: Immaculate Conception of the B.V.M.	98			
Thanksgiving Day (Lectionary psalms)	1 Chron	113	138	145
Thanksgiving Day (C.E. alternate psalm)**	67			
Anniversary of Dedication of a Church, option 1	1 Chron			
option 2	46			
option 3	84			
option 4	95			
option 5	122			

* (**18 OT C** was Psalm 95 in original 1970 Lectionary)

** C.E. = *Celebrating the Eucharist*

+ Psalm 147a is Ps 146 in the Vulgate; Psalm 147b is Ps 147 in the Vulgate. We have treated them as separate psalms.

Index of First Lines of Psalm Extracts

Entries are in strictly alphabetical order, ignoring any punctuation or gaps between words

References are to Psalm numbers, not page numbers
Where a psalm has several extracts, the first line of each one is listed if it begins differently

Canticles are Ex 15 (Exodus), 1 Chron (1 Chronicles), Is 12 (Isaiah), Dan 3 (Daniel), Lk 1 (Luke)

22	All who see me scoff at me	121	I lift up my eyes toward the mountains
47	All you peoples, clap your hands	116	I love the Lord, because he has heard
42-3	Athirst is my soul	18	I love you, O Lord, my strength
80	A vine from Egypt you transplanted	31, 71	In you, O Lord, I take refuge
		69	I pray to you, O Lord
132	Behold, we heard of it in Ephrathah	122	I rejoiced because they said to me
119	Blessed are they whose way is blameless	92	It is good to give thanks to the Lord
Dan 3	Blessed are you, O Lord, the God of our fathers	34	I will bless the Lord at all times
128	Blessed are you who fear the Lord	145	I will extol you, O my God and King
146	Blessed he who keeps faith for ever	30	I will extol you, O Lord, for you drew me clear
1 Chron	Blessed may you be, O Lord	22	I will fulfil my vows before those who fear the Lord
128	Blessed is everyone who fears the Lord	138	I will give thanks to you, O Lord, with all my heart
41	Blessed is the one who has regard for the lowly and the poor	85	I will hear what God proclaims
32	Blessed is the one whose fault is taken away	Ex 15	I will sing to the Lord, for he is gloriously triumphant
1	Blessed the man who follows not		
103, 104	Bless the Lord, O my soul	16	Keep me, O God, for in you I take refuge
137	By the streams of Babylon		
		145	Let all your works give you thanks, O Lord
95	Come, let us sing joyfully to the Lord	118	Let the house of Israel say
		107	Let the redeemed of the Lord say
145	Every day I will bless you	24	Lift up, O gates, your lintels
33	Exult, you just, in the Lord	112	Light shines through the darkness for the upright
69	For your sake I bear insult	67	May God have pity on us and bless us
		Lk 1	My soul proclaims the greatness of the Lord
118, 136	Give thanks to the Lord, for he is good	84	My soul yearns and pines
105	Give thanks to the Lord, invoke his name		
29	Give to the Lord, you sons of God	54	O God, by your name save me
147b	Glorify the Lord, O Jerusalem	72	O God, with your judgment endow the king
Is 12	God indeed is my savior	63	O God, you are my God whom I seek
46	God is our refuge and our strength	16	O Lord, my allotted portion and my cup
50	God the Lord has spoken and summoned the earth	104	O Lord, my God, you are great indeed
		131	O Lord, my heart is not proud
51	Have mercy on me, God, in your goodness	139	O Lord, you have probed me, you know me
78	Hearken, my people, to my teaching	62	Only in God is my soul at rest
17	Hear, O Lord, a just suit	80	O shepherd of Israel, hearken
84	How lovely is your dwelling place	130	Out of the depths I cry to you, O Lord
116	How shall I make a return to the Lord		
		117	Praise the Lord, all you nations
116	I believed, even when I said	147a	Praise the Lord, for he is good
89	I have made a covenant with my chosen one	113	Praise, you servants of the Lord
119	I have said, O Lord, that my part		
40	I have waited, waited for the Lord	25	Remember that your compassion, O Lord

Index of First Lines of Psalm Extracts, pg. 2

40	Sacrifice or offering you wished not	24	The Lord's are the earth and its fullness
66	Shout joyfully to God, all the earth	89	The promises of the Lord I will sing forever
100	Sing joyfully to the Lord, all you lands	45	The queen takes her place at your right hand
98	Sing to the Lord a new song	107	They who sailed the sea in ships
98	Sing praise to the Lord with the harp	123	To you I lift up my eyes
81	Take up a melody, and sound the timbrel	33	Upright is the word of the Lord
90	Teach us to number our days aright	78	What we have heard and know
146	The God of Jacob keeps faith for ever	8	When I behold your heavens, the work of your fingers
19	The heavens declare the glory of God	4	When I call, answer me, O my just God
68	The just rejoice and exult before God	126	When the Lord brought back the captives of Zion
19	The law of the Lord is perfect	15	Whoever walks blamelessly and does justice
33	The Lord brings to nought the plans of the nations	15	Who walks blamelessly and does justice
145	The Lord is gracious and merciful		
93	The Lord is king, in splendour robed	65	You have visited the land and watered it
97	The Lord is king; let the earth rejoice	86	You, O Lord, are good and forgiving
27	The Lord is my light and my salvation	25	Your ways, O Lord, make known to me
23	The Lord is my shepherd; I shall not want	90	You turn man back to dust
146	The Lord God keeps faith for ever	91	You who dwell in the shelter of the Most High
146	The Lord keeps faith for ever		
110	The Lord said to my Lord		

Index of First Lines of Responses

Entries are in strictly alphabetical order, ignoring any punctuation or gaps between words
References are to Psalm numbers, not page numbers
Canticles are Ex 15 (Exodus), 1 Chron (1 Chronicles), Is 12 (Isaiah), Dan 3 (Daniel), Lk 1 (Luke)

97	A light will shine on us this day
4, 16, 23, 30, 33,	
47, 66, 97, 98, 100,	
103, 104, 107, 112,	
113, 116, 117, 118,	
145, 146, 147a,	
147b	Alleluia (*once, twice or three times*)
98	All the ends of the earth
51	Be merciful, O Lord, for we have sinned
91	Be with me, Lord, when I am in trouble
146	Blessed are the poor in spirit
84	Blessed are they who dwell in your house
119	Blessed are they who follow the law of the Lord
1	Blessed are they who hope in the Lord
128	Blessed are those who fear the Lord
128	Blessed are those who fear the Lord and walk in his ways
33	Blessed the people the Lord has chosen
51	Create a clean heart in me, O God
Is 12	Cry out with joy and gladness
78	Do not forget the works of the Lord
31	Father, into your hands I commend my spirit
90	Fill us with your love, O Lord
89	Forever I will sing the goodness of the Lord
118	Give thanks to the Lord, for he is good
107	Give thanks to the Lord; his love is everlasting
Dan 3	Glory and praise for ever
68	God, in your goodness you have made a home
47	God mounts his throne to shouts of joy
136	God's love is everlasting
117	Go out to all the world
84	Here God lives among his people
40	Here I am, Lord; I come to do your will
15	He who does justice will live in the presence of the Lord
84	How lovely is your dwelling-place
27	I believe that I shall see the good things of the Lord
90	If today you hear his voice
95	If today you hear his voice
18	I love you, Lord, my strength
90	In every age, O Lord
138	In the sight of the angels
131	In you, O Lord, I have found my peace
139	I praise you, Lord, for I am wonderfully made
23	I shall live in the house of the Lord all the days of my life
32	I turn to you, Lord, in time of trouble
34	I will bless the Lord at all times
30	I will praise you, Lord, for you have rescued me
22	I will praise you, Lord, in the assembly of your people
145	I will praise your name for ever, Lord
145	I will praise your name for ever, my king and my God
51	I will rise and go to my father
71	I will sing of your salvation
116	I will take the cup of salvation
116	I will walk before the Lord
72	Justice will flourish in his time
66	Let all the earth cry out to God with joy
66	Let all the earth cry out to God with joy, alleluia
137	Let my tongue be silenced
24	Let the Lord enter; he is king of glory
95	Let us come before the Lord
122	Let us go rejoicing
Ex 15	Let us sing to the Lord
42-3	Like a deer that longs for running streams
31	Lord, be my rock of safety
146	Lord, come and save us
40	Lord, come to my aid
72	Lord, every nation on earth will adore you
32	Lord, forgive the wrong I have done
132	Lord, go up to the place of your rest
41	Lord, heal my soul, for I have sinned against you
119	Lord, I love your commands
138	Lord, I thank you for your faithfulness and love
69	Lord, in your great love, answer me
92	Lord, it is good to give thanks to you
85	Lord, let us see your kindness
4	Lord, let your face shine on us
33	Lord, let your mercy be on us
80	Lord, make us turn to you
138	Lord, on the day I called for help

Index of First Lines of Responses, pg. 2

104	Lord, send out your Spirit
85	Lord, show us your mercy and love
24	Lord, this is the people that longs to see your face
17	Lord, when your glory appears
86	Lord, you are good and forgiving
19	Lord, you have the words of everlasting life
138	Lord, your love is eternal
16	Lord, you will show us the path of life
67	May God bless us in his mercy
128	May the Lord bless us
22	My God, my God, why have you abandoned me
63	My soul is thirsting for you
Lk 1	My soul rejoices in my God
25	No one who waits for you, O Lord
104	O bless the Lord, my soul
67	O God, let all the nations praise you
8	O Lord, our God, how wonderful your name
116	Our blessing-cup is a communion
123	Our eyes are fixed on the Lord
121	Our help is from the Lord
147b	Praise the Lord, Jerusalem
146	Praise the Lord, my soul
147a	Praise the Lord, who heals the broken-hearted
113	Praise the Lord who lifts up the poor
25	Remember your mercies, O Lord
62	Rest in God alone, my soul
71	Since my mother's womb
98	Sing to the Lord a new song
81	Sing with joy to God our help
34	Taste and see the goodness of the Lord
25	Teach me your ways, O Lord
34	The angel of the Lord will rescue those who fear him
67	The earth has yielded its fruit
33	The earth is full of the goodness of the Lord
145	The hand of the Lord feeds us
19	Their message goes out through all the earth
112	The just man is a light in darkness

98	The Lord comes to rule the world
78	The Lord gave them bread from heaven
126	The Lord has done great things for us
98	The Lord has revealed to the nations
103	The Lord has set his throne in heaven
34	The Lord hears the cry of the poor
103	The Lord is kind and merciful
103	The Lord is kind and merciful, slow to anger
93	The Lord is king; he is robed in majesty
97	The Lord is king, the most high over all the earth
27	The Lord is my light and my salvation
23	The Lord is my shepherd
145	The Lord is near to all who call upon him
105	The Lord remembers his covenant
103	The Lord's kindness is everlasting
54	The Lord upholds my life
29	The Lord will bless his people with peace
15	The one who does justice will live in the presence of the Lord
19	The precepts of the Lord give joy to the heart
45	The queen stands at your right hand
46	There is a stream whose runlets gladden the city of God
65	The seed that falls on good ground
118	The stone rejected by the builders
80	The vineyard of the Lord is the house of Israel
46	The waters of the river gladden the city of God
147b	The Word of God became man
118	This is the day the Lord has made
23	Though I walk in the valley of darkness
50	To the upright I will show the saving power of God
25	To you, O Lord, I lift up my soul
69	Turn to the Lord in your need
100	We are his people, the sheep of his flock
1 Chron	We praise your glorious name
24	Who is this king of glory
130	With the Lord there is mercy
110	You are a priest for ever
16	You are my inheritance, O Lord
25	Your ways, O Lord, are love and truth
19	Your words, Lord, are Spirit and life
Is 12	You will draw water joyfully